CAWNPORE

CAWNPORE

G. O. TREVELYAN

GYAN

Published by

Gyan Publishing House
5, Ansari Road
Daryaganj, New Delhi-110002
Phone: 011-47034999, 9811692060
E-mail: books@gyanbooks.com

Distribution Network
gyanbooks.com
India, USA, Canada, UK, Australia, France

ISBN : 978-81-212-3199-2 (PB)
First Published, London, 1865

2nd Impression 2020

Printed at: Gyan Press, Delhi.

Cawnpore
Author: G. O. Trevelyan

It is good that the house and the well of horrors have been replaced by a fair garden and a graceful shrine.

Vincent Brooks, litho.

SACRED TO THE PERPETUAL MEMORY
OF A GREAT COMPANY OF CHRISTIAN PEOPLE
CHIEFLY WOMEN AND CHILDREN

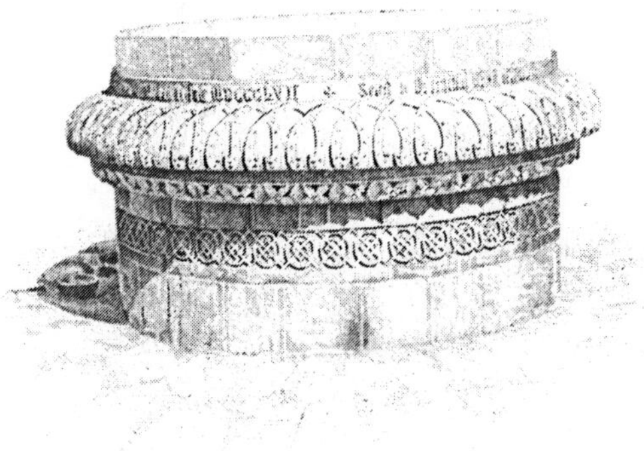

XVI DAY OF JULY MDCCCLVII

CONTENTS.

PREFACE.

THE Author of this work has made it his aim to preserve a scrupulous fidelity to the original sources of his information. The most trivial allusions, the slightest touches, are equally authentic with the main outlines of the story. The authorities most frequently consulted are:

1. The Depositions of sixty-three witnesses, Natives and Half-castes, taken under the directions of Colonel Williams, Commissioner of Police in the North-West Provinces.

2. A Narrative of Events at Cawnpore, composed by Nanukchund, a local lawyer.

3. Captain Thomson's Story of Cawnpore.

4. The Government Narratives of the Mutiny, drawn up for the most part by the civil officers

in charge of the several districts. The Author returns his most hearty thanks to Sir John Lawrence and the authorities of the Calcutta Home Office, who, at the cost of great trouble to themselves, supplied him with the copies of these invaluable documents reserved for the use of the Indian Government.

8, Grosvenor Crescent,
March, 1865.

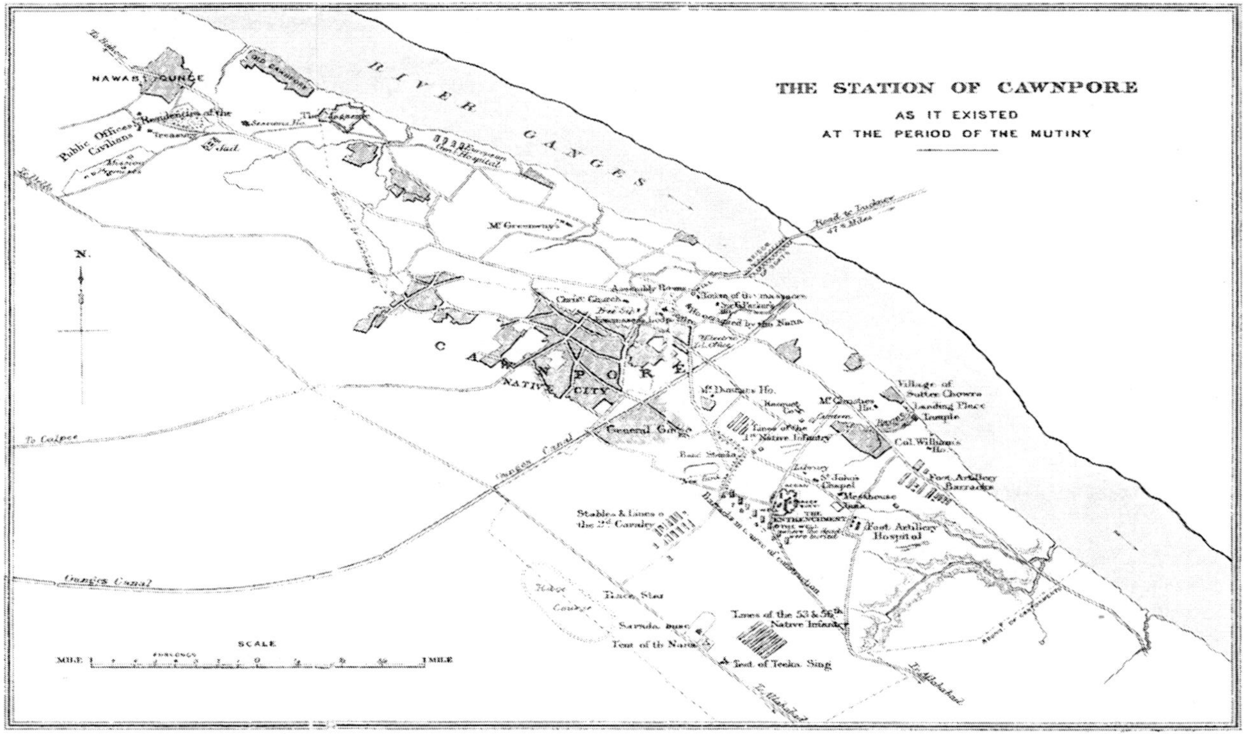

Stanford's Geog! Estab! London

London & Cambridge. Mac llan & Co.

CAWNPORE.

CHAPTER I.

THE STATION.

THE city of Cawnpore lies on the south bank of the Ganges, which at that spot is about a quarter of a mile in breadth, and this too in the dry season; for, when the rains have filled the bed, the stream measures two thousand yards from shore to shore. And yet the river has still a thousand miles of his stately course to run before that, by many channels and under many names, he loses himself in the waters of the Bay of Bengal. In old times an officer appointed to Cawnpore thought himself fortunate if he could reach his station within three months from the day he left Fort William. But tow-ropes and punt-poles are now things of the past, and the traveller from Calcutta arrives at the end of his journey in little more than thirty hours.

By the treaty of Fyzabad, in 1775, the East Indian Company engaged to maintain a brigade for the defence of Oude. The revenues of a rich and extensive tract of country were appointed for the maintenance of this force, which was quartered at Cawnpore, the principal town of the district. In 1801, Lord Wellesley, who loved to carry matters with a masterful hand, closed the mortgage, and the territory lapsed to the Company, who accepted this new charge with some diffidence. Indeed, they were not a little uneasy at the splendid rapacity of their high-souled servant. No one understood better than he the full meaning of the finest lines of that poet whose graceful diction none like himself could imitate :—

> " Tu regere imperio populos Romane memento :
> " Hæ tibi erunt artes : pacisque imponere morem ;
> " Parcere subjectis, et debellare superbos."

But that policy which suited the temper of the Senate of old Rome was not exactly of a nature to please the Directors of a Joint Stock Company. It was very well for statesmen and generals to look for their reward in the pages of history. It behoved City men to keep an eye on the fluctuations of the Share list.

Thus it happened that, ever since the beginning of the last quarter of the eighteenth century, Cawnpore had been a first-class military station. In the spring of 1857 it had attained an importance to which the events of the following summer gave a fatal shock. The recent annexation of Oude was an additional motive for keeping a strong hold on Cawnpore; for that city commanded the bridge over which passed the high road to Lucknow, the capital of our newly acquired province. At that time the station was occupied by three regiments of sepoys, the First, the Fifty-third, and the Fifty-sixth Bengal Infantry. The Second Cavalry, and a company of artillerymen, brought up the strength of the native force to three thousand men. Of Europeans and persons of European extraction, there were resident at Cawnpore more than a thousand. There were the officers attached to the sepoy battalions; sixty men of the Eighty-fourth regiment of the British Line; seventy-eight invalids belonging to the Thirty-second regiment, then quartered at Lucknow, and destined to pass through the most fearful trial from which ever men emerged alive; fifteen of the Madras Fusileers; and fifty-nine of the Company's artillerymen: in all, some three hundred soldiers of English birth. Then there were the covenanted civilians, the aristocracy of Indian society; the lesser officials attached to the Post-office, the Public Works, and the Opium Departments; the Railway people; the merchants and shopkeepers,—Europeans some, others half-castes, or, as they would fain be called, Eurasians. There, too, (alas!) were the wives and little ones of the men of all these classes and grades, and in no slender proportion; for among our countrymen in India the marriage state is in special honour. There likewise were a great number of half-caste children belonging to the Cawnpore school, who were soon to buy at a very dear price the privilege of having been begotten by a European sire.

The military quarter was entirely distinct from the native city. And here let the English reader divest himself at once of all European ideas, and keep clear of them, as much as in him lies, during the whole course of this narrative. Let him put aside all preconceived notions of a barrack,—of a yard paved with rough stones, and darkened by buildings four stories high, at the windows of which lounge stalwart warriors in various stages of *déshabille*, digesting their fresh boiled-beef by the aid of a short pipe and a languid gossip. Let him try to form to himself a picture of a military station in Northern India, for it was within the precincts of such a station that was played out the most terrible tragedy of our age.

The cantonments lay along the bank of the river, over a tract extending six miles from northwest to southeast: for, wheresoever in Hindostan Englishmen make their homes, no regard is had to economy of space. Each residence stands in a separate "compound," or paddock, of some three or four acres, surrounded by an uneven, crumbling mound and ditch, with here and there a ragged hedge of prickly pear. For all over India fences appear to exist rather for the purpose of marking boundaries than for any protection they afford against intruders. The house, like all houses outside the Calcutta Ditch, consists of a single story, built of brick, coated with white plaster; the whole premises, if the owner be a bachelor or a subaltern, in a most shabby and tumble-down condition. A flight of half a dozen steps leads up to a verandah which runs round three sides of the building. The noticeable objects here will probably be a native tailor, working in the attitude adopted by tailors in all lands where men wear clothes; a wretched being, squatted on his haunches, lazily pulling the string of a punkah that passes through a hole in the brickwork into the Sahib's bedroom, a monotonous occupation, which from time to time he sweetens by snatches of sleep; a Madras valet, spreading butter on the Sahib's morning toast with the greasy wing of a fowl; and, against the windward wall, a row of jars of porous red clay, in which water is cooling for the Sahib's morning bath.

The principal door leads at once into the sitting-room, a spacious, ill-kept, comfortless apartment; the most conspicuous article being a huge, oblong frame of wood and canvass suspended across the ceiling, and the prevailing impression an overwhelming sense of the presence of cobwebs. The furniture, which is scattered about in most unadmired disorder, is in the last stage of dilapidation. Every article in an Anglo-Indian household bears witness to the fact that Englishmen regard themselves but as sojourners in the locality where fate and the quartermaster-general may have placed them. A large rickety table in the centre of the room is strewn with three or four empty soda-water bottles, a half-emptied bottle of brandy, a corkscrew, glasses, playing-cards, chessmen, an Hindostanee dictionary, an inkstand, a revolver, a bundle of letters, a box of cigars, the supplement of *Bell's Life*, and a few odd volumes from the regimental book-club ;—of no very seductive quality, like enough, for the colonel's lady has kept the new novels, and the doctor, who is secretary to the club, has impounded the biographies, so that our ensign is fain to put up with "Aids to Faith," and the third volume of the "History of the Inductive Sciences." Then there are eight or ten chairs, a good half of which might well claim to be invalided on the score of wounds and long service; a couch with broken springs; a Japanese cabinet, bought as a bargain when the old major was sold up; and an easy cane chair of colossal dimensions, the arms of which are prolonged and flattened, so as to accommodate the occupant with a resting-place for his feet. In one corner stands a couple of hog-spears, supple, tough, and duly weighted with lead and barbed with steel of proof; a regulation sword; a buggy-whip; a hunting-crop; a double-barrelled rifle and a shot-gun—weapons which the owner depreciates as archaic, expressing his intention of providing himself during his first visit to Europe, with "By Jove, a complete "outfit from Purdey, two double-barrelled breech-"loaders, and a breech-loading rifle." On nails driven into the plaster hang a list of the men in the company to which the young fellow is attached; a caricature of the paymaster; a framed photograph of the cricket eleven of the public school where he was educated; and, if he be of a humorous turn, the last wigging, or letter of admonition and reproof, received from the colonel of his regiment.

In such a scene, and amidst such associations, does the English subaltern wear out the weary hours of the interminable Indian day; smoking; dozing; playing with his terrier; longing for the evening, or for a call from a brother-officer, with whom he may discuss the Army List, and partake of the ever-recurring refreshment of brandy and soda-water; lazily endeavouring to get some little insight into the languages of the hateful East by the help of a fat fawning native tutor, and a stupid and indecent Oordoo work on mythology; pondering sadly on home landscapes and home recollections, as he gazes across the sharply-defined line of shadow, thrown by the roof of the verandah, into the outdoor heat and glare; with no pleasanter object of contemplation than the Patna sheep belonging to the Station Mutton Club, and his own modest stud, consisting of a raw-boned Australian horse and an old Cabul pony picketed under a group of mango-trees near the gate of the compound.

The centre apartment is flanked on either side by a smaller chamber; both of which are employed as bed-rooms, if, for the sake of company or economy, our young friend is keeping house with some Addiscombe chum. Otherwise, the least desirable is set apart as a lumber-room; though, to judge from the condition of the articles in use, it is hard to imagine what degree of shabbiness would qualify furniture to become lumber in Bengal. The door into the Sahib's bedroom stands open, like every other door in British India; the multitude of servants, and the necessity for coolness, forbidding the very idea of privacy. There stands a bedstead of wood, worm-eaten, unplaned, unpolished; inclosed on all sides with musquito-curtains of white gauze, the edges carefully tucked in beneath the mattress, through which is dimly seen the recumbent form of the Sahib, clad in a silk shirt and linen drawers, the universal night-dress of the East. The poor boy is doing his best to recover, during the cooler morning hours, the arrears of the sleepless night, which he has passed in a state of feverish irritation—panting, perspiring, tossing from side to side in desire of a momentary relief from the tortures of Prickly Heat, the curse of young blood; anon, sallying into the verandah to rouse the nodding punkah-puller, more happy than his wakeful master. Little of ornament or convenience is to be seen around, save a capacious brass basin on an iron stand, and half a dozen trunks, of shape adapted to be slung in pairs on the hump of a bullock. An inner door affords a view into a bath-room, paved with rough bricks; the bath consisting of a space surrounded by a parapet some six inches high, in which the bather stands while his servant sluices him with cold water from a succession of jars. It may be that on a shelf at the bed's head are treasured some objects, trifling indeed in value, but made very dear by association; a few school prizes and leaving-books; a few sheets of flimsy pink paper, closely written, soiled, and frayed at every fold; one or two portraits in morocco cases, too sacred for the photographic album, and the inspection and criticism of a stranger. There is something touching in these repositories, for they tell that, however much the lad may appear to be absorbed in the pursuits and pleasures of the mess-room, the parade-ground, the snipe-marsh, and the race-course, his highest thoughts and dearest hopes are far away in that land where he is never again to abide, until those hopes and thoughts have long been tamed and deadened by years and troubles.

Such are the quarters of a British subaltern. The home of a married pair may be somewhat more comfortable, and the residence of a man in high office considerably more magnificent; but the same characteristics prevail everywhere. A spirit of scrupulous order, and a snug domestic air, are not to be attained in an Indian household. At best a semi-barbarous profusion, an untidy splendour, and the absence of sordid cares, form the compensation for the loss of English comfort. Still, the lady must have her drawing-room, where she can display her wedding presents, and the purchases which she made at the Calcutta auctions during the cold season before last. The Commissioner must have his sanctum, where he can wallow in papers, and write letters of censure to his collectors, letters of explanation to the Revenue Board, and letters of remonstrance to the local military authorities. The epicure cannot do without a roofed passage leading from his kitchen to his parlour; nor the sporting man without a loose box for the mare which he has entered for the Planter's Plate at Sonepore. Then, too, gentlemen of horticultural tastes like to devote a spare hour to superintending the labours of their gardeners: and the soil at Cawnpore well repays attention. Most kinds of European vegetables can be produced with success, while peaches and melons, shaddocks and limes, grow in native abundance: together with those fruits which an old Qui-hye loves so dearly, but which to a fresh English palate are a poor substitute indeed for hautboys and ribstone pippins;—the mango, with a flavour like turpentine, and the banana, with a flavour like an over-ripe pear; the guava, which has a taste of strawberries, and the custard-apple, which has no perceptible taste at all.

None of those institutions which render the ordinary life of the English officer in India somewhat less monotonous and objectless were wanting at Cawnpore. There was a church, whose fair white tower, rising among a group of lofty trees, for more than one dull and dusty mile greets the eyes of the traveller on the road from Lucknow. That church, which has stood scatheless through such strange vicissitudes, will soon be superseded by a more imposing temple, built to commemorate the great disaster of our race. There were meeting-houses of divers Protestant persuasions, a Roman Catholic chapel, and a mission of the Society for the Propagation of the Gospel. There was a race-course, as there is in every spot throughout the East, where a handful of our countrymen have got together; a theatre, where the ladies of the garrison with good-natured amusement witnessed cornets and junior magistrates attempting to represent female whims and graces; a Freemason's lodge, where the work of initiation and instruction went merrily on in a temperature of 100° in the shade. There was a racket-court, and a library, and news-rooms, and billiard-rooms. There were the assembly-rooms, where dinners were given to passing Governors-General, and balls to high official dames, where questions of precedence were raised, and matches made and broken. There was a breakfast club, whither men repaired after their ride to discuss the powers that be over their morning toast, at that meal so dear to Britons from the Himalayas to Point de Galle, and from the Sutlej to Hong-Kong, whether, as throughout Bengal, it be termed "little "breakfast," or, as at Madras, it be known by the title of "early tea." There was the band-stand, the very heart and centre of up-country fashion, where the wit and beauty and gallantry of the station were nightly wont to congregate. There was the ice-club, for the manufacture and supply of that luxury which becomes a necessity under the tropic of Cancer;—which more favoured Calcutta obtains straight from the Canadian lakes, with Newfoundland codfish and Pennsylvanian apples embedded in the crystal mass. The markets were well supplied with fish, flesh, and fowl, at a cost that would gladden the heart of an English housewife, though Anglo-Indians complain loudly of the rise in prices, and grumble at being forced to pay sixpence a pound for mutton, and three shillings for a fat turkey. In the game season, quails, wild ducks, snipe, and black partridges were cheap and abundant; and a dish of ortolans, a treat which in Europe is confined to Italian tourists and Parisian millionaires, was a common adjunct to the second course at Cawnpore dinner-tables.

The quarters of the native troops presented a very different appearance from the English bungalows. Sepoy lines, generally speaking, consist of long rows of huts built of mud on a framework of bamboos, and thatched with straw. Every soldier has his own doghole, in which he keeps an inconceivable quantity of female relations, from his grandmother downwards. There he rules supreme, for no Sahib, be he ever so enthusiastic on the subject of sanitation and drainage, would care to intrude upon the mysteries of a sepoy household. At the ends of each row stand the habitations of the native officers attached to the company: two or three cabins round a tiny court-yard, fenced in with a mud wall a few feet in height. The sepoy, unlike a European soldier, never becomes wholly military in his tastes and habits. The dearest ambition of a villager is to increase the number of huts on his little premises, and that ambition is not to be quenched even by drill and pipe-clay.

Each of the regiments had a bazaar peculiar to itself, crowded with people employed in supplying the wants, and ministering to the pleasures of the battalion which honoured them with its patronage. Sutlers, corn-merchants, rice-merchants, sellers of cotton fabrics, of silver ornaments, of tobacco and stupefying drugs, jugglers, thieves, swarms of prostitutes, fakeers, and Thugs retired from business, made up a motley and most unruly population, which was with difficulty kept in some show of order by the energy of Sir George Parker, the cantonment magistrate. The united crew of these dens of iniquity and sedition did not fall short of forty thousand in number.

The sepoys were tall men, the average height in a regiment being five feet eight inches, and, seen from a distance, in their scarlet coats and black trousers, they presented a sufficiently military appearance. But, on nearer inspection, there was something in the general effect displeasing to an eye accustomed to the men of Aldershot and Chalons. No Oriental seems at ease in European costume,—least of all in the English uniform so dear to the heart of the old tailor colonels. The native soldier in full dress wore a ludicrous and almost pathetic air of uneasiness and rigidity. His clothes hung on him as though he were a very angular wooden frame. Whether from consciousness of the figure which he cut in his red tunic, or from an instinctive fear of the contamination contained in Christian cloth, the sepoy was no sooner dismissed from parade or relieved from guard than he hastened to doff every shred of the dress provided by Government. Clad in the unprofessional but more congenial costume of a very scanty pair of linen drawers, he might be seen now seated over a pile of rice or a huge bannock, cooked for him by the women of his family; now, performing the copious ablutions, the obligation to which constitutes the single virtue of his national religion; now, submitting the crown of his head to the barber for a periodical shave; now, perchance, discussing with a circle of comrades the probability of the Emperor of the Russians joining with Brigadier Napoleon and the King of Roum in a scheme for destroying the power of the East Indian Company.

His pay was seven rupees, or fourteen shillings, a month. Small as this sum may appear to us, it was amply sufficient to endow the sepoy with far higher social consideration than is enjoyed by a private soldier in European countries. The purest of pure Brahmins, his faith forbade him from spending much money on the gratification of his appetite. The most confirmed gourmand in the battalion could never dream of a better dinner than some coarse fish from a neighbouring tank, flavoured by a handful of spices ground between two fragments of a gravestone abstracted from the last English cemetery on the line of march. Such luxuries as these could be procured at a rate that left even the private soldier a large margin whence to provide for any other calls that might be made upon his purse. He accordingly was regarded as a very considerable personage by the native populace. A peasant-proprietor or small shopkeeper thought it no small honour to receive an offer of marriage for his daughter from a gentleman serving in the ranks of the Company's army, and the sepoy was not slow to make use of his matrimonial advantages. A column of native troops on the march was accompanied from station to station by an endless string of small carts, each containing one or two veiled ladies, presumably young and pretty; one or two without veils, very indubitably old and ugly; together with a swarm of dusky brats with enormous stomachs, stark naked, with the almost nominal exception of a piece of tape fastened round the loins.

In spite of his excellent pay, the native soldier was almost invariably deep in debt. A strong sense of family ties, an extreme generosity towards poor connexions, is a marked trait in the Hindoo character, amiable indeed, but not encouraging to the student of Social Science. Whenever an Indian official steps into an income, relations of every degree flock from all parts of the continent to prey upon his facile affection, and the prospect of sharing the corner of a sepoy's hut and the parings of his pay proved sufficiently attractive to bring into cantonments herds of country cousins from Rohilcund and Shahabad. Neither would seven rupees a month adequately defray the occasional extravagances enjoined by "dustoor" or custom: dustoor, the breath of a Hindoo's nostrils, the motive of his actions, the staple of his conversation, the tyrant of his life. It has frequently happened that a private soldier has celebrated a marriage feast at a cost of three hundred rupees, to obtain which he must sell himself body and soul to one of those griping ruthless usurers who are the bugbears of Oriental society.

At the commencement of 1857, the condition of the native army was unsatisfactory in the highest degree. An impartial observer could not fail at every turn to note symptoms which proved beyond the possibility of a doubt that a bad spirit was abroad. But, unfortunately, those who had the best opportunity for observing these symptoms were not impartial. The officers of the old Bengal army regarded their soldiers with a fond credulity that was above suspicion and deaf to evidence: and no wonder: for on the fidelity of that army was staked all that they held most dear—professional reputation, social standing, the means of life, and finally, life itself. It was in deference to their pardonable but most fatal prejudices that on this ominous subject silence was enforced during the years which preceded the outbreak. It was to please their pride of class that the tongues of more discerning men were tied, and their pens blunted. It was in vain that General Jacob, the stout Lord Warden of the Scinde Marches, wrote and expostulated with all his native energy and fire.

Threatened and frowned on by his employers, sneered at by his fellow officers as an agitator and a busy-body, he was at length brought to acknowledge that the tone of the Bengal army was a matter on which a wise man did well to hold his peace. That great commander, whose excellent military judgment, matured in European camps, revolted at a state of things so fraught with peril and scandal, learned too late that not even the audacity of a Napier, not even the glory of Meeanee could protect him from the consequences of having presumed to call in question the faith of the sepoy. As the only apparent effect of his admonitions the turbulent and warlike province of Oude was annexed to our territory, and the ranks of our army were swelled by the addition of thousands of disaffected native mercenaries.

That discipline was lax, that insubordination was a-foot had long been known by many who dared not speak out the truth. As far back as the year 1845 there occurred a case in which a regiment broke into open mutiny, and pelted its officers through cantonments with the material employed in road-mending, a customary missile in Bengalee riots. A party of native infantry on a night march presented an appearance, absurd indeed, but to a thoughtful spectator not without serious significance. The men straggled along, carrying in their hands some beloved pipe, their most treasured possession, while their muskets were carelessly flung into the bullock-carts, in which not a few sepoys were snoring comfortably amidst the baggage. Even those on foot dozed as they walked, with that unaccountable capacity, common to all Hindoos, of going to sleep under the most adverse circumstances; the collar of their great-coat turned up and kept in its place by a strip of calico; their ears protected by folds of cloth passed underneath the chin and fastened over the top of the head, with a regimental forage-cap perched on the summit of this unsightly and unmartial head-gear. In some corps men had so little respect for military rule and custom as to strip off their uniforms even when on guard. There were those who in great part attributed these irregularities to the abolition of corporal punishment effected by Lord William Bentinck, that wise and true friend of the native population of India. It is to be hoped, for the cause of humanity and enlightenment, that men who so think are mistaken in their opinion. It cannot, however, be denied that, whatever be the reason, there was truth in the words spoken to a civilian by an old pensioned native officer :—"Ah Sahib!" said the veteran, "The army has ceased to fear."

At the siege of Mooltan, where native troops from all parts of India were collected into one army, the vile temper of the Bengal sepoys and the extraordinary indulgence displayed towards them by their officers became painfully apparent. These insolent high-caste mercenaries positively refused to labour in the trenches, and endeavoured to induce or force the modest and trusty Bombay soldiers to follow their example. On one occasion a mob of these rascals, being unable to persuade a fatigue-party of Bombay men to strike work, proceeded to revile and at length to stone their worthier comrades. A captain in a rifle regiment marked the ringleaders, but the Bengal officers flatly declined to take any steps in the matter, and the story was hushed up in order that their feelings might be spared. When the Sixty-sixth Native infantry mutinied, their chiefs endeavoured to palliate the guilt of the regiment; but Sir Charles Napier refused to see with any eyes save his own, and promptly disbanded the corps, which was replaced by an excellent levy of the valiant Highlanders of Nepaul. Sir Charles expressed great displeasure at the report sent in by the commanding officer of the regiment, and especially at a sentence which characterised what was in fact a shout of defiance as a "a murmur of discontent." To the very last, at a time when mutiny and murder were rife from Peshawur to Dacca, each particular colonel was firmly impressed with the idea that his battalion would be the Ariel of the army, faithful only it to its oath and salt, to the recollections of bounty-money and the hopes of pension. "Pity," writes an officer of the Sixty-fifth regiment, "that Europeans abusing a corps cannot be strung up." On the twenty-second of May a letter appeared in the *Englishman* newspaper from Colonel Simpson, who commanded the Sixth Bengal Infantry at the all-important station of Allahabad. He was very indignant at the suspicions which had been expressed concerning the intentions of the men under his charge, who, according to him, "evince the utmost loyalty. So far from being mis- "trusted, they are our main protection." Not many days after he was glad to escape into the fort with a ball through his arm, while his officers were being butchered by the men on whom he had placed so unbounded a reliance. The "staunchness" of the sepoys was at that time so common a topic with their chiefs that the expression became a byword among Calcutta people; for at whatever station the colonel most loudly, pertinaciously, and angrily declared his regiment to be "staunch," it was to that quarter that men looked for the next tidings of massacre and outrage. It was not till he saw his own house in flames, and the rupees from the Government treasury scattered broad-cast over the parade-ground—it was not till he looked down the barrels of sepoy muskets, and heard sepoy bullets whizzing round his ears, that an old Bengal officer could begin to believe that his men were not as staunch as they should be; and yet, as will be seen in the course of this narrative, there might exist a degree of confidence and attachment which was proof even against that ordeal.

Respect for the obligations of blood-relationship is so strong in the Hindoo mind, that jobbery and nepotism flourish in Oriental society to an extent which would seem inconceivably audacious to the colder imagination of a western public servant. The system of family patronage runs through all ranks and classes. The Indian judge loves to surround himself with kindred clerks of the court and consanguineous ushers. The Indian superintendant of police prefers to have about him inspectors and sergeants, bound to his interest by nearer ties than those of official dependence. The head bearer fills his master's house with young barbarians from his native village; and, in like manner, the veteran sepoys took measures to keep the regiment supplied with recruits from the neighbourhood in which they themselves had been born and bred. No strapping young Tewarry, or Pandy, who had a mind to shoulder a Company's musket and touch the Company's rupees, had long to wait for a place in the section of which the sergeant was his uncle and the corporal his brother-in-law. On the other hand, a stranger was soon driven from the regiment by that untiring and organized social oppression, in which, if we are to believe the daily press, military men of all nations and grades are such admirable adepts. And so it came to pass in the course of time, that the company partook of the nature of a family, and the battalion of the nature of a clan. The consequence was, that there existed a sympathy and free-masonry throughout the ranks of quite another tendency from that tone of regimental patriotism and martial brotherhood, known in European armies by the title of "*esprit-de-corps*." Such a state of things afforded peculiar facilities for conspiring. A disaffected body of sepoys possessed the power of a host, and the discretion of a clique. The most extensive and perilous designs could be matured in perfect secrecy, and carried into effect by the weight of a vast and unanimous multitude.

The real motive of the mutiny was the ambition of the soldiery. Spoilt, flattered, and idle, in the insolence of its presumed strength that pampered army thought nothing too good for itself, and nothing too formidable. High caste Brahmins all, proud as Lucifer, they deemed that to them of right belonged the treasures and the empire of India. Hampered with debt, they looked for the day of a general spoliation. Chafing under restraint, they panted to indulge themselves in unbridled rapine and licence. They were bent upon the foundation of a gigantic military despotism. They looked forward to the time when Soubahdars and Jemmadars should be Maharajas and Nawabs; when the taxes should be collected by sepoy receivers-general, and paid into sepoy treasuries; when every private should have his zenana full of the loveliest daughters of Lahore and Rohilcund; when great landholders from Bundelcund and Orissa should come with cases of diamonds to beg a favourable decision from Mungul Pandy; when great merchants from Liverpool and Marseilles should come with bags of sovereigns to ask leave of Peer Bux to establish a factory at Mutlah or Chandernagore. They evinced an equal contempt for all the other classes of the inhabitants of India. They despised the excellent armies of Bombay and Madras, and their insolence was requited with bitter aversion. They looked down on the Ghoorkas as savages, and presumed to regard the heroes of Chillianwallah and Ferozeshah as a conquered race; as if, forsooth, it was sepoy prowess which, after more than one series of fierce and dubious battles, had at length prevailed over the brave and haughty warriors of the Punjaub. And at length, in the plenitude of their pride and folly, they began to call in question the efficacy of the English name.

We had, indeed, been negligent. We had been improvident even unto madness. Some twenty thousand European troops were scattered over the continent of India; for the security of which seventy thousand are now held to be barely sufficient. In the May of 1857, from Meerut in the North-west, to Dinapore in the South-east, two weak British regiments only were to be found. In these days, a battalion of English infantry may be placed at any important city in our dominions within the twenty-four hours. Then, all the field-batteries throughout the entire region of Oude, with a single exception, were manned by native gunners and drivers. Now, in every station on the plains, the artillerymen, the trained workmen of warfare, without whom in modern times an armed force is helpless, are one and all our own countrymen. Then, our only communication was along roads which the first rains turned into strips of bog, and up rivers treacherous with crossing current and changing sandbanks. Now, through the heart of every province, there runs, or soon will run, those lines of rail and lines of wire, which defy alike season and distance.

The natives of India possess a sharp insight into matters that come within the limits of their own sphere, but are strangely ignorant of all that passes beyond those limits. The sepoy ringleaders knew to a man the strength, or rather the weakness, of European forces in the North of India. But, incredible as it may appear, they were firmly impressed with the idea that they saw with their eyes the whole extent of our resources. Public opinion in Hindostan placed the population of the British Isles at something over a hundred thousand souls. This error was so universal that a native who did not share in the hallucination was sure to be a man of superior discernment and rare strength of mind. Hyder Ali and Runjeet Sing, the Hannibal and the Mithridates of India, had often in their mouths the same phrase concerning the power of the Company. They feared, they would say, not what they saw, but what they did not see. Jung Bahadour, the far-famed Mayor of the Palace of Nepaul, when the first dull rumour of the coming crisis began to be bruited, paid a visit to England on purpose to learn for himself what the state of the case really was; and returned firmly resolved not to take part against a power which could raise at a pinch hundreds of millions of money, and hundreds of thousands of men. On one occasion during the troubles, a party of sepoys attacked some guns worked by Sikh artillerymen, only to be beaten off with heavy loss. The officer in charge of the battery was much amused at hearing one of the men say to his comrades, "If those fools of pandies had "ever been at Battses' Hotel, Vere Street, Oxford "Street, they would not have come on so boldly." On inquiry, it appeared that this judicious Punjabee had gone to London in the service of some Anglo-Indian; where, as he stood at the mouth of Vere Street, he might see passing to and from Hyde Park in a single day as many Sahibs as would stock two such towns as Loodianah or Umritsur.

The conviction that all our available male population was already in India began to be shaken as, regiment after regiment, brigade upon brigade, angry fighting men of Saxon race came pouring up from Calcutta in a continuous stream, by road, by rail, and by river. And yet that conviction lingered long. When the magnificent array collected for the final siege of Lucknow passed through Cawnpore, our Sikh allies would have it that Sir Colin, like the stage manager at Astley's theatre, marched his men in at one end of the town and out at the other, and then brought them back outside the walls to repeat the same manœuvre. When the mutineers first caught sight of the Highland costume, they cried with joy that the men of England had been exhausted, and that the Company had been reduced to call out the women. They soon had reason to repent their mistake, and thenceforward adopted a theory more consistent with the fact, for they held that the petticoats were designed to remind their wearers that they had been sent to India to exact vengeance for the murder of the English ladies.

The insolence and greed of the soldiers, their impatience of discipline, and their lust of power, were the effective causes of the outbreak. But the proximate cause was the fancied insult which had been offered to their national religion. Upon this most vexed question, a distinguished civil servant, who held high office in Calcutta during those eventful months, is wont to say that he could never trust the judgment of a man who maintains that the greased cartridges had little to do with the mutiny. There are a class of our countrymen who delight in stigmatizing the natives of India as hypocrites and infidels. These men affect to disbelieve in the sincerity of the religious professions of any Mussulman who cannot resist the temptation of iced champagne, or of any Hindoo who indulges himself in a quiet slice of the joint which has appeared at his master's table. As if the men who are foremost to avenge the wrongs of their creed and to thrust it down the throats of their neighbours were always the most scrupulous in their obedience to its precepts. As if History was not full of covetous Fathers of the Church and polygamous Defenders of the Faith. Jehu was zealous to destroy the priests of the House of Baal, and to burn his images with fire: howbeit he departed not from the sins of Jeroboam, the son of Nebat, who made Israel to sin. Archbishop Laud was emphatically a good Churchman, and yet he too often forgot the blessing pronounced upon the merciful by the Divine founder of his Church, and the curse uttered against those who lade men with burdens grievous to be borne.

The mind of the sepoy reeked with religious prejudice. He had adopted his profession in accordance with the dictates of his superstition. He belonged to a sacred order, and his life was one long ceremony. He could not prepare his simple food without clearing for himself a separate plot of ground secure from the intrusion of others. Should a stranger step into this magic ring, the food which he had cooked was thrown untasted away. When some Bengal regiments were serving in China, it occasionally happened that an unlucky native of the country, intent on theft or barter, set his profane foot within the hallowed circle, and was immediately saluted with a volley of threats and missiles from the outraged soldier whose meal he had spoiled. The bewildered wretch would take to flight across the camping-ground, plunging through the kitchens, defiling dinners by the score, and, in whatever direction he turned, rousing about his ears a swarm of indignant hungry Brahmins. Even if the sepoy was inclined to become lax in his observances, there were not wanting ghostly advisers to check his latitudinarian tendencies. A battalion on march was usually preceded by two or three fakeers, the bloated, filthy, sensual wandering friars of the East; wild-looking fellows, in orange or salmon-coloured linen, if by good luck they deigned to wear any clothes at all; their locks of long hair matted in strange fashion with grease and dirt; their bodies sprinkled with ashes and daubed with coarse paint. So pernicious and irregular a custom was not tolerated in the Presidencies of Bombay and Madras: but in Bengal these fellows were highly regarded by the soldiers, and did duty as unofficial regimental chaplains.

Five parts tallow, five parts stearine, and one part wax, were the ingredients of that unsavoury composition, the memory of which will henceforward never perish as long as England has history and India has tradition. Captain Boxer, of the Royal Laboratory at Woolwich, was quite unable to offer any decided opinion as to the particular description of animal from which the tallow was derived, but was certain that the mixture was innocent of hog's lard. Not so thought the Brahmins of the regiments stationed in the vicinity of the capital. About the middle of January, 1857, amidst the frivolous and ill-natured gossip which is the chief material of Calcutta journalism, there peer out certain vague and uncomfortable paragraphs. "A rumour has been current among "the sepoys at Dumdum and Barrackpore that they "are to be baptized, and we hear that they are greatly "alarmed in consequence. It should be explained to "them that the only ceremony of the kind to which "soldiers are required to submit is the baptism of "fire." Again, a letter from Barrackpore announces that "bungalows here are set fire to every night." On the 10th of February, "a Hindu" solemnly warns the Governor-General thus: "My Lord, this is the "most critical time ever reached in the administra-"tion of British India. Almost all the independent "native Princes and Rajahs have been so much "offended at the late Annexation policy, that they "have begun to entertain deadly enmity to the "British empire in India. Moreover, as for the "internal defences of the empire, the cartridge "question has created a strenuous movement in "some portions of the Hindu sepoys, and will "spread it through all their ranks over the whole "country to the great insecurity of British rule." These notices, which we now read by the light of a terrible experience, appear side by side with satirical poems on their more fortunate comrades by military officers who cannot get civil employ; advertisements of a fancy fair for the advancement of native female education; and a proposition to appoint a committee of "eligible young civilians" to indemnify the ladies whose Europe bonnets have been ruined by the dust on the course. Ere many months were flown, eligible young civilians had far other matters to occupy their attention.

At length, on the 26th of February, the Nineteenth Bengal Native Infantry, quartered at Berhampore, being directed to parade for exercise with blank ammunition, refused to obey the command, and in the course of the following night turned out with a great noise of drumming and shouting, broke open the bells of arms, and committed other acts of open mutiny. By order of the Governor-General the regiment was disarmed, marched down to Barrackpore, a distance of something over a hundred miles, and there disbanded by Major-general Hearsey, who performed his trying task with energy, discretion, and courage. As yet there had been no blood shed; but far worse was soon to come. The Thirty-fourth Native Infantry had for some time past been ripe for revolt. There were nearly six hundred high-caste men in the ranks, and the corps was stationed among local associations which fostered the most lively emotions in the minds of men in a state of high religious excitement. In the year 1825, Barrackpore had been the scene of a military tumult which had been repressed with timely severity. One of the ringleaders, a Brahmin sepoy, had been hanged in the presence of his comrades. This man was regarded as a martyr; the spot where he met his fate, on the edge of a large tank, was still pointed out to each new-comer, and the brass implements with which he performed his acts of worship had been preserved in the quarter-guard as relics of the departed saint. Unfortunately the regiment was commanded by an officer who thus describes himself in honest and manly language: "I beg to state that "it has been my invariable plan to act on the broad "line which Scripture enforces, that is, to speak "without reserve to every person. When I therefore "address natives on the subject of religion, whether "individually or collectively, it has been no question "with me whether the person or persons I addressed "belonged to this or that regiment, or whether he is "a shopkeeper, merchant, or otherwise, but I speak "to all alike, as sinners in the sight of God; and I "have no doubt that I have often in this way "(indeed, am quite certain,) addressed sepoys of my "own regiment, as also of other regiments at this "and other stations where I have been quartered. ". . . . As to the question whether I have en- "deavoured to convert sepoys and others to Christi-

"anity, I would humbly reply that this has been my "object; and, I conceive, it is the aim and end of "every Christian who speaks the Word of God to "another, namely, that the Lord would make him "the happy instrument of converting his neighbour "to God." Did not this good Colonel forget who it was who bade us give not that which is holy unto the dogs, neither cast our pearls before swine, lest they trample them under their feet, and turn again and rend us?

On the 29th of March, a private of the Thirty-fourth, Mungul Pandy by name, under the combined influence of religious frenzy and intoxicating drugs, took into his head to swagger about in front of the lines, musket in hand, bawling: "Come out, you "blackguards! The Europeans are upon us! From "biting these cartridges we shall become infidels! "Get ready! Turn out, all of you!" This conduct in the course of time brought down upon him the Adjutant and the Sergeant-major, which in no wise disconcerted Mungul Pandy. He shot the officer's horse, disabled his bridle arm, and finally, with the assistance of some of the boldest among his comrades, desperately wounded and drove off both the Europeans. The Colonel next appeared on the stage. Here again it may be best to quote his own words: "The native officer at length ordered the guard to "advance. They did so, six or seven paces, and "halted. The native officer returned to me, stating "that none of the men would go on. I felt it was "useless going on any further in the matter. Some "one, a native in undress, mentioned to me that the "sepoy in front was a Brahmin, and that no one "would hurt him. I considered it quite useless, and "a useless sacrifice of life, to order a European "officer with the guard to seize him, as he would, no "doubt, have picked off the European officer, without "his receiving any assistance from the guard. I then "left the guard, and reported the matter to the "Brigadier."

Fortunately there was at hand a man who had no scruple about the life of at least one European officer. Before many minutes had elapsed General Hearsey rode on to the parade-ground, and found it already covered with an agitated mob of sepoys, amongst whom might here and there be seen an English officer doing his best to prevent his men from following the example of Mungul Pandy, who had by this time reloaded his musket, and was now stalking about in the presence of his regiment, which had got together round the quarter-guard, brandishing his dripping sword, and shouting: "You have "excited me to do this, and now, you blackguards, "you will not join me!" An officer called out to

Hearsey, "Have a care! His musket is loaded!" The General replied, "Damn his musket!" an oath concerning which every true Englishman will make the customary invocation to the Recording Angel.

Hearsey summoned the guard to advance, but the native officer answered as before. The General, however, by a significant motion of his revolver, gave the Jemmadar to understand that this time he had to deal with a man of very different kidney from the Colonel. The guard, accordingly, went forward; the Jemmadar in front, watched on either side by a young Hearsey, pistol in hand. Their sire himself rode straight at the mutineer, who, seeing that the game was up, turned the muzzle to his own breast, touched the trigger with his toe, and fell, severely hurt. He was secured, and conveyed to the hospital; and the concourse dispersed quietly to their lines, after having been roundly taken to task by the General for their cowardice and unsoldierlike behaviour in standing by without moving a finger, while their officers were being cut to pieces.

Mungul Pandy was condemned by court-martial, and duly hanged on the 8th of April. At first there was some difficulty about finding an executioner. Public opinion had become less squeamish before the year was out. From this miserable fanatic was taken the name of "Pandy," which in Anglo-Indian slang signified mutineer. There were those who loved to apply the horrible nickname of "white "Pandies" to those wise and good men who, amidst the general frenzy, preserved some spark of justice and humanity; who would not lend their countenance to a barbarous policy dictated by cruelty and craven fear; who refused to devastate provinces and depopulate cities, to butcher the women of Delhi and torture the shopkeepers of Allahabad, to confound innocent and guilty in one vast proscription and one universal massacre: just as, at the end of the last century, there were those who stigmatized as "Jacobins" the English statesmen who could not be reviled or shocked out of the belief that the king and the nobility of France had been less sinned against than sinning; and that, in any case, it was not our business to avenge the wrongs of alien dukes and marquises upon the senators who had abolished their privileges, the peasants who had shot their game, and the board which was busily engaged in dividing their provinces into departments.

Seven companies of the Thirty-fourth regiment were disbanded, after all pecuniary claims had been discharged. The closing effect was dramatic enough. General Hearsey made the men a spirited harangue, reminding them of their misdeeds, and giving some hints as to their future conduct which they would have done well to have laid to heart. Then came the parting; not without tears, it is said, on both sides. The sepoys stripped off their accoutrements, and were ferried across the river, bag and baggage, in Government steamers, and there sent about their business. In order to disprove the report that the Company had designs against their religion, they were informed that every facility would be afforded them for visiting Hindoo shrines of repute before they bent their steps towards their villages in Oude and Bahar.

Unfortunately for themselves, the men of the two regiments broken up at Barrackpore were bent upon doing a far less innocent service to the cause of their faith than that of feeing, out of the arrears of their pay, the priests of Juggernauth and Tripety. The most active and determined among their number deliberately proceeded to spread over the whole continent of India the tidings of the late occurrences, told with more than Oriental exaggeration, and received with more than Oriental credulity. No society of rich and civilized Christians, who ever undertook to preach the gospel of peace and goodwill, can have employed a more perfect system of organization than was adopted by these rascals, whose mission it was to preach the gospel of sedition and slaughter. By twos and threes, in various disguises, and on divers pretexts, they found their way to every native regiment in the three Presidencies. Wherever they went they related how the Queen of England had commanded that the Hindoos and Mussulmans of India should be made Christians, come what might; how the Governor-General, the Great Lord Sahib, had remonstrated with her, saying that he must first slay three hundred thousand holy and learned men of both religions; how the Queen had rejoined, "Let it then be done;" how the Great Lord Sahib had resolved to begin with the army, and had ordered the troops to bite cartridges smeared with the fat of cow and pig; how the sepoys at Barrackpore had bravely resisted the tyrannous and accursed mandate; how some had testified to the death, and some had suffered bonds and scourging, and all had been deprived of their rank and calling, and robbed of the pensions which they had earned by valour and fidelity and ancient service. Then their hearers were warned that a like fate was in store for all; that a strenuous and united effort could alone save their freedom and their religion; and that the hour was fast approaching when the Brahmins of the army must rule, or be for ever slaves and Christians. Sometimes, it was a couple of fakeers perched on an elephant; sometimes, a party of country-people on their way to the Ganges for their annual dip in the sacred stream; a gang of gipsies; a string of camel-drivers; or a troop of musicians escorting a celebrated nautch-dancer to her home in Cashmere, after a successful season in Bengal. However it might be, it invariably happened that, a few hours after the strangers had entered the station, the bazaar and the cantonments were in a ferment of gossip and conjecture; the sepoys at once grew sulky and idle; the Mahomedans of the town became insolent, and the Hindoos pert. The very domestic servants appeared to share the contagion; the cooks got drunk, and the grooms stupid; the water-carrier omitted to fill the bath, and the butler to ice the Moselle; the peon spent twice his usual number of hours in conveying a note to the next compound but one; while the bearers delighted to insult their mistress by smoking under her window, and coming bareheaded into her presence, whenever the Sahib and his horsewhip were well out of the way.

To us, who from the standing-point of complete and certain knowledge look back upon that March and April pregnant with a great and sombre future, it seems indeed miraculous that our countrymen then resident in India should not have entertained a suspicion of what those months would bring forth. It appears incredible that the officers should have lived their ordinary lives; hunting; dining; dancing; speculating on the probable height of the thermometer, and the possible chances of promotion; while within a few yards of their quarters the men were debating the programme of the coming mutiny; arranging who was to shoot down the adjutant, and who was to fire the thatch of the colonel's bungalow; discussing their hopes of assistance from Gwalior, Nepaul, and St. Petersburg. Can it be believed that morning after morning our countrymen looked down the row of dark faces and gleaming eyes, and never dreamed that in all that array, so fair and orderly to view, any heart beat with a loftier ambition than could be satisfied by a stripe or an epaulette; with a deadlier malice than might be gratified by the disappointment of some rival in the good opinion of the soubahdar? And yet, so it was. In spite of all that was said and written concerning the childlike docility of the affectionate sepoy, confidence and regard did not exist between the officer and the soldier. That the case had once been far otherwise was acknowledged on all sides, and the change was noted by military men of the old school with regret, qualified by a slight tincture of self-satisfaction. Young subalterns retorted that the ancient intimacy between superior and inferior was connected with the loose habits which disgraced

Anglo-Indian society in days gone by, when the soldier pandared to the vices of his officer, or, at any rate, was cognisant of their existence. Those who have studied cause and effect will be slow to accept the theory that this estrangement between the mess-room and the lines was in any great measure due to the increased morality of the Indian army.

The root of the evil lay in the withdrawal of officers from regimental duty for employment on the staff and in the civil posts; a custom so dear to all who bore the great and time-honoured names, which had been conspicuous in the Court of Directors and at the Calcutta Council-board as far back as the time of Barwell and Warren Hastings. And yet, though family interest received due consideration from those who dispensed the good things of the service, it was unfortunate for the efficiency of the Bengal Army that merit did not go without a share in the loaves and fishes. A young man on the threshold of his profession was recommended by his father, and entreated by his sisters, skilled like all Anglo-Indian ladies in the inscrutable mysteries of official success, to get away from his regiment as early as possible. The teaching of his relations was enforced by the golden words which dropped from the lips of the Chairman of the

Honourable Court, when, on the prize-day at Addiscombe, the lad stood forth blushing with modest pride, the Pollock medal in his hand, the sword of honour under his arm, and a pile of military histories, emblazoned with the arms of the academy, on the table before him. After his arrival on Indian shores, the same advice was impressed upon him by his uncle the Sudder judge, his cousin the junior secretary, and his school-chum the probationary-sub-assistant-commissary-general.

Rich were the prizes open to the aspiring cadet:—rich, but far from rare. There were the political agencies at the courts of Holkar and Scindiah; at the seats of the ancient and romantic dynasties of Rajpootana; at that European station whence, in dangerous proximity, an English resident still watches with anxious glance the intrigues and feuds which agitate the nest of Arab and Rohilla cut-throats, who protect and terrify the Nizam of Hyderabad. There were the Deputy Commissionerships of Oude and the Punjaub, whose occupants enjoyed a salary almost equal to that of a Collector in the more settled provinces, with a far greater share of power and responsibility. There were the posts in the branches of administration more exclusively military: the Departments of the Adjutant-General, the Quarter-Master-General, the Commissary-General, and the Judge-Advocate-General. Finally, there were the numerous irregular corps in the Deccan and on the North-west Frontier, to each of which were attached some three or four captains and subalterns, who fully appreciated the increase of their pay, and the excitement afforded by their critical and interesting duties. In short, appointments which enabled officers to make money and reputation faster than was possible for their less fortunate brethren who remained in the line, were so numerous that, after family claims had been satisfied, the surplus sufficed to absorb all the most promising and pushing youngsters in the Bengal Military Service.

It was not only that this system drained the army of individual zeal and talent. The professional spirit of the mass could not thrive under so blighting an influence. The officers present with the corps gradually ceased to take pride in the conscientious performance of their regimental duties; for their employment upon those duties was a standing proof that they were wanting in ability and high official connexion. It was very difficult to throw much energy and enthusiasm into such work as escorting treasure, guarding jails, inspecting the cross-belts and listening to the grievances of Sepoys, while a junior lieutenant in the same battalion was coercing refractory Rajahs, or scouring the border at the head of five hundred wild Pathan horsemen. What wonder if, under these circumstances, men became sick at heart? Disgusted at their position, they no longer made the welfare and happiness of their soldiers an all-important object: and neglect often deepened into aversion and contempt. The cadets, as was only too natural, caught the prevailing tone. Young men fresh from home are so shocked at the apparent deficiency in the Hindoo character of manliness, honesty, and self-respect, the qualities, which Englishmen most regard, that, so to speak, their better impulses are apt to render them careless of the rights and sentiments of the native population. "Do I not well to be insolent?" is a question asked daily, in a more or less logical form, by the majority of our countrymen in India. It requires a larger stock of philosophy than generally falls to the share of a lad of nineteen in a new red coat, with his first month's pay in the pocket, to realize the conviction that an imperial people, who undertake to govern others, must first govern themselves; and that it is the height of folly and cruelty to subjugate a hundred millions of men, and then abuse them because they are as God made them, and not as we would fain have them.

And so it came to pass that to be sent back to

head quarters was "a shame," regimental duty was "a bore," and the sepoys were "niggers." That hateful word, which is now constantly on the tongue of all Anglo-Indians, except civilians and missionaries, made its first appearance in decent society during the years which immediately preceded the mutiny. The immorality of the term is only equalled by the absurdity. To call the inhabitants of Hindostan "niggers," is just as unreasonable as it would be for Austrian officials to designate the subject populations of Venetia and Hungary by the collective title of "serfs." In the eyes of an English planter, or railway-contractor, there is no distinction of race or rank. Khoonds and Punjabees, Pariahs and Coolin Brahmins, bazaar-porters and Rajahs with a rent-roll of half a million, and a genealogy longer than that of Howards and Stanleys, are "niggers" alike, one and all, with the prefix of that profane epithet, which has been the Shibboleth of the Englishman abroad since the days of Philip de Comines. And so, in a Bengal corps, whether he were a grey-bearded Mahomedan soubahdar, the arbiter and exponent of regimental custom and tradition, or a high-caste Rajpoot, or a Sikh veteran marked with the scars of Sobraon; every man knew well that he was dubbed "nigger" by some slip of an ensign, who could not tell his right hand from his left in any Oriental language. In such an atmosphere how could mutual attachment exist, or mutual confidence? How could there not exist dislike and disaffection; the bitterness of injured pride, and of feelings misunderstood or heedlessly contemned?

There were usually some eight or nine officers actually doing duty with a battalion. A colonel and doctor, three or four captains and lieutenants, and three or four ensigns, formed what was in those days considered to be a very respectable complement. The other members of the mess were far away from head-quarters, inditing minutes at Calcutta, deciding suits in some distant non-regulation province, or tracking the course of the Nile through the deserts of Nubia. Such, however, was not universally the case. Here and there might be found a corps where the regimental tone, that unwritten and impalpable law, not passed in words, nor enforced by overt penalties, but obeyed in silence and without question, had ordained that staff employment was not a legitimate object of ambition. The officers plumed themselves upon keeping all together, and rising one with another in the ordinary course of promotion. They shot tigers, and speared hogs, and played whist and billiards, and meanwhile looked well after their companies, and contrived to know something about the private history and character of every man under their command. They voted it unfashionable to attempt the pass examination in Hindoostanee, success in which was an indispensable qualification for the staff: an ordeal familiarly known as the P. H.; that pair of consonants which are seldom far from the lips, and never out of the thoughts of the more aspiring subalterns of the Bengal army. And yet, averse as they were to grammars and dictionaries, these men spoke the vernacular languages with rare facility. But not even to such officers as these was breathed a syllable of that fearful secret, which England would have cheaply bought at the price of a million pounds for a single letter. Their soldiers entertained towards them a strong and genuine regard. It was not among the ranks which they commanded, that the spirit of sedition was born and nurtured. But in the day of wrath there was no distinction of person. When the baneful sirocco of mutiny, called by the imaginary Hindoo "the Devil's Wind," was abroad in the air, all milder influences yielded before its withering blast. The consciousness of the authority of the "Fouj ki Bheera," or "general will of the army," was to individual men, or regiments, almost irresistible. Some troopers in Fisher's Irregular Cavalry performed a signal act of gallantry at Lucknow, during the early days of the outbreak, for which they received a handsome reward. While waiting for their money in the verandah of the commissioner's house, they fell into conversation with certain of their fellow-villagers among his servants. "We like our colonel," said they, "and will "not allow him to be harmed; but if the whole "army turns, we must turn too." A week elapsed, and these men looked quietly on from their saddles, while Colonel Fisher was shot to death by a scoundrel in the lines of the military police. Then they threw aside all semblance of discipline, murdered the second in command, and shouted to the adjutant, who was a general favourite, to ride and begone, if he desired to spare them the pain of taking his life. At one large station the men were in open mutiny, and the officers had grouped themselves in front of the battalion, expecting every moment the fatal volley. They agreed, however, not to abandon hope until they had witnessed the effect produced by the presence of a captain of old standing in the service, who was apparently loved and trusted by the whole regiment, and especially by the grenadier company, to which he had been attached for many years. When his approach was announced, every eye turned towards his bungalow, which stood on the parade-ground, close to that flank where the grenadiers were stationed. He had not gone ten paces down the line before he fell dead, pierced by a bullet from the ranks of his own command.

In every regiment there was a Soubahdar major, or native colonel; and in every company a Soubahdar, who answered to a European captain, and a Jemmadar, who answered to a European subaltern. These were the commissioned officers, who wore swords and sashes, sat on a court-martial, and were saluted by the rank and file. They had one and all carried the musket, and there was no approach to friendship or even to familiar intercourse between them and their Saxon brethren in arms, who considered that, if they offered their soubahdar a chair during an interview on regimental business, quite enough had been done to mark the difference between a commissioned and a non-commissioned Sepoy. The sergeant and the corporal were represented by the havildah and the naick; titles which make the list of killed and wounded in Indian battles so bewildering to an English reader. Thus the Brahmin battalion had a complete outfit of Brahmin officers, and this it was that rendered the rebellious army so terribly efficient for evil. When every Englishman in a corps had been murdered or scared away, the organization none the less remained intact. The regiment was still a military machine finished in every part, compact, flexible, and capable as ever of a great and sustained exertion of strength and courage. This imperfect, but it is to be feared, tedious sketch of the composition of our native force, as it existed before the mutiny, may well be closed with the oracular words of Sir Charles Napier, the Cassandra of the old Bengal army: "Your young, "independent, wild cadet, will some day find the "Indian army taken out of his hands by the sou-"bahdars. They are steady, respectful, thoughtful, "stern-looking men; very zealous and military: the "sole instructors of all our soldiers."

The native town of Cawnpore contained sixty thousand inhabitants. It possessed no architectural beauties worthy to detain the traveller who, from those stately landing-places whence rise, tier above tier, the shrines and palaces of Benares, was hurrying on towards the ineffable glories of Agra. The most remarkable feature was a spacious boulevard, more than a hundred feet in breadth, called the Chandnee Choke, or street of silver. This name, common to the principal avenue in all the great cities of the north west, is a monument of the days of bad government, and a primitive commercial system. When banks were few and robbers bold and numerous, men preferred to have some part of their wealth about their persons, and in a portable form. A minister at a native court, however rich the harvest he might gather in during the fitful sunshine of royal favour, thought it well to keep a handful of diamonds and rubies in his girdle, as a provision against the day of disgrace and flight. Now, by the help of a bill of exchange and a single trusty agent, he may store up his gains in European stocks and debentures far out of reach of the greediest Nizam or the neediest Maharaja. In like manner, in old times, farmers and shopkeepers were wont to convert their superfluous rupees into ornaments of fantastic design for themselves, their wives, and their children. The unceasing flow of silver towards the east, which affords to political economists a constant sensation of pleasing bewilderment, is attributed in part to the fact that the Indian peasant still continues to invest his earnings on the wrists and ancles, the ears and noses of his family. Cawnpore was noted for the excellence and cheapness of all articles made of leather—saddlery, boots and shoes, bottle-covers, helmets, and cheeroot-cases. The manufacture was introduced by a colony of Chinese, the frugal and industrious Lombards of India, who settled in the Bazaar many years ago. A subaltern could buy a set of harness for his buggy at something under three pounds, and thoroughly equip his hack for half that sum: and, if he was not very particular about shape and colour, he might pick up a serviceable country-bred horse for a hundred rupee note.

The city had an evil reputation. Situated on the frontier of two distinct jurisdictions, it swarmed with rascals from Oude, on their way to seek obscurity in British territory, and rascals from our north-west provinces, on their way to seek impunity in the dominions of the Nawab. Oonao, the half-way house on the road which led from Cawnpore to Lucknow, gave a name to a class of murders of peculiar atrocity. On and about that highway were constantly found the dead bodies of travellers; sepoys, for the most part, returning to their villages with their savings and the voucher for their pension. In most cases a rope was drawn tightly round the neck, but the surgeons who conducted the inquests gradually came to be of opinion that the victims had been poisoned, or, at any rate, stupified, by being induced to smoke tobacco mixed with a noxious drug. The police exerted themselves in vain to obtain a clue to the mystery. Whenever a fresh officer of note was appointed to the district, the murderers made a point of presenting him with a "nuzzur," or "offering," in the shape of a larger than usual batch of corpses. The difficulty of detection was increased by an odious custom well known to all Anglo-Indian magistrates, which here flourished with extraordinary vigour. A malicious Hindoo will deliberately mangle the body of a person who has died from a natural cause, and fling it on the ground of some neighbour to whom the scamp may happen to bear a grudge. The unfortunate recipient finds himself involved in the consequences dreaded by the poor people in the Arabian Nights, when the hunchback was choked by a fishbone beneath their hospitable roof.

Bajee Rao, the Peishwa of Poonah, was the last monarch of one of those great Mahratta dynasties which long shared the sovereignty of the Central Highlands and the plunder of all Hindostan. So near a neighbour could not fail to be guilty of the "amount of "treachery," "faithlessness," and "bad "internal government," necessary to justify the annexation of his dominions. Urged by that painful necessity of taking what belongs to others, which is the inevitable result of all our dealings with Oriental powers, we dethroned Bajee Rao, confiscated his territories, and assigned him a residence at Bithoor, a small town twelve miles up the river from Cawnpore. Here he lived until his death in princely state, inasmuch as the Company always behaved with great generosity towards the princes whom it had plundered, after the manner of those open-handed thieves of fiction who fling back a couple of broad pieces to the traveller whom they have eased of his purse and watch. Bithoor was pleasantly situated upon the banks of the sacred stream, and was peculiarly suited to be the Saint Juste in which a retired Brahmin ruler might be content to end his days; for the spot was held in singular favour by Brahma. Here, after the creation had been accomplished, the deity had sacrificed a hecatomb, in token that his great work was good. The pin which fastened the divine sandal was picked up in after days, and inserted in the steps of the principal landing-place, where it may still be seen by the incredulous. At the full moon in November, prodigious crowds of pilgrims assemble from all parts of India to celebrate the present god with frankincense, and flowers, and barbarous music, and drunken frenzy. With his traditions and his greyhounds, his annuity of eighty thousand pounds, and his host of retainers, Bajee Rao led a splendid and not unhappy existence. But the old Mahratta had one sore trial. He had no son to inherit his possessions, perpetuate his name, and apply the torch to his funeral pyre: for the last office, so the inflexible law of his religion ordained, might be performed by none other than a filial hand. In this strait he had recourse to adoption, a ceremony which, by Hindoo law, entitles the favoured person to all the rights and privileges of an heir born of the body. His choice fell upon an individual who, according to some, was the son of a Poonah corn-merchant, while others say that he was born in great poverty at a miserable village in the vicinity of Bombay. The name of this man was Seereek Dhoondoo Punth: but the execration of mankind has found his cluster of titles too long for use, and prefers the more familiar appellation of "the Nana."

Bajee Rao died in 1851, and the heir forthwith put in a demand for the continuance of the pension which the Company had granted to his adopted father.* The claim was disallowed, and the Nana,

* To give the Nana his due, we must not forget that his was no fancied grievance. We must read his story by the light thrown on Oriental customs and habits of thought by an Englishman imbued throughout his nature with the spirit of the East. Before the name of Nana Sahib was heard of in this country, Mr. Urquhart had already written as follows concerning the Hindoo system of adoption:

"It may well be imagined how incomprehensible was such a "system to western conquerors—what difficulties it occasioned them "when they sought to do right—what facilities it afforded them "when they intended to do wrong! It may well be imagined how, "in the one case and in the other, the heart of a whole people could "be sickened with disgust, or aroused in indignation, by acts which "presented to the dispassionate or conscientious observer or judge "at home no character of offence.

"Of this we have an instance in the case of the late Raja of "Sattara, the deprivation of whose property vitiated his adoption, "and consequently, according to his belief and that of his fellow-"countrymen, consigned his soul to eternal damnation.* The

* The "Raja of Sattara" is no other than Bajee Rao.

who at length began to despair of prevailing upon the Calcutta authorities, determined to go to the fountain-head, and accordingly despatched an agent to London. For this purpose he selected his confidential man of business, Azimoolah Khan, a clever adventurer who began life as kitmutgar, or footman, in an Anglo-Indian family. In spite of his disadvantages, he acquired a thorough acquaintance with the English and French languages. He sub-

"adopted son was placed in the same predicament, being cut off "from both stocks. This was the great wrong which he suffered; "which all India felt; which no man in England could comprehend; "and which, from the incompatibility of ideas, no one belonging to "the one country could render intelligible to the people of the other.

"Had this happened under a Hindu government, the case would "have been provided for. In the event of succession by the prince, "(for confiscation is wholly prohibited by their law,) he was bound to "appoint the proper officer to perform in his name the Sráddha, and "could only hold the property on that condition. No doubt under "the Mussulman system, as it always conformed to existing usages, "provision had been made for similar contingencies; an eastern "people could not be ignorant of usage, far less contemptuous of it; "and though Islam has put an end to the ancestral oblation, the "professors of that creed retained its impress in all their ideas, and "in many of their customs.

"I have not alluded to the merits of the case; but how much is "the character of the penalty aggravated in the mind of the people "of India, who know, if we do not, what England owes to the act "of this prince, and what had been his devotion to her. What "worse fate can England's foes experience? What is to be gained "by being her friend? That one Englishman may become surreptitiously rich, the fountain of justice is polluted, and an empire "endangered."

sequently became a pupil, and thence a teacher, in the Government School at Cawnpore; in which position he attracted the notice of the Nana. Azimoolah arrived in town during the height of the season of 1854, and was welcomed with open arms by that portion of society which makes no inquiries into the antecedents of an aspirant to its favour, provided he be not a fellow-countryman or Christian. According to the creed of this class, every Hindoo was necessarily a prince, just as every Maronite is a martyr, and every Pole a patriot. Azimoolah speedily became a lion, and obtained more than even a lion's share of the sweetest of all flattery. The ladies voted him charming. Handsome and witty, endowed with plenty of assurance and an apparent abundance of diamonds and Cashmere shawls, the ex-kitmutgar seemed as fine a gentleman as the prime minister of Nepaul, or the Maharaja of the Punjaub. On the first day of the great vengeance, when Havelock's forlorn hope came to Bithoor, grim and eager, straight from the brink of the fatal well, our soldiers discovered amongst the possessions of this scoundrel letters from more than one titled lady couched in terms of the most courteous friendship. An indiscretion for which a sneer would be too severe a punishment, at such a moment excited bitter and painful emotion.

Great as were the successes which the agent of the Nana gained on his own account in Mayfair, he was able to effect very little for his master in Leadenhall Street and Westminster. In the reports which he transmitted to Bithoor he attributed his failure to the bribes which the Board of Control and the Privy Council had eaten at the hands of the East Indian Company; an explanation which appeared satisfactory to the Maharaja. On his way home Azimoolah passed through Constantinople at the time when our fortune in the Crimea was at the lowest ebb. During the mid-gloom of that terrible winter there was much talk among those who did not love us concerning the decadence of England and the youthful vigour of the Russian power. Of such gossip the clever Asiatic collected an ample budget, in order to console his baffled employer with cheery vaticinations relating to the approaching downfall of the British rule

Although the Nana had failed in his attempt on the public purse, his wealth was still conspicuous even among the colossal incomes of Indian landholders. He had contrived to secure to himself the whole property of the ex-Peishwa, and strange stories were told about the means by which this end had been accomplished. The nephew of Bajee Rao started a claim for one half of his uncle's estate, which moiety he valued at more than three millions.

The suit was dismissed, and the plaintiff never ceased to affirm that "the palm of the judge had been "greased by the Nana:" but too much attention must not be paid to this declaration; for, whenever a native accuses the bench of corruption, he simply means that he has lost his case. It is certain that the Maharaja kept in confinement against their will the widows of his predecessor; for whose younger daughter he planned a marriage inconsistent with the rules and traditions of the family; an act of outrageous tyranny in the estimation of High Brahmins. He wedded the eldest sister to a husband whom she was never allowed to see; and, when her death occurred after no long interval, it was whispered about the neighbourhood that there had been very foul play in every sense of the word. Those fictitious tales of vice and atrocity, with which literary hacks of the vilest class feed the corrupt imaginations of their readers, too often find a parallel in the realities of a great oriental household. The doctrine of personal rights has no existence within the walls of a zenana. Nowhere was the mystery of iniquity deeper and darker than in the palace of Bithoor, which was indeed a worthy nest for such a vulture. There were rooms in that palace horribly unfit for any human eye, where both European and native artists had done their best to gratify a master who was willing to incur any expense for the completion of his loathsome picture-gallery.

In the apartments open to the inspection of English visitors there was nothing which could shock either modesty or humanity, though a Sahib of fastidious taste might take exception to the arrangement of the furniture and the decorations. The habits of an Oriental are so simple, his wants so few, that the most Anglified Hindoo gentleman can never acquire himself, and still less impart to his servants a thorough acquaintance with our complicated domestic appliances. There is something very droll in the sanctum occupied by the eldest son of a rich native family; where, by a display of Western art and civilization, "Young Bengal" excites the envy of his contemporaries, and scandalises those among his relatives who belong to the old school. A cast from an exquisite statuette of Thorwaldsen stands side by side with a gilt shepherdess, or Highlander, or other specimen of that vulgar ware which with us has long been banished from the farmhouse to the cottage. A copy of some Roman or Florentine Madonna hangs next to a coloured print of a ballet-dancer; while a proof signed by Holman Hunt or Millais is flanked by "Facing a Bullfinch" and "Swishing a Rasper" from the classical collection of Mr. Fores, of Piccadilly. Over a sideboard of carved oak has long ceased to tick a veneered clock, daubed with the representation of the Exchange at Philadelphia; and round the tent-table of some deceased or insolvent ensign are gathered half a dozen chairs which once graced the boudoir of a vice-regal dame. No Eastern Anglo-maniac possessed a more heterogeneous collection than the Nana, who, living far from Calcutta, the centre of exotic fashion, was reduced to content himself with whatever treasures might come into the market at casual up-country sales. A gentleman of some literary reputation, who was entertained by the Maharaja in days gone by, thus describes the Bithoor ménage:—"I sat down "to a table twenty feet long (it had originally "been the mess-table of a cavalry regiment) which "was covered with a damask table-cloth of Euro-"pean manufacture, but instead of a dinner napkin "there was a bed-room towel. The soup—for the "steward had everything ready—was served up in "a trifle-dish which had formed part of a dessert "service belonging to the Ninth Lancers—at all "events the arms of that regiment were upon it; "but the plate into which I ladled it with a broken "tea-cup was of the old willow pattern. The pilau "which followed the soup was served upon a huge "plated dish, but the plate from which I ate it was "of the very commonest description. The knife was "a bone-handled affair; the spoon and fork were "silver, and of Calcutta make. The plated side-"dishes, containing vegetables, were odd ones; one "was round, the other oval. The pudding was "brought in upon a soup-plate, of blue and gold "pattern, and the cheese was placed before me on "a glass dish belonging to a dessert service. The "cool claret I drank out of a richly cut champagne "glass, and the beer out of an American tumbler "of the very worst quality."

The Maharaja had a large and excellent stable of horses, elephants, and camels; a well-appointed kennel; and a menagerie of pigeons, falcons, peacocks, and apes, which would have done credit to any Oriental monarch, from the days of Solomon downwards. His armoury was stocked with weapons of every age and country, from a masterpiece of Purdey, to the bow and arrows used by the Hillmen of Orissa. His reception-rooms sparkled with mirrors and chandeliers that had come direct from Birmingham; and his equipages had stood within the twelvemonth in the warehouses of Longacre. He possessed a vast store of gold and silver plate; and his wardrobe overflowed with shawls and jewellery, which on gala days were regarded with longing eyes by the Cawnpore ladies. Nor did they lack frequent opportunities of contemplating the

Maharaja in his panoply of kincob and Cashmere scarfs, crowned with a tiara of pearls and diamonds, and girt with old Bajee Rao's sword of state, which report valued at three lacs of rupees. For the Nana seldom missed an occasion for giving a ball or a banquet in European style to the society of the station; although he would never accept an entertainment in return, because our Government, which refused to regard him as a royal personage, would not allow him the compliment of a salute. Nor did he treat his guests with the semi-barbarous discourtesy evinced by some native hosts, who pass the evening seated among a group of courtiers, scrutinizing the dancers through a lorgnette, and apparently regarding the whole proceeding as a ballet arranged for their individual amusement. The Maharaja mixed freely with the company; inquired after the health of the Major's lady; congratulated the judge on his rumoured promotion to the Sudder Court; joked the assistant magistrate about his last mishap in the hunting-field; and complimented the belle of the evening on the colour she had brought down from Simla. His wealth was abundant enough to allow of any vagaries of hospitality and personal extravagance, and does not seem to have been seriously impaired even by the expense entailed by a crowd of lazy myrmidons whom he kept about his person; a folly common to all high-born and opulent Hindoos. Every native landlord, who can induce his neighbours to dignify him with the title of Rajah, delights in flourishing about the country under the escort of a host of blackguards—the horsemen armed with lances and old cavalry swords, and mounted on raw-boned, long-tailed horses, smeared with coarse paint—the infantry straggling along under the weight of clubs, partizans, brass blunderbusses, and long matchlocks, of which the stock is studded with glass beads, and the muzzle shaped into the semblance of a dragon's mouth. The Nana kept several hundreds of these scamps in idleness and insolence. He provided them with four rupees a month, and a suit of clothes once a year; an allowance which they eked out by plundering the peasants for twenty miles round, and extorting an intermittent blackmail from the tradesmen of Cawnpore.

At the time of the mutiny the Nana was about thirty-six years of age. His complexion was sallow; his features strongly marked, and not unpleasing. Like all Mahrattas, both head and face were shaven clean. He was fat, with that unhealthy corpulence which marks the Eastern voluptuary. The circumstances under which a young Rajah comes to maturity leave him very scant chance of obtaining perfection, moral or physical. From his earliest years he is surrounded by flatterers and pandars. While still a child in the harem, it is the object of every one, beginning with his own mother, to obtain his ear by adulation, and by the freemasonry of corrupt discourse. During his boyhood he has no little peers on whom to exert his faculties for emulation and self-denial, and, when he has arrived at man's estate, he may look in vain for any object of honourable ambition amidst the dead level of national dependence. He never walks, save from his divan to his bath; never mounts one of the huge cream-coloured steeds, which on high feast-days amble behind his palanquin in melancholy cavalcade; never knows the sensation of honest fatigue and wholesome hunger. No whim ungratified; every propensity cherished and pampered; incapable of effort; incognizant of duty; he is vicious with deeper than Parisian immorality, and listless with more than Belgravian ennui. Long before the age at which a high-born Englishman makes his choice of Hercules between balls and blue-books, the effete sensuality of a Hindoo noble is reduced to seek gratification in the illicit charms of Indian hemp and French brandy. What wonder that in middle life he is flabby and gross beyond hope and compass; too feeble for manly exercise, too self-indulgent to practise a self-denying regimen? It is to be presumed that a long course of lentil diet and hill-climbing in Nepaul has by this time reduced that superfluous bulk which may yet grace a Cawnpore gallows.

The Maharaja of Bithoor exhibited a lively interest in the proceedings of our Government at home and abroad, in our history, our arts, our religion, and our customs; although he was entirely ignorant of our language. He subscribed to all the leading Anglo-Indian journals, which were translated to him daily by an individual who had been unlucky enough to exchange a situation on the East Indian Railroad for the post of English Professor in the household of the Nana. The Rajah played billiards admirably, while he was yet slim enough to bend over the table without inconvenience. He especially delighted in the game, because it afforded him an opportunity for mixing on familiar terms with the officers of the garrison. Nothing could exceed the cordiality which he constantly displayed in his intercourse with our countrymen. The persons in authority placed an implicit confidence in his friendliness and good faith, and the ensigns emphatically pronounced him a capital fellow. He had a nod or a kind word for every Sahib in the station; hunting-parties and jewellery for the men, and picnics and shawls for the ladies. If a subaltern's wife required change of air, the Rajah's carriage was at the service of the young couple, and the European apartments at Bithoor were put in order to receive them. If a civilian had overworked himself in court, he had but to speak the word, and the Rajah's elephants were sent on to the Oude jungles. But none the less did he never for an instant forget the grudge which he bore our nation. While his face was all smiles, in his heart of hearts he brooded over the judgment of the Company, and the wrong of his despised claim. From his hour of repulse to his hour of vengeance, his life was one long irony. Thenceforward his story would more fitly be told in the wild and mysterious rhythms of the old Greek drama than in sober English prose; for in truth that story finds no parallel, save in the ghastly tales which hang like a mist of blood round the accursed house of Pelops. The lads who, with his sapphires and rubies glistening on their fingers, sat laughing round his Thyestean table, had one and all been doomed to die by a warrant that admitted of no appeal. He had sworn that the injustice should be expiated by the blood of women who had never heard his grievance named; of babies who had been born years after the question of that grievance had passed into oblivion. The great crime of Cawnpore blackens the page of history with a far deeper stain than Sicilian Vespers, or September massacres; for this atrocious act was prompted, not by diseased and mistaken patriotism, nor by the madness of superstition, nor yet by incontrollable fear that knew not pity. The motives of the deed were as mean as the execution was cowardly and treacherous. Among the subordinate villains there might be some who were possessed by bigotry and class-hatred, but the chief of the gang was actuated by no higher impulses than ruffled pride and disappointed greed.

CHAPTER II.

THE OUTBREAK.

DURING the spring of 1857 the native society of Hindostan presented those remarkable phenomena which, in an Asiatic community, are the infallible symptoms of an approaching convulsion. The atmosphere was alive with rumours, of the nature peculiar to India ;—strange and inconsequent fragments of warning or prediction, which, with reverent credulity, are passed from mouth to mouth throughout a million homesteads. No one can tell whence the dim whisper first arose, or what it may portend ; it is received as a voice from heaven, and sent forward on its course without comment or delay ; for the Hindoo people, like the Greeks of ancient time, hold Rumour to be divine. Some of these unwritten oracles undoubtedly grew spontaneously from the talk of men, and were to be regarded merely as indications of the agitated and uneasy condition of the public mind ; but, beyond all question, some secret influence was at work to advertise, so to speak, the mutiny. The ringleaders of that gigantic conspiracy advisedly undertook to impress upon the world at large the idea that something was coming, the like of which had not been known before. Manifold and variously expressed as were the prevailing reports, all had one and the same tendency. With a thousand tongues, and in a thousand forms, they spoke of a great trial that awaited the national religions; a trial from which they were eventually to emerge unscathed and victorious. A prophecy had long been current, that the hundredth year from the battle of Plassey would witness the downfall of the English rule; and the hundredth year had arrived. A mandate had of late gone forth from the palace of Delhi, enjoining the Mahommedans at all their solemn gatherings to recite a song of lamentation, indited by the royal musician himself, which described in touching strains the humiliation of their race, and the degradation of their ancient faith, once triumphant from the Northern snows to the Southern strait, but now trodden under the foot of the infidel and the alien. In January, the peasants of Bengal were repeating to each other a sentence apparently devoid of meaning, "Sub lal hoga hi," "everything is to become red." Some referred this dubious announcement to the probable extension of our empire over the whole continent, when the scarlet coats of our soldiers would be seen at Hyderabad and Khatmandoo, in Cashmere and Travancore; while others hinted that there was something thicker than water, and of a deeper crimson than a British uniform. Side by side with like ambiguous sayings, were more plain-spoken assertions concerning cartridges smeared with lard, and flour mixed with the ground bones of cow and pig, and other treacherous devices by which the demon who swayed the sceptre of Hindostan, the impalpable but omnipotent Kumpani, aimed at the destruction of sect and caste, and the universal establishment of Christianity. . And, finally, during the early days of March, every hamlet in the Gangetic provinces received from its neighbour the innocent present of two chupatties, or bannocks of salt and dough, which form the staple food of the population. This far-famed token, the fiery cross of India, had no definite signification. It notified generally that men would do well to keep themselves prepared, for that something was in the air. In after days, one who had learned their effect by bitter experience, likened the chupatties to the cake of barley-bread which foreshadowed the destruction of the host of Midian. And so, from hand to hand, and from house to house, and from village to village, the mysterious symbol flew, and spread through the length and breadth of the land confusion and questioning, a wild terror, and a wilder hope. Truly, it may be said that, as in Judæa of old, there was distress of nations, and perplexity; men's hearts failing them for fear, and for looking after those things that were coming on the earth.

Meanwhile, at Cawnpore, people ate, and drank, and married, and gave in marriage, and led the ordinary life of an up-country station. The magistrate grumbled because the judge acquitted too large a per centage of his committals; and the collector pronounced himself ill-used because the revenue board would not allow him an additional lac of rupees for his pet embankment; and the subalterns complained that the police-magistrate did not permit them to impress men to act as beaters at less than the market rate of wages; and the captains by the aid of the mess-room army-list, made those intricate calculations which are the delight of military men and the despair of civilians; and the ladies, those, at least, on whom during the past cold season Fortune and Hymen had smiled, began to allow that the weather had grown too warm for dancing, though still eminently favourable for morning calls; and one talked of sending her children home; and another of going herself to the hills; and, towards the end of April, a party of disbanded Brahmins of the Nineteenth regiment came from the west, and spread through the Sepoy lines strange tales of greased cartridges, and gibbets, and midnight tumults, and officers cut down in the midst of the parade-ground.

Before the month of May was half over, the English residents at Cawnpore were beginning to be made uneasy by the disagreeable character of the intelligence from Agra. Something had happened at Meerut, and it was feared that something had happened at Delhi. Guns had been heard all the night of the tenth. European travellers from the north-west, whose arrival had been confidently expected, did not make their appearance. A party of the police had gone out to look for them, but met nobody except a young sepoy trotting down the road on a cavalry troop-horse, who refused to answer any questions. But in the meanwhile, by those secret channels through which in eastern regions bad news travels with more than proverbial celerity, it was well known in the bazaar that the Third Light Cavalry had turned upon their officers; that murder and arson had been the order of the day; that the vast native garrison of Delhi had risen to a man, and had butchered every Englishman on whom they could lay their hands; that mutiny had gotten to itself a nucleus and a stronghold in the capital of the Mogul.

These tidings caused great excitement throughout the cantonments, and, especially, in the lines of the Second Cavalry, to whose regiment the corps which had set the example of sedition stood next on the rolls of the Bengal army.

The officer in command of the Cawnpore division was Major-General Sir Hugh Wheeler, K.C.B. At the outbreak of the troubles, many of our most important stations were entrusted to the charge of men who had won their spurs at Seringapatam, and might well have been content to have closed their career at Mooltan. It was to our shame as a military nation that, during such a crisis, the fortunes of England too often depended on the anility of invalids who should have been comfortably telling their stories of the Mahratta war in the pump-rooms of Cheltenham and Buxton. History blushes to chide these veterans for shortcomings incidental to their age. It is hardly just to blame them for prating of Lord Lake, and whimpering about the unsoldierlike appearance which the troops presented without their stocks and with their sun-helmets, at a time when younger warriors would have been disarming, and blowing from guns, and securing treasure, and throwing up earthworks, and sending the women and children down the river to Calcutta. In his second half-century of Indian service, Sir

Hugh was among the oldest members of the old school of Bengal officers. He worshipped his sepoys; spoke their language like one of themselves; and, indeed, had testified to his predilection for the natives of Hindostan by the strongest proof which it is in the power of a man to give. Short and spare, he still rode and walked like a soldier; and appears to have been capable of as much exertion as could reasonably be expected from an Englishman who had spent beneath an Indian sun more than two-thirds of his seventy-five years. On the eighteenth of May, he despatched the following message to the seat of Government:

"All well at Cawnpore. Quiet, but excitement "continues among the people. The final advance "on Delhi will soon be made. The insurgents can "only be about 3,000 in number, and are said to "cling to the walls of Delhi, where they have put "up a puppet-king. I grudge the escape of one "of them. Calm and expert policy will soon re-"assure the public mind. The plague is, in truth, "stayed."

The reader need not be alarmed at the length of the telegraphic news from Cawnpore. There is but little more to come. For in truth the plague was very far from stayed. The soldiery knew their own strength, and were well inclined to turn the knowledge to profit. There were schoolmasters who might have taught them a lesson of quite another description: but it was a far cry to Barrackpore, and there was no Hearsay at hand. It happens that a native lawyer, Nanukchund by name, took the precaution to keep a full and faithful journal, from the fifteenth of May onwards. This man was bound to our interest by the indissoluble tie of a common fear. A personal enemy of the Nana, he was actually engaged in conducting the suit instituted by the nephew of Bajee Rao to establish his claim to the half of his uncle's estate. With genuine Hindoo sagacity, he foresaw the approaching struggle, and the ultimate triumph of the English power; and conjectured that a record of events compiled with accuracy, slightly tinged by a somewhat ostentatious loyalty, would certainly procure him credit, and, possibly, a comfortable official income. Two days before Sir Hugh made his cheerful report to the Governor-General, Nanukchund looked in on a friend employed at the Treasury, and there heard the native officers of the guard uttering traitorous language, while their men amused themselves by quarrelling with the townsfolk who went to the Treasury on business. They detained people who came out with money or stamp-papers, and would not release them till ordered to do so by the

Soubahdar. "It began to be evident," says this shrewd observer, "that nobody had any authority "but the Soubahdars and the sepoys."

At length the symptoms of the growing malady became too patent to be disregarded even by the most sanguine physician. It came to the ears of the General that the son of a trooper in the Second Cavalry had been boasting to his schoolfellows that he was in the secret of what his father's regiment intended to do for the good cause. And, about the same time, one Khan Mahomed, a sepoy of the Fifty-sixth, took upon himself to assert that on the fifth of the next month the native troops were to be deprived of their arms, assembled under the pretence of getting their pay, and then and there blown up from a mine constructed by the European officers in the intervals of billiards. This singularly unpleasant prophet seems to have been without honour in his own battalion. His comrades brought information to the adjutant, who gave himself no trouble about the matter, beyond telling them that the story was all a lie. Thereupon Khan Mohamed went to the cavalry lines, where he found an audience more ready to accept his tale. On this occasion he imported some squadrons of English troopers, who were to be equipped with the swords and horses of his hearers. The regiment was soon in a panic of rage and fear. It became necessary to take immediate measures. The incendiary was put in irons, and an urgent application for aid telegraphed to Lucknow. Sir Henry Lawrence was roused from his bed at midnight, and by break of day all the available post-carriages in the station were rolling along towards Cawnpore, crammed inside and out with English soldiers.

But, in an hour of evil omen, Sir Hugh bethought himself of invoking the assistance of a more dubious ally. The Nana had lately paid a visit to the capital of Oude, under pretence of seeing the lions of the place. The arrogance of his manner, and the discourtesy of his sudden and unannounced departure, had attracted the attention of Mr. Gubbins, the Financial Commissioner, who communicated to General Wheeler his suspicions, backed by the opinion of Sir Henry Lawrence. It may be that the fatal step was first suggested by the warning of wiser men. It may be that the idea had long been familiar to the mind of the infatuated veteran. At all events, the sole answer to the remonstrance from Lucknow was a message, dated the twenty-second of May, stating that "two guns, and three hundred men, "cavalry and infantry, furnished by the Maharaja of "Bithoor, came in this morning."

On their march to Cawnpore, these scoundrels furnished a striking proof of their discipline and good faith. Chimna Apa, a man of some property, who supplied the nephew of Bajee Rao with the means of carrying on his lawsuit, was driving out of town in the direction of Bithoor, when he unexpectedly came upon this formidable array, commanded by the rival litigant. Apa, like a sensible fellow, jumped off his conveyance, and ran into a neighbouring ravine. The Nana's people appropriated a valuable sword and five hundred rupees, which the fugitive had left behind in his haste, cudgelled the servants, and went off declaring that the master had better look to himself, as the British rule would only last a few days longer. This specimen of the services which these new protectors were likely to render to the cause of law and order was brought to the notice of the authorities; but they had gone too far to draw back. The Nana took up his quarters in the midst of the houses occupied by the civilians and their families; the Treasury, which contained upwards of a hundred thousand pounds, was put under the custody of his body-guard; and it was even proposed that the ladies and children should be placed in sanctuary in Bithoor palace.

There were some, however, who scrupled to entrust the honour of England and the lives of her daughters to the exclusive guardianship of a discontented Mahratta. At their instigation the General set to work in a dilatory spirit to provide an asylum where, if the worst should befall, we might shelter, for a while at least, the relics of our name and power. He does not appear to have thought of the magazine, which was admirably adapted for defence. A mud wall, four feet high, was thrown up round the buildings which composed the old dragoon hospital, and ten guns of various calibre were placed in position round the intrenchment, by which name the miserable contrivance was dignified. Orders were given to lay in supplies for twenty-five days. The stock of rice, butter, salt, tea, sugar, rum, beer, and preserved meats looked well enough on paper. But the master's eye, which in India is even more essential than elsewhere, was entirely wanting. The contractors behaved after their kind. Peas and flour formed the bulk of the supplies, and even these were ridiculously insufficient. The regimental officers, who had no very lively confidence in Sir Hugh as a caterer, sent in large contributions of liquor and hermetically-sealed tins from their mess-stores. The tangible results of a fortnight's labour and supervision, at a time when every hour was precious, and every day priceless, consisted in a few cart-loads of coarse native food, and a fence not high enough to keep out an active cow. Utterly inefficient as they were, the sight of these preparations had a most unfortunate influence upon the minds of the sepoys. The timid were seriously alarmed by the hostile attitude adopted by our countrymen. The bolder spirits rejoiced to witness so plain a confession of apprehension on the part of their officers, while the more honest and trustworthy among their number would say to each other: "The sahibs "have lost all confidence in us, and we shall never "get over it." Where there is a will, there is a way, even in such a strait. And where there is half a will, there is a way likewise; but it leads whither it is not good that brave men should go, to disaster and discomfiture, to bootless sacrifice and inglorious ruin. During these days Azimoolah, while walking with a lieutenant who had been a great favourite at Bithoor, pointed to the fortification which was then in progress, and said:—

"What do you call that place you are making out "in the plain?"

"I am sure I don't know," was the reply.

Azimoolah suggested that it should be called "The Fort of Despair." "No, no;" answered the Englishman, "we will call it the Fort of Victory:" an observation that was received by his companion with an air of incredulous assent, which he must have acquired in West End drawing-rooms.

And now ensued a period of ceaseless dread, of suspicion that never slumbered, of suspense hardly preferable to the most terrible certainty. The women and children spent the nights within the circuit of the intrenchment, while their husbands, with devotion that merited a better reward, pitched their tents among the sepoy huts, and so took what sleep they might. On the twentieth of May, flames broke out after dark in the lines of the First Native Infantry. In a moment the station was on the alert. Men hurried on their clothes, and clutched revolvers from under their pillows. Guns loaded with grape were trundled down to a preconcerted rendezvous. It was no easy matter to persuade people that so ill-timed a conflagration could be altogether accidental. The twenty-fourth of the month was the festival of the Eed; a season which Mahommedans celebrate with the blood of sheep and goats, though on this occasion there was serious cause to apprehend lest, in their religious enthusiasm, they should pant for nobler victims. Sir Hugh telegraphed to Lucknow his belief that nothing could avert a rising. The feast, however, passed off without any disturbance. The Mussulmans in our ranks paid their respects to their officers; acknowledged with apparent gratitude the customary present of a fat Patna sheep; and protested that, come what might, they would be faithful to their leaders:—a statement that was accepted for as much as it was worth. But these alternations of confidence and alarm gradually settled down into chronic gloom. On the return of the Queen's birthday the usual compliment was omitted, lest the natives should interpret the firing of the salute as a signal for revolt. Even military loyalty dared not do honour to our sovereign in a garrison that was still nominally her own. A sergeant's wife was making some purchases in the bazaar, when a man, whose martial gait and spruce appearance clearly proclaimed the sepoy in undress, accosted the poor woman in these words:—"Ah! "you will none of you come here much oftener; "you will not be alive another week." Our countrymen began to keep watch all night by turns, armed to the teeth. As on a burning ship, when the sea runs high, and the last boat has been swamped or dashed to pieces, the crew wait with clenched teeth till the fire has reached the magazine, and say, "Now it is coming;" or again, "Now;" so the Englishmen at Cawnpore, ignorant what each day might bring forth, certain only that the catastrophe was not remote, sat, pistol in hand, and expected the inevitable. Some families endeavoured to get down to Allahabad ere it was yet too late. But the roads swarmed with rebellious peasantry, and liberated jail-birds: the shallows in the river forbade all passage in this the eighth month of the annual drought; and escape was found to be impracticable. Whatever destiny might have in store was to be shared by all alike.

During the closing days of May, people were writing hard to catch the Home Mail: and they did well, for it was the last. Strange, beyond conception of poet strange and sad, must have been the contents of that Cawnpore mail-bag. Imagine Colonel Ewart seated at his desk in a tent surrounded by line behind line of huts and camp-fires, in and about which are swaggering hundreds of insolent, faithless mercenaries. Picture that scene, and then read: "I do not wish to write gloomily, " but there is no use in disguising the fact, that we " are in the utmost danger; and, as I have said, if " the troops do mutiny, my life must almost certainly be sacrificed; but I do not think they will " venture to attack the intrenched position which " is held by the European troops, so I hope in God " that my wife and child will be saved.

" And now, dear A——, farewell. If, under " God's providence, this be the last time I am to " write to you, I entreat you to forgive all I have ever

" done to trouble you, and to think kindly of me. I " know you will be everything a mother can be to my " boy. I cannot write to him this time, dear little " fellow. Kiss him for me. Kind love to my brothers."

So spoke the stout soldier, fearing not for himself, but for a wife who was worthy of the husband, as her own words show. " My dear child," she says, " is looking very delicate. My prayer is that she " may be spared much suffering. The bitterness of " death has been tasted by us many times during " the last fortnight, and, should the reality come, " I hope we may find strength to meet it with a " truly Christian courage. It is not hard to die " oneself, but to see a dear child suffer and perish, " that is the hard, the bitter trial, and the cup " which I must drink, should God not deem it fit " that it should pass from me. My companion, " Mrs. Hillersdon, is delightful. Poor young thing, " she has such a gentle spirit, so unmurmuring, so " desirous to meet the trial rightly, unselfish and " sweet in every way. She has two children, and " we feel that our duty to our little ones demands " that we should exert ourselves to keep up health " and spirits as much as possible." That is the temper with which the mothers of Englishmen should die, if die they must.

"Such nights of anxiety," she continues, "I would

" never have believed possible, and the days are full " of excitement. Another fortnight, we expect, will " decide our fate ; and, whatever it may be, I trust " we shall be able to bear it. If these are my last " words to you, you will remember them lovingly, " and always bear in mind that your affection and " the love we have ever had for each other is an " ingredient of comfort in these bitter times." Such was the tone of the letters which, thence and at that season, went forth to spread a terrible solicitude through many an English household. Very different from the tender confidences and innocent gossip, the reminiscences of sick leave and the anticipations of furlough, the directions to milliners and the inquiries about boarding-schools, which are the ordinary materials of the Home Correspondence from an Indian station.

Meanwhile, the Nana was in intimate communication with the ringleaders of the Second Cavalry. The black sheep of the regiment were wont to hold meetings at the quarters of a trooper named Shumshoodeen Khan, and of Teeka Sing, a Hindoo Soubahdar, who, by his audacity and energy, had gained an ascendancy among his colleagues. These gatherings were attended by Jwala Pershad, a hanger-on at Bithoor Palace, and Muddud Ali, who had lately resigned the service of the Maharaja and taken to horse-dealing, but who still used to visit his former master in the way of business. At length, Teeka Sing had the honour of an interview with the Nana himself, during which, according to the story current among his comrades, the Soubahdar spoke to this effect: "You have come to take "charge of the magazine and treasury of the English; "we all, Hindoos and Mahommedans, have united "for our religions, and the whole Bengal army has "become one in purpose. What do you say to it?" The Nana replied, "I, also, am at the disposal of "the army." This very essential question having been so frankly answered, arrangements were made for a final consultation. One June evening, after dusk, the Maharaja, accompanied by his brother Bala and the ubiquitous Azimoolah, repaired to a landing-place on the Ganges, whither his emissaries had conducted Teeka Sing and his associates. The whole party seated themselves in a boat, and talked earnestly for the space of two hours. They appear to have arrived at a satisfactory conclusion; for, next day, Shumshoodeen wetted his prospective honours at the house of Azeezun, a favourite courtesan of the Second Cavalry troopers. In his tipsy fondness he told the girl that in a day or two the Nana would be paramount, and promised to stuff her house with gold mohurs from roof to cellar.

The Maharaja endeavoured to conceal his movements by shifting his residence to and fro between Bithoor and the cantonments; but he was closely watched by the spies of those among his own countrymen who had reason to dread his elevation. If British authority were to perish, if the sepoys and their new ally were in power but for a single week, it would go ill indeed with all who had ever crossed the Nana in love, law, or speculation. And, especially, any who had concern in the great law-suit would do well to look to themselves, litigant, pay-master, witness, and counsel alike. As early as the twenty-sixth of May, the sharp-sighted advocate, whose diary has been already quoted, drew up an account of the embryo conspiracy, and sent it in the form of a petition to the magistrate of the Station; "Who," says Nanukchund, "gave no heed to my petition, and "got so vexed with me that I cannot describe his "anger. He said to me, 'You have all along been "'speaking ill of the Nana, and filing suits against "'him in the civil courts. I cannot pay attention to "'any representation from a person so hostile to the "'Nana.' I replied that those affairs had no connexion "with the present question, that the Nana had long "harboured enmity to the Government, and a great "number of rascals belonged to his party; that he "(the Magistrate) would remember my caution, and "that I had obtained certain intelligence, as the "men of the Nana's household communicated it to "Chimna Apa, my client. The Magistrate would "listen to nothing. In despair, I did nothing fur- "ther than keep a copy of the petition in my book. "It is a hopeless case. Let us see what will be the "end of all this neglect." A dramatist of ancient Greece would have attributed such obstinate blindness to the malice of some injured deity, misleading to their bane those whom he had marked for destruction. There is a Goddess of Delusion in the eternal order of things no less than in the Æschylean mythology.

The last mail had already left Cawnpore. At nine o'clock on the night of the third of June, went forth the last telegraphic message that ever reached the outer world. Thus it ran:—

"*Sir Hugh Wheeler to the Secretary to the* "*Government of India.*

"All the orders and proclamations have been "sent express, as the telegraph communication be- "tween this and Agra is obstructed.

"Sir Henry Lawrence having expressed some "uneasiness, I have just sent him by post car- "riages out of my small force two officers and "fifty men of Her Majesty's 84th Foot; convey- "ance for more not available. This leaves me "weak, but I trust to holding my own until more "Europeans arrive."

So it was. Prompted by a genuine sentiment of chivalry, Sir Hugh not only sent back the Lucknow reinforcement that had arrived during the previous week, but increased it by a detachment from his own scanty command. He doubtless considered that, at such a time, a loan of English bayonets should bear high interest. And it was well for these men that they were removed from the doomed garrison to a field where they might fight not without some prospect of life, some hope of victory. Those who were marked to remain and die were enough to do their country loss.

As in a frame predisposed to disease the slightest irregularity is productive of fatal results, so now at Cawnpore the smouldering fires of discontent and distrust were inflamed by an incident which at ordinary times would have passed almost without remark. There was resident at the station a cashiered subaltern whom it would be cruel to name; one of those miserable men who had sought relief from the mental vacuity and physical prostration of an Indian military life in the deadly solace of excess. This officer, whether in the wantonness of drink, or the horror of shattered nerves, fired a shot at a cavalry patrol who challenged him as he reeled out of his bungalow into the darkness. He missed his aim, as was natural under the circumstances; but the trooper lodged a complaint in the morning, and a court-martial was assembled which acquitted the Englishman, on the ground that he was intoxicated at the time, and that his musket had gone off under a mistake. The sepoys, familiar as they were with the brutality of low Europeans and the vagaries of military justice, would at a less critical season have expressed small surprise either at the outrage or the decision. But now their blood was up, and their pride awake, and they were not inclined to overrate the privileges of an Anglo-Saxon, or the sagacity of a military tribunal. The men of the Second Cavalry muttered angrily that possibly their own muskets might go off by mistake before very long, and this significant expression became proverbial throughout the whole native force. Additional point was given to the grim humour of the soldiery by the unwonted sight of the corpses of an English lady and gentleman, which, floating down the river from some distant scene of death, had turned aside into the canal that traversed the city of Cawnpore. Ganges was yet to bear many such dire burdens. Though wires had been cut, and mails burnt, and every road blockaded, these silent but unimpeachable messengers, in virtue of the safe-conduct granted to them alone, were long destined to carry from station to station the tidings of woe and dismay.

The end was not remote. That despair deferred, which had long made sick the hearts of our countrymen; that great fear which was their companion day and night, had now reached their consummation. On Thursday, the fourth of June: while far away on the banks of pleasant Thames, Eton was celebrating the birthday of her patron monarch, with recitations from Julius Cæsar, and copious libations of unwonted champagne: at Cawnpore the men of the Second Cavalry were sharpening sabres, and distributing ammunition, and secreting their families and their property in the back-slums of the native city. In the mid-darkness of the succeeding night, when men were in their first sleep, three reports of a pistol, and a sudden and brilliant conflagration, showed that the hour had arrived. Teeka Sing, who was on picket duty with his troop, set the example of sedition, which was speedily followed by the entire corps. Some ran to set alight the house of the English riding-master; some to make a bonfire of the horse-litter; others to secure the treasure-chest and the colours. These last were stoutly opposed by the old Soubahdar-major, or native Colonel, who was cut down at his post after a gallant resistance. Then the regiment, mounted and accoutred, drew up on the high road. A bugle sounded, and two horsemen left the ranks, and went towards the lines of the First Native Infantry, and there cried in a loud voice through the gloom: "Our Soubahdar-major "sends his compliments to the Soubahdar-major of "the First, and wishes to know the reason of this "delay, as the cavalry are drawn up on the road." Hereupon the sepoys, ignorant that the man in whose name they were invoked was at that moment lying senseless and bleeding in the quarter-guard as a punishment for his loyalty—ignorant of this, and perhaps not much caring—began to load their muskets, and hurry on their cross-belts, and pack up their valuables. Colonel Ewart was at once on the spot, and in vain endeavoured to recall his soldiers to their allegiance, saying to them in the Hindoostanee tongue: "My children! my children! this is not "your usual conduct. Do not so great a wicked-"ness!" But it was too late for argument or entreaty. The battalion turned out in a body, fraternized with the mutinous troopers, and marched off in their company towards Nawabgunge, the North-west suburb of Cawnpore, where lay the Treasury and the Magazine.

Meanwhile the alarm spread through the station. The Adjutants of the Fifty-third and Fifty-sixth regiments got their sepoys together on the parade-ground, and kept them under arms till the sun was well above the horizon. Then the Colonel of the Fifty-sixth marched his battalion down to the deserted lines of the Second Cavalry, collected and secured the horses and arms which had been left behind by the mutineers, and finally permitted his men to doff their uniforms and cook their breakfasts. The Major of the Fifty-third likewise dismissed his regiment, and at the same time summoned into the entrenchment all his native officers, commissioned and non-commissioned. At such a crisis it was singularly injudicious to leave the men to themselves, especially as in this corps the Soubahdars and Jemmadars were for the most part free from the taint of disaffection, and might have done much towards keeping the rank and file to their allegiance. During their absence a trooper of the Second Cavalry rode in among the huts with a message from the company of the Fifty-third which was posted at the Government Treasury, to the effect that the guard would allow no division of the spoil until their own regiment was on the spot to claim its share. Ere long four or five grenadiers of the Fifty-sixth were observed to steal across to the neighbouring lines, and soon after they were seen talking eagerly and in a low voice with a sergeant and private of the light company.

Presently these two men shouted out: "Glory be to "the great God! Gentlemen, prepare for action!" and a rush was made on the quarter-guard. The sergeant broke open the treasure-chest, and the private seized the colours. The native Captain who was in charge of the precious deposit stood his ground like a man; but he was fired at, hustled, and overpowered by numbers. In an instant all was uproar, confusion, and terror. The sergeant of the fourth company burst into tears, and ran to fetch the Adjutant; the soldiers of the fifth and light companies flung on their coats, loaded their muskets, and crammed their girdles with the regimental rupees; while the remainder of the corps came of their own accord on to the parade-ground with the intention of placing themselves under the command of their officers. Unfortunately at this moment Sir Hugh Wheeler, prompt with an ill-timed energy, and wary with a misplaced distrust, ordered the guns of the intrenchment to open fire upon the wavering multitude. At first the sepoys of the Fifty-third seemed unwilling to believe that their commander had adopted this cruel and uncourteous method of intimating to them that he dispensed with their services: but the third round proved too strong a test for their loyalty. They broke and fled along the main road: the greater part never stopping until they had joined the mutineers at Nawabgunge: though a considerable number preferred to conceal themselves in an adjacent ravine until such time as it should please Sir Hugh to allow them to come within gun-shot of their own officers.

So went the Fifty-third. The story of the revolt of the Fifty-ninth is told with characteristic Hindoo simplicity by Khoda Bux, a commissioned officer of that regiment. He says, "I was sleeping in my "house between twelve and one A.M., when Hossain "Bux, Havildar, Grenadier Company, came and "awoke me, and said, 'What? Are you not awake? "'There is a row in the cavalry lines, three reports "'of a pistol, and the Quarter-master Sergeant's bun- "'galow is on fire.' I was astonished, and ordered "the regiment to turn out, and went to give in- "formation to the Adjutant. He came out of his "tent, and went with me to parade, and asked if the "regiment was ready. I said, 'Yes, it is ready.' "He said, 'Where is it?' I said 'In front of the "'bells of arms.' He ordered them to form up in "front of the quarter-guard. I formed them up, "and made them ready. I received orders that, "if any cavalry man came, he was instantly to "be shot. In this way we passed the night with "our officers. No one took off his uniform. The "cavalry having mutinied went away to Delhi. In

" the morning the Adjutant ordered us to take off " our uniforms, and eat our dinners. Then the " guards were placed, and we took off our uniforms. " The colonel came to us, and asked what Naick was " on duty at the elephant sheds, as the cavalry and " First Native Infantry wanted four elephants, which " were under a guard of a Naick and four sepoys " of the regiment, and he was greatly pleased they " had refused to give them up, and that he was " so content with the Naick that he should make " him an Havildar. I said it was Gunga Deen, Naick, " First Company. The First Regiment mutinied " like the cavalry, and went away. After this the " Colonel said, 'Bhowany Singh, Soubahdar, has been " 'wounded by these mutineers. I will go and see " 'him." I and Annundeedeen, Havildar Major, " went with the Colonel to the Cavalry Hospital, and " saw Bhowany Singh, who was wounded. The " Colonel was very much pleased with him. The " Colonel then went to his bungalow, and I and " Annundeedeen went to our lines, and, having " taken off our uniforms, began to smoke; when " Chain Singh, Havildar, came and said, 'Jemmadar, " 'the regiment is turning out.' I asked by whose " orders, and why. He said, 'I don't know.' I " went outside, and saw that the Havildar was " dreadfully frightened, and was buttoning his coat.

"I went with him to my company, and saw some "of the men in the tent packing up their clothes, "and others throwing them away. I asked them "what was the matter, and why they were getting "ready. They said, 'The Fifty-third regiment is "'getting ready, and so are we.' I said 'Your "'regiment is the Fifty-sixth; what have you to "'do with the Fifty-third? It would be better for "'you first to shoot me, and then to do what you "'like afterwards.' Many of the men said, 'You "'are our senior officer; we will not kill you. Come "'with us.' I said, 'Very well; I will get ready, "'and come with you.' I went out of the tent "very slowly for about a hundred yards, and then "ran as fast as I could to the intrenchment, and "told the Colonel and Adjutant that the regiment "had mutinied. They said, 'Come with us, and "'we will see.' I said, 'Oh, gentlemen, all the "'regiment has mutinied, and are your enemies. It "'is not right for you to go to them.'"

While Khoda Bux was in search of his Colonel it happened that one of the round shots, fired with a view of frightening away the Sepoys of the Fifty-third, rolled among the camp-kitchens of the Fifty-sixth. Hereupon Gunga Rai, a grenadier of an excitable and suspicious temperament, called out that they were all going to be killed, and took to his heels in the direction of Nawabgunge, followed by the whole mob of his comrades.

And now the ship had struck the reef towards which she had long been drifting, and had gone to pieces in the twinkling of an eye. It only remained for the crew to provision the boats and knock together some sort of a raft, as in that hour of sudden and bewildering peril best they might. Our officers at once proceeded to gather up the relics of the native force. Some went the round of the huts, while others, by the aid of a bugler, ferretted out the men who had sought a hiding-place in the ravine. There were found in all some eighty soldiers whose sense of duty had been stronger than their fear of the English nine-pounders. During the rest of the day, these sepoys were employed in carting and conveying within the intrenchment the muskets, ammunition, and accoutrements which were lying about in the lines. Meanwhile many of our countrymen commenced preparations for instant flight. All that day a stream of luggage and furniture was passing to and fro between the European quarter and the principal landing-places. In that season of uncertainty and danger, natives who followed the calling of porters and carriers could not be procured in the bazaar, so the work had to be done by the domestic servants. A sense of comparative relief now began to prevail throughout the community. Our officers felt that the time had arrived when they might consult without dishonour the security of themselves and their families. Their occupation was gone; and it seemed very well that their lives had not gone likewise. The blow had fallen; and they survived. They knew the worst; and that worst was better than the best which they had foreseen. Their military pride had been hurt by the sight of their battalion running from them like a parcel of street-boys at the appearance of a policeman; but in the cowardice of the sepoys lay the salvation of the officers. Besides, not only was it extremely improbable that the mutineers would ever venture again within range of Sir Hugh's artillery, but there existed a powerful attraction to draw them in quite another direction. Delhi was the centre towards which gravitated all the wandering atoms of sedition. There the green flag of the prophet had been unfurled, and the ancient imperial faith was again dominant. There, on his ancestral throne, sat the descendant of Shah Jehan, *roi fainéant* no longer, but endowed with a lurid splendour of princely independence. There, with arms dyed to the elbows in European blood, mustered the heroes of the great outbreak—the men who had hated with the deepest hate, and dared with the most headlong and effectual daring. Thither, to swell the ranks of that Prætorian guard, swarmed from every corner of Northern India all who had reason to covet the ruin of England, or to dread her triumph. And thither, as our countrymen were well aware, the Cawnpore mutineers designed to go without delay. Under a firm impression that all instant risk was at an end, a considerable number of officers passed the night of the fifth July in their private residences without the circuit of the intrenchment. Confidence had succeeded to distrust, cheerful activity to sombre and passive expectation. The faces of the sepoys were turned towards far Delhi. On the way to Allahabad, by road or by river, there was nothing which could stop armed and determined men. Their professional feelings wounded, but their throats uncut and their honour untarnished, there was good hope that within a month they might be smoking their cheroots in the verandah of the United Service Club in safe and luxurious Calcutta.

But it was not so to be. The rebellion had already gotten to itself a chief, and the chief had matured for himself a policy. When the mutineers had arrived at Nawabgunge they were given to understand that the Nana was in the neighbourhood. Accordingly he was waited on by a deputation of native officers and troopers who addressed him in these words: "Maharaja, a kingdom awaits you if "you join our enterprise, but death if you side with "our enemies." The ready reply was, "What have "I to do with the British? I am altogether yours." The envoys then requested him to lead the troops to Delhi. He assented to their desire; and ended by placing his hand on the head of each of the party, and swearing fidelity to the national cause. Then the rebels returned to their comrades, and the business of spoliation began. The mutineers first marched in a body to the Treasury: the keeper of the keys was terrified into surrendering his charge: the doors were unlocked, and silver to the value of near a hundred thousand pounds sterling was distributed among the ranks of the four regiments. Then the concourse dispersed in search of plunder and mischief. Some broke open the jail, and turned loose upon society the concentrated rascality of one of the most rascally districts in our Eastern dominions. Others set fire to the magistrate's office and the Court House; and, in a fit of irrational malice, made a bonfire of all the Records, civil and criminal alike. Others again, after parading about with a flag hoisted upon the back of an elephant, vented their spite by cutting the cables of the bridge of boats, great part of which floated down the river. All European houses at the west end of the station were burned and sacked. An unhappy overseer of highways was fired upon, not without effect, and hunted along the road, the construction of which he had been engaged in superintending. When they had done as much damage as could be got into a single morning the mutineers packed their more valuable booty about their persons; filled a long caravan of carts with their property, their domestic gods, and their female relations of every degree; set forth on their adventurous journey; and, after a very easy afternoon's march, halted at Kullianpore, the first stage on the Delhi road.

But as soon as the deputation from the rebel army had left the presence of the Nana his most trusted advisers unanimously adjured him to give up the idea of accompanying the march on Delhi; and especially his âme damnée, Azimoolah, urged that if he allowed himself to be absorbed into the court of the Mogul he would lose all power and influence: that it would be far more politic to bring into subjection the country round Cawnpore, and so command all the avenues by which the English reinforcements could penetrate into the heart of the disaffected regions: that when once possessed of the keys of Delhi and the Punjaub he might bargain with the rebels for the captain-generalship of their armies, and the universal sovereignty of the north of India; and then, with twenty myriads of bayonets and sabres at his back, he might sweep down the valley of the Ganges, and wreak, once and for ever, his vengeance on the detested race; fight, on this its hundredth anniversary, a Plassey very different from the last; renew the Black Hole of Calcutta under happier auspices, and on a far more generous scale; and so teach those Christian dogs what it was to flout a Mahratta and cheat a Brahmin of royal blood. The eloquence of the ci-devant footman fired the Maharaja, who accordingly ordered his elephants and pushed on for Kullianpore, attended by his brothers Bala and Baba Bhut, and the indispensable Azimoolah. The ringleaders of the mutiny expressed their pleasure in being blessed once more with the light of his countenance, but displayed very little inclination to give up the idea of Delhi. On the contrary, they suggested that the Nana should stay behind at Cawnpore, and garrison the Magazine with his own retainers, while they themselves prosecuted their expedition towards the North West. To this Bala, a man of execrable temper, which, however, he appears to have been able to curb on occasion, replied that Sir Hugh Wheeler and his Europeans would make themselves very unpleasant to the defenders of the Magazine, and proposed that the Mutineers should first return and clear out the intrenchment and then go off to Delhi. At this point the Maharaja threw in a prospect of unlimited pillage and an offer of a gold anklet to each sepoy, which produced an instant and favourable effect upon his audience. The mutineers agreed to retrace their steps, and not leave the station until they had put all the English to the sword. As a pledge of their earnest intention to carry out his desires they unanimously saluted the Nana as their Rajah, and proceeded forthwith to choose leaders who should command them in the field. Soubahdar Teeka Sing, the prime mover of the revolt, was appointed chief of the cavalry, with the title of General. Jemmadar Dulgunjun Sing became Colonel of the Fifty-third, and Soubahdar Gunga Deen Colonel of the Fifty-sixth.

There is a certain significance in these names: for they indicate that, in the opinion, at any rate, of the mutineers themselves, the boldest and most active among the authors of the mutiny were not Mussulmans, but Hindoos. The belief that such was in fact the case is now very generally entertained by our most thoughtful and observant public servants: but that belief is singularly unpalatable to the mass of the Anglo-Indian community. It was the fashion at the time to attribute the outbreak to the machinations of the Mahomedan population. Those ambitious zealots (such was the creed of the day) had never forgiven us for ousting them from their ancient pre-eminence. It was said that the professors of a proselytizing faith would never be reconciled to Nazarene domination; that the professors of an aggressive faith would never brook that others than they should assert the lofty privileges of an imperial race. And so our countrymen contended that every follower of the prophet was at heart a rebel and a traitor, and, therefore, must necessarily be at the bottom of all the rebellion and treachery in the land. The habit of assuming that men who hold certain opinions must be bent upon a certain course of action, and the habit of using that assumption to justify our own injustice is, and always has been, peculiarly English. Our ancestors took it for granted that their Roman Catholic countrymen were haunted by an incessant longing to compass the death of their own sovereign, and insisted upon treating as fanatics and assassins honest north-country squires who desired to compass nothing except the death of a bitch-fox. Our grandfathers took it for granted that every radical was a Jacobin, and that every Jacobin slept upon thorns as long as clergymen kept their glebes, and marquises kept their heads. Our fathers, and, it is to be feared, not a few of our brothers, took it for granted that every Jew fixed his hopes exclusively upon the day when his venerable faith should again flourish in its pristine haunts, and regarded England as a place of pleasant but not unprofitable exile; and, as a fitting corollary to so plausible a proposition, we deduced the conviction that Baron Rothschild would sacrifice the prosperity of his constituency to the interests of the New Jerusalem.

In the year 1857, our passion for visiting upon people the crimes which we thought they were bound by their tenets to commit ran riot throughout the north of India. Our proverbial tendency to give a dog a bad name and hang him was most barbarously and literally exemplified in the case of the unfortunate Moslem. After the capture of Delhi, every member of a class of religious enthusiasts named Ghazees were hung, as it were, *ex-officio;* and it is to be feared that a vindictive and irresponsible judge, who plumed himself upon having a good eye for a Ghazee, sent to the gallows more than one individual, whose guilt consisted in looking as if he belonged to a sect which, probably, was hostile to our religion. It would have been equally humane and logical if the ministers of Queen Elizabeth had burned as a Jesuit every one who was bald on the crown of his head. The city of Patna, where the Mahomedan element was large and influential, was the favourite bugbear of the Calcutta alarmists. Happily for them, the officer in charge of that city shared their suspicions and prejudices, and afforded them inexpressible delight by discovering secret meetings, by intercepting treasonable correspondence, and by arresting leading bankers on the charge of harbouring mutineers. And yet, while tumult and massacre were rife in the great towns of Oude and the North-west, the disturbances in Patna were confined to one partial *emeute,* and one unpremeditated murder. At length the Governor of Bengal, tired of requesting to be informed why people had been executed in an irregular manner; sick of listening to the complaints of shopkeepers who were not allowed to leave their houses after nine at night, and disciples of Mahomedan professors whose studies were interrupted by the incarceration of their teachers, superseded the Commissioner, and appointed a successor, who at once gave his confidence to an able official of the Mahomedan persuasion. From that day forward Patna was as quiet as Madras. No act of fidelity or self-sacrifice could exempt a Mussulman from the hatred and distrust of a large section of Anglo-Indian society. Syed Azimoodeen, whom Lord William Bentinck had thought worthy of his friendship and esteem, was among the defenders of the house at Arrah. The besiegers had set a price on his head, and had offered to spare the lives of the little garrison if he and one other were surrendered to their vengeance. As a reward for his loyalty, he became for some months subsequently the popular theme of abuse in the Anglo-Saxon papers. "Is it, or is it not the fact," so writes a correspondent, "that Syed Azimoodeen "supplied the mutineers with information as to the "hiding-places of English fugitives? Is it, or is it "not the fact that Coer Sing gave particular injunc-"tions to the sepoys, that, when the house was "stormed, Syed Azimoodeen should be excepted "from the slaughter?" This production proved too strong for the digestion even of the constant reader of a Calcutta journal. A few days afterwards there appeared a communication inquiring whether it was or was not the fact that Coer Sing had given particular orders that the bullets fired against the house should not hit Azimoodeen, and that, when the mine exploded, he should be dropped on to a feather-bed placed in the middle of the compound. But who can wonder at any excess of folly and ferocity in a publication which could stoop to insert a letter recommending the rack for "respectable Mahome-"dans?" When there were some hopes that an overflow of the river would complete the desolation of our Gangetic provinces, an Englishman was found blasphemous enough to put these words on paper: "we accorded great favours to the rascally Mussul-

" mans, but the rains are acting so as to nullify all " our indulgences."

During the progress of the revolt, the apprehensions of our countrymen always became more intense at the approach of the great anniversaries of the Mahomedan religion. In the early summer, the festival of the Eed was to many an Anglo-Indian household a season of unspeakable anxiety, for men dreaded lest to themselves, as to the Egyptians in old time, the ceremony should prove a veritable Passover, solemnized by the death of their firstborn. Later in the year came the Mohurrum, the most august and touching of all Oriental rites. It is impossible even for a Christian and an European to look on without emotion when the insignia of the mighty dead are borne along,—the crimson standard of the brother who perished by the sword, and the green standard of the brother who perished by poison:—when, midst a forest of silver staves and silken banners, are led the chargers of the heroes; while behind streams along a dense multitude, beating their breasts, and reciting in sad cadence the immutable formula of lamentation. Though nigh twelve hundred years have passed since the tragedy was enacted, the unfeigned earnestness and melancholy of the mourners excite in the spectator sympathy far more acute than is accorded even to the funeral of a contemporary. In the year 1857, Englishmen sat booted and spurred, pistol in belt and saddle on horse; and listened, as the tramp of feet, mingled with the clapping of hands and the dull murmur of "Ah me, for Hosein! Ah me, for "Hassan!" died away in the distance. And yet the Eed and the Mohurrum passed without bloodshed; and men ceased to fear for their lives, and began to tremble for their cherished theory. And, in truth, it was just as probable that the Mahomedans of India should succeed in inciting to rebellion a hundred thousand Brahmin sepoys, by working upon their religious susceptibilities, as that the Orangemen of Ireland should organize and direct the Roman Catholic population in a crusade against the English Crown. However little may be the love lost between the rival creeds in the Emerald Isle, there is quite as little waste of that sentiment in the case of the rival superstitions of our Eastern dominions. On this question, so important when viewed with respect to the relations between ourselves and the class of our subjects most worthy of our consideration and regard, the eyes of our compatriots might have been opened at an early stage of the troubles, by the report of a Court of Inquiry, which sat upon the disturbance at Barrackpore. That court, "from the evidence before them, are of "opinion that the Sikhs and Mussulmans of the "Thirty-fourth Regiment of Native Infantry are "trustworthy soldiers of the State, but that the "Hindoos generally of that corps are not trust- "worthy." But there is a blindness which it is idle to foment with the application of common sense, or to couch with the incisive point of fact; the blindness of terror and rage, and vengeance seeking in the dark for a victim and a pretext.

At dawn on the morning of the sixth of June, Sir Hugh Wheeler received a letter, in which the Nana announced his intention of at once commencing the attack. Our officers were summoned within the intrenchment, where, for a fortnight past, the women and children had already been in sanctuary. The order was obeyed with soldier-like promptitude, intensified by the consciousness of imminent peril. It fared ill with those who had indulged in a fond anticipation that their next change of lodging would be to Allahabad and Calcutta. With no notice of quarter, or month, or week; with no valuation for fixtures, or inventory of furniture, they were called upon to shift to a residence held on short and uncertain tenure, and at a fearful rent. There was no time for packing, or even for selection. There was not leisure to snatch a parting cup of coffee, or a handful of cigars, or an armful of favourite books, or a pith-helmet that had been tested by many a long day's tiger-shooting under the blazing Indian sun. All possessions, however hardly earned and highly prized; all dear memorials of home and love; were to be alike abandoned to the coming foe. He who, in that close and burning night of the mid summer, had on his house-top courted a little air and sleep, might not stay to take anything out of his house. He who had been on some early service in the field might not return back to take his clothes. Few and happy were they who had secured a single change of raiment; and those who, in the hurry of the moment, had stayed to dress themselves from head to foot, were by comparison not unfortunate. Half-clad, unbreakfasted, confused, and breathless, our countrymen huddled like shipwrecked sea-farers into the precincts of the fatal earthwork, which they entered only to suffer, and left only to die.

For that fortification had been erected under evil auspices. As of Hiel the Bethelite, so it may be said of poor Sir Hugh, that he marked out the ground in his first-born, and set up the épaulement in the youngest of his household. A chief, whose military eye had not been dulled by age, would have discerned the rare capabilities for defence afforded by the magazine, which consisted of an immense walled inclosure, containing numerous buildings and an inexhaustible store of guns and ammunition. The position was watered, and at the same time protected in the rear, by the Ganges. The public offices and the treasury were in the immediate vicinity, so that the records and the money might have been placed in safety at the cost of a few hours' labour. The doors of the jail would have been commanded by our cannon, and at least one tributary to the flood of disorder pent within its bounds. The native government officials, who for the most part resided at Nawabgunge, might have remained in communication with the civil authorities within the fortress; and the garrison could have been readily supplied with provisions from the loyal villages in the neighbourhood, and, indeed, from the city itself; which, says our old friend Nanukchund, "was like a certain wife "who used to act up to the wishes of her husband, "because she feared him, and then could also "protect herself; but, when her husband died, she "found herself under other people's control, and "lived in licence." He further observes that "the "Sahibs did the reverse of wisdom. They made "the intrenchment far out in the plain and outside "the city, without reflecting that, in case of mutiny "breaking out, it would be surrounded by the "rebels on all four sides, who would be assisted "by the artillery of the Magazine, and the Government treasure so temptingly thrown in their way. "Thus, to illustrate the proverb, the Sahibs put "a sword into the enemy's hand, and thrust their "own heads forward."

Such was indeed the case. If the choice of the site for our place of refuge had been confided to Azimoolah and Teeka Sing, they could not have selected one more favourable for the attack. The Dragoon hospital stood in the centre of a vast open space, flat with the flatness of Bengal, on the south bank of the canal which separated the military quarter from the Native city, the bridge of boats, the civil station, and the magazine. The establishment consisted of two single-storied barracks surrounded by spacious verandahs; each intended to afford accommodation for a company of a hundred men. The building that was somewhat the larger of the two was thatched with straw, which circumstance alone rendered the position untenable. The other was roofed with concrete, a condition usually expressed by the word "pucka;" that ubiquitous adjective which is the essential ingredient of Anglo-Indian conversation. Both houses were constructed of thin brickwork, hardly proof against the rays of an Eastern sun, and far too frail to resist a twenty-four pound shot. The hospital was provided with a due modicum of cooking sheds and servants' huts; and in front of the thatched barrack was a well, protected by a slight parapet. By order of Sir Hugh these premises had been inclosed in a mud-wall of the shape of a rectangular parallelogram; four feet in height; three feet in thickness at the base; and twenty-four inches at the crest, which was, therefore pervious to a bullet from an Enfield rifle. The batteries were constructed by the very simple expedient of leaving an aperture of a size proportioned to the number of the guns: so that our artillerymen served their pieces, as in the field, with their persons entirely exposed to the fire of the enemy.

Behind those slender bulwarks was gathered a mixed and feeble company, to the full sum of a thousand souls. Of these, four hundred and sixty-five were men, of every age and profession. Their wives and grown daughters were about two hundred and eighty in number, and their little ones at least as many. All who were able to bear arms, twenty score by tale, were at once called together, and told off in batches under their respective officers. The north side of the intrenchment, facing the river, was strengthened by a poor little triangular outwork, which our garrison entitled "the Redan;" as if to cheer themselves, during their cruel and inglorious struggle, with a reminiscence of chivalrous European warfare. This important post was entrusted to Major Vibart, of the Second Cavalry, assisted by Captain Jenkins. At the north-eastern corner, Lieutenants Ashe and Sotheby superintended a battery of one twenty-four pounder howitzer and two nine-pounders. Captain Kempland had charge of the east curtain, while at the south-eastern angle stood three nine-pounder guns under the charge of Lieutenants Eckford, Burney, and Delafosse; of whom one was destined to show upon happier fields of battle how the soldiers of Cawnpore fought and bled. Next in order came the main-guard, held by Lieutenant Turnbull, and flanked by a tiny rifled piece carrying a three-pound ball, which was manned by a detachment under the orders of Major Prout. Towards the north, Lieutenants Dempster and Martin directed the working of three nine-pounders; and their next neighbour was Captain Whiting, who felt the Redan with his right, and thus closed the circuit of the defence. The general supervision of the artillery devolved upon Major Larkins; but that officer was incapacitated by illness from taking a very active part in the operations.

There was no time to be lost. While the commanders of the various posts were choosing their parties, and placing their sentries, and dispensing their share of the arms and ammunition, already the roar of great guns, and the clouds of black smoke rising fast and frequent in the north-west quarter, told them that the warning of the Nana was no empty menace. As when, during some great hurricane, such as of late passed o'er pale Calcutta, the tidal wave comes surging up the river, unlooked for and irresistible, leaving in its track desolation and ruin, the wrecks of ships and the corpses of men—so on that morning, over doomed Cawnpore, swept the returning flood of mutiny and misrule. At break of day the whole rebel array poured down the Delhi road in a compact body, with the Maharaja at their head, who had good reason to be proud of his following. It was a force which would have done credit to any Mahratta chief in the palmiest days of that redoubted race. There was an entire regiment of excellent cavalry, well-mounted and equipped. There was a detachment of gunners and drivers from the Oude Artillery, who had been despatched as a loan from Lucknow to Cawnpore, just in time to enable them to take part in the revolt. There were the Nana's own myrmidons, who made up by attachment to his cause what they wanted in military skill. Lastly, there were three fine battalions of Bengal sepoys, led by experienced sepoy officers, armed with English muskets, and trained by English discipline. When the mutineers arrived at the outskirts of the station, Teeka Sing, the General, postponing his private gain and malice to the public good, repaired at once to the magazine, and spent the morning in securing a fleet of thirty boats which lay beneath the walls, laden with shot, shell, and heavy cannon. The guns in serviceable order he sent off towards the intrenchment on carriages drawn by Government bullocks; and those which were not in condition for immediate use, he compelled the artificers of the establishment to brush up on the Government lathes. But the main body of the insurgents displayed no such foresight or self-control. They kept close order no longer, but spread themselves out to the right and left, and, robbing, burning, and murdering as they went, bore southwards over the civil quarter and the native city. Sir George Parker and a party of his friends, who, inobservant of the coming storm, were lingering over their last breakfast in his pleasant villa, had barely time to fly for their lives. Four office-clerks, who lived together in a shop on the banks of the canal, after a valiant resistance, were smoked out of their lodging, and slain as they fled. The troopers of the Second Cavalry galloped up and down the lanes of the black town, hunting for Englishmen; and the low-caste Mahomedans of the bazaar—the sword-polishers, the cotton-spinners, and the dealers in silver ornaments —joined eagerly in the chase. One European was run down and worried to death in a garden. Another, a gentleman advanced in age, had concealed himself in a hut near the posting-house, in company with his wife, his little daughter, and his son, a boy of sixteen years. The wretched family were tracked to their hiding-place, arrested, and dragged before the Nana, who ordered them for instant execution; and they were happy at least in this, that they died together, and without delay. Proclamation was made that every building in which shelter had been given to Europeans, Eurasians, or Christians of any extraction, should first be plundered, and then razed to the ground. This announcement provided the rebels with a pretext for breaking open and ransacking the dwellings of many respectable natives. Buddree Nath, the commissariat contractor, who was accused of secreting Lady Wheeler and her daughters, lost the savings of a lifetime in the course of a single hour. The scum of the city made the most of their period of licence, and, when any portable property came in their way, took good care not to inquire very closely into the creed of the owner. Among others, the King of Oude is supposed to have suffered a heavy loss. Forty thousand rupees belonging to a Hindoo merchant were taken from a cart which stood in the premises of the post-office, and removed into the most blackguard districts of the neighbourhood. A gang of cavalry soldiers went down the Street of Silver, the main thoroughfare of the town, beating in the doors of the cloth-merchants and money-changers, insulting the trembling tradesmen, and carrying off all the valuables on which they could lay their hands. Meanwhile, those mutineers whose religious spite overcame their desire for lucre, were deriving intense enjoyment from the occupation of cannonading the church. Another large company of Brahmin sepoys, whose orthodox indignation took a more practical turn, and could not content itself with the somewhat tame pastime of persecuting senseless brick and plaster, marched off to the Mahomedan quarter; bombarded the residence of the Nunhey Nawab, the most influential Mussulman noble of the vicinity; blew open the gates; smashed the glass-ware and the porcelain; appropriated the contents of the wardrobe and the plate-chest; and told the master of the house to consider himself a prisoner. They then proceeded to take into custody other leading gentlemen of the same persuasion, and returned to the Nana loaded with spoil, and followed by a line of sedan-chairs containing the persons of their captives.

As the morning advanced, the reports of the

musketry and the tumult of voices grew more and more distinct to the ears of our countrymen. Nearer and ever nearer rolled the flames of the blazing houses, and the white puffs which betokened the presence of artillery. At length, stung by a generous impatience, Lieutenant Ashe took out his guns to reconnoitre, accompanied by some five and twenty volunteers. The party had barely gone forward a quarter of a mile, when they caught sight of the rebel van, which had already passed the canal, and occupied in force the neighbourhood of the bridge. Our people returned faster than they went, and not all; for one, at least, Lieutenant Ashburner, was never again seen or heard of; and poor Mr. Murphy, of the East Indian Railway, brought back with him a wound, to which he succumbed before the day was out. He enjoyed the melancholy honour of being buried in a solitary coffin which had been found in a corner of the hospital; and shared with one other, a lady who died of fever, enviable in that she was the first, the privilege of being decently interred within the precincts of the intrenchment. There soon came to be scanty leisure for funeral rites. At ten o'clock the mutineers fired their first shot, from a nine-pounder gun, which they had brought down to the vacant lines of the First Infantry. The ball struck the crest of the mud wall, and glided over into the smaller barrack, where it broke the leg of an unhappy native footman, who breathed his last in the course of the afternoon. This terrible and unwonted visitor, the precursor of many, scared indoors a large assembly of ladies and children who were sitting and playing in and about the verandahs; and sent to their posts the fighting men, most of whom had now their earliest experience of the sensation produced by the whizzing rush of a round shot; an ominous sound, which, ere long, became familiar to them as the click of the billiard-ball to a marker, or the buzz of the tennis-ball to an *habitué* of Princes' Club.

And so the siege had begun. The first stroke had been played in that momentous contest, of which the stake was a thousand English lives; since nothing remained for our countrymen to protect save their bare existences and the empty shadow of the British rule. The first game had gone against us. The Nana had won the regiments; and the regiments had won their colours, their weapons, and their pay. Why needed they to grudge the losers their breath? Why, for a possession of no value, except to the owner, should they deliberately commence a hazardous and protracted game of double or quits? Power and authority, treasures and munitions, the sinews and the muscles of war, had alike passed over to the sepoys. What temptation was there to run the manifold public chances of battle, and incur the personal risk which none can avoid who bring angry Englishmen to bay, in order to destroy a handful of disheartened invalids and civilians; scarcely numerous enough to escort their women and children in safety to Allahabad through the perils of eddies, and quicksands, and bands of highwaymen recruited and emboldened in those months of general anarchy?

But it came to pass that their heart was hardened, and they would not let our people go. The ringleaders of the mutiny knew well that their position was one of utmost hazard. They had been too criminal to be forgiven, and too successful to be forgotten. Henceforward their aim was to implicate their comrades beyond the hope of pardon; to place between them and their former condition of life a gulf filled with English blood. And when the Nana exhorted his followers to slay and spare not, he spoke to willing ears; for between them and our countrymen there existed a degree of mutual distrust which could only end in mutual extermination. The minds of men were so agitated and disordered by anger and uneasiness, that the sole chance of life for either party lay in the utter destruction of the other. Already quarter was no longer given, and, indeed, could hardly be said to be worth the asking.

A European knew that, if one set of Pandies entertained any qualms of compassion or gratitude, the next squad who came across him would infallibly cut his throat; and a sepoy knew that, if his captors took the trouble to drag him about in their train for a few days, the magistrate at the first station on the road would have him hung before the officer in command of the party had emerged from the bath-room. This was no generous rivalry of national vigour and skill and prowess. Little of military science was here, and less of military courtesy. With clenched teeth and bated breath, the Brahmin and the Saxon closed for the death-grapple; well aware that, when once their fingers were on each other's throats, one only of the combatants would ever rise from the trampled sand.

As soon as the Rubicon of insurrection had been passed; as soon as the gauntlet of sedition had been thrown; the first care of the mutineers was to get rid of all who had been the witnesses of their guilt, and who might hereafter be the judges. No sepoy felt secure of his neck and plunder as long as one solitary Englishman remained on Indian soil; for our revolted mercenaries shared to the full that strange mixture of veneration, bewilderment, aversion, and terror, with which our Eastern subjects still regard that extraordinary people who, in the course of a single decade, expanded from a handful of clerks and factors to a galaxy of warriors and pro-consuls. It is hardly possible for a man brought up amidst European scenes and associations to realize the idea conceived of him and his countrymen by a thorough-bred Hindoo. On the one hand, the natives must acknowledge our vast superiority in the arts of war and rule. Our railways, and steamships, and Armstrong guns, are tangible facts which cannot be slighted. They must be perfectly alive to the knowledge that we have conquered them, and are governing them in a more systematic and downright manner than they have ever been governed before. But, on the other hand, many of our usages must appear in their eyes most debased and revolting. It is difficult to imagine the horror with which a punctilious and devout Brahmin cannot but regard a people who eat the flesh of cow and pig, and drink various sorts of strong liquors from morning till night. It is at least as hard for such a man to look up to us as his betters, morally and socially, as it would be for us to place among the most civilized nations of the word a population which was in the habit of dining on human flesh, and intoxicating itself daily with laudanum and salvolatile. The peculiar qualities which mark the Englishman are peculiarly distasteful to the Oriental, and are sure to be widely distorted when seen from his point of view. Our energy and earnestness appear oppressive and importunate to the languid, voluptuous aristocracy of the East. Our very honesty seems ostentatious and contemptible to the wily and tortuous Hindoo mind. That magnificent disregard of *les convenances*, which has rendered our countrymen so justly beloved by all the Continental nations, is inexplicable and hateful to a race who consider external pomp and reticent solemnity to be the necessary accompaniments of rank, worth, and power. Add the mysterious awe by which we are shrouded in the eyes of the native population, which very generally attributes to magic our uniform success in everything we take in hand, and you will have some notion of the picture presented to the Brahmin imagination by an indefatigable, public-spirited, plain-spoken, beer-drinking, cigar-smoking, tiger-shooting, public servant. We should not be far wrong if we were content to allow that we are regarded by the natives of Hindostan as a species of quaint and somewhat objectionable demons, with a rare aptitude for fighting and administration; foul and degraded in our habits, though with reference to those habits not to be judged by the same standard as ordinary men; not altogether malevolent, but entirely wayward and unaccountable; a race of demi-devils, neither quite human, nor quite supernatural; not wholly bad, yet far from perfectly beneficent; who have been settled down in the country by the will of fate, and seem very much inclined to stay there by our own. With this impression on his mind the Bengal sepoy desired with a nervous and morbid anxiety to get quit of the Sahibs by fair means or foul. He did not care to expose us to unnecessary misery and humiliation; to torture our men, or to outrage our women. His sole object was to see the last of us: to get done with us for good and for ever. Ignorant beyond conception of European geography and statistics, he had convinced himself that, if once the Anglo-Indians of every sex and age were killed off, from the Governor General to the serjeant-major's baby, there did not exist the wherewithal to replace them. And therefore he said in his heart: "Come, and let us destroy "them together. Let us cut them off from being a "nation, that their name may be no more in remem-"brance." He conceived that Great Britain had been drained dry of men to recruit the garrison of our Asiatic empire; that our home population consisted of nurses and children, of invalids who had left the East for a while in quest of health, and veterans who had retired to live at ease on their share of the treasures of Hindostan. He fancied that the tidings of a general massacre of our people would render our island a home of helpless mourners: he found that those tidings changed it into a nest of reckless and pitiless avengers. He believed our power to be a chimera, and he discovered it to be a hydra. He learned too late that he had digged a pit for himself, and had fallen into the ditch which he had made; that his mischief and his violent dealings had come down upon his own head: that Englishmen were many, and that, when the occasion served, their feet too were not slow to shed blood: that our soldiers could kill within the year more heathen than our missionaries had converted in the course of a century: that our social science talk about the sacredness of human life, and our May Meeting talk concerning our duty towards those benighted souls for whom Christ died, meant that we were to forgive most of those who had never injured us, plunder none but such as were worth robbing, and seldom hang an innocent Hindoo if we could catch a guilty one: that the great principles of mercy and justice and charity must cease to be eternally true until the injured pride of a mighty nation had been satisfied, its wrath glutted, and its sway restored.

But though apprehension and dislike had inspired the rebels with a determination to destroy every Englishman off the face of the land, had they no feeling of ruth for the sufferings and the fate of our women? Never in European warfare has the sword been deliberately pointed at a female breast; save during those rare seasons, indelible from memory and inexpiable by national remorse, when, after the mad carnage of a successful escalade, drunkenness and licence have ruled the hour. If the Nana knew the valour and strength of our officers too well to allow him to be merciful, how came it that he did not respect the weakness of our ladies? No one can rightlyread the history of the mutineers unless he constantly takes into account the wide and radical difference between the views held by Europeans and Asiatics with reference to the treatment and position of the weaker sex. We, who still live among the records and associations of chivalry, horrify Utilitarians and Positivists by persisting in regarding women as goddesses. The Hindoos, who allow their sisters and daughters few or no personal rights; the Mahomedans, who do not even allow them souls; cannot bring themselves to look upon them as better than playthings. The pride of a Mussulman servant is painfully wounded by a scolding from the mistress of the house, and he takes every opportunity of showing his contempt for her by various childish impertinences. Among the numberless symptoms of our national eccentricity, that which seems most extraordinary to a native is our submitting to be governed by a woman. And as a Hindoo fails to appreciate the social standing of an English lady, so it is to be feared that he gives her little credit for her domestic virtues. Her free and unrestrained life excites in his mind the most singular and unjust ideas. To see women walking in public, driving about in open carriages, dining, and talking, and dancing with men connected with them neither by blood nor marriage, never fails to produce upon him a false and unfortunate impression.* And therefore it happened that a sepoy corporal, whose estimate of an European lady was curiously compounded of contempt, disapprobation, and misconception, was little adapted to entertain those sentiments of knightly tenderness and devotion which Petrarch and Cowley have handed down to us from the days

* In "The Mirror of Indigo;" a vernacular drama which has gained for itself a niche in Indian history, and contributed a rather remarkable page to the Law Reports of the Calcutta tribunals; the following passage occurs in a conversation between two native women :—

Reboti. Moreover, the wife of the Indigo-planter, in order to make her husband's case strong, has sent a letter to the Magistrate, since it is said that the magistrate hears her words most attentively.

Adwie. I saw the lady. She has no shame at all. When the magistrate of the district (whose name occasions great terror) goes riding about through the village, the lady also rides on horseback with him. Riding about on a horse! Because the aunt of Kezi once laughed before the elder brother of her husband all people ridiculed her: while this was the magistrate of the district.

of Bayard and Henry of Navarre. In the eyes of such a man every Englishwoman was but the mother of an English child, and every English child was a sucking tyrant. The wolves, with their mates and whelps, had been hounded into their den, and now or never was the time to smoke them out, and knock on the head the whole of that formidable brood. And so, on the first Saturday of that June—these, bent on a wholesale butchery; those, prepared to play the man for their dear life, and for lives dearer still,—with widely different hope, but with equal resolution, on either side of the meagre rampart besiegers and besieged mustered for the battle.

CHAPTER III.

THE SIEGE.

THE intelligence of the revolt speedily travelled over all surrounding districts, and attracted to the spot the entire available blackguardism of the neighbourhood. The disloyal and insolvent landholders for thirty miles about called out their tenantry and retainers, and made the best of their way to Cawnpore. As when the redoubted Hebrew captain founded an Asylum in the cave of Adullam, so now unto the leaders of the mutiny gathered themselves every one that was in distress, and every one that was in debt, and every one that was discontented. Thus immutable is the constitution of Oriental society:—unchanged by thirty centuries; unchangeable, perchance, by thirty more. Some chieftains brought two hundred armed followers; others four hundred. One Rajah came with a tail of forty score: while Bhowany Sing, whom Nanukchund designates as "that old and notorious "scoundrel," marched into the rebel camp at the head of twelve hundred matchlockmen. No one seems to have entertained any doubt as to the final extinction of our sway. The old order of things had disappeared for ever, and it behoved any feudal leader who had ambition or necessities to be present and ready to assert himself ere the new order was definitely established. The Nana was first to seize the occasion by the forelock. A trusty adherent was sent to Bithoor with an escort of twenty horse to announce the commencement of the Mahratta rule. It was a terrible hour for the personal enemies of him who had assumed the prime authority. As soon as it became known that their master was in power, the idle ruffians who swarmed in his palace at once proceeded to gratify his spite and their own wanton cruelty. They forced the doors of Goordeen, who acted as agent to the widows of Bajee Rao, the late Peishwa; knocked down his house about his ears; slew his people; and ended by blowing him from the mouth of a cannon. They seized the attendants of Chimna Apa, who pulled the strings of the law-suit brought against the Maharaja by his cousin; loaded them with chains; and informed them that they were to be put to death as soon as the captors could find leisure to cut off their hands and noses. Nanukchund, who had been the leading counsel in the case, was warned in time of the impending danger. He sent word to his juniors to provide for their own safety, and himself sought concealment in an unfurnished house belonging to one of his friends, whence he observed the progress of the insurrection with a penetration that was occasionally distorted by present terror and the anticipation of future advancement.

On the morning of Sunday, the seventh of June, a proclamation in two languages was issued at Cawnpore from the press of a schoolmaster, and distributed by his pupils, adjuring all true Hindoos and Mussulmans to unite in defence of their religions, and rally round the person of the Nana. Neither Mussulmans nor Hindoos were slow to obey the call. The residents of the Butcher's Ward forthwith set up the green standard, and were joined by the dregs of the population. Respectable Mahomedans at first held aloof; but next day the banner was removed to an open square, south of the canal, whither a large and influential body of the faithful repaired to do homage to the symbol of their religion. Azeezun, the Demoiselle Théroigne of the revolt, appeared on horseback amidst a group of her admirers, dressed in the uniform of her favoured regiment, armed with pistols, and decorated with medals. A priest of high consideration seated himself beneath the flag, rosary in hand, and endeavoured by prayer and meditation to ascertain whether the day was propitious for an attack upon the stronghold of the infidel. His piety, however, was cut short by a round-shot from Lieutenant Dempster's battery, which sent the assemblage of believers scuttling to the nearest cover: upon which the holy man bundled together his beads, tucked up his robes, and made off with a precipitation not altogether consistent with the doctrine of fatalism.

Meanwhile throughout and around the town were being gathered in the gleanings of that harvest of murder. A miserable family of the name of Mackintosh was discovered lurking under a bridge disguised in native clothes, their faces stained with pitiful want of skill in imitation of the Hindoo complexion. A road overseer was caught with his wife and children to the north of the station; and another person employed in the same department, who had found a temporary refuge beneath the roof of an individual whom he had formerly obliged with a contract, was now turned adrift, and taken by the bloodhounds who were scouring the city. To each and all of these capture was death, instant, inexorable. The Maharaja had despatched a party of sepoys to the residence of Mr. Edward Greenway, a man of considerable property, who had given shelter to an officer recently cashiered by court-martial. This gentleman now proved that in whatever military qualities he might have been deficient, courage, at least, was not amongst them; for he defended the threshold of his host until the last cartridge had been expended, and then walked in among the assailants, and bade them cut his throat: an invitation to which they eagerly responded. They then secured Mr. Greenway, his wife, his sister, and his little ones, and brought them as prisoners to the Nana; who ordered them into confinement with the expectation of obtaining a ransom, and the intention of killing them whether or not the money was forthcoming. He for one had no notion of permitting his avarice to clash with his barbarity.

As the excitement of tracking down and unearthing Englishmen began to languish on account of the growing scarcity of victims, the mutineers gradually betook themselves to the more serious business of the siege. During the whole of Saturday Teeka Sing had been hard at work in the Arsenal, mounting the great guns, and despatching them successively to the scene of action. As fast as each piece arrived, it was placed in position, and manned by a party of volunteers. By noon on Sunday the cordon of batteries was complete, and our intrenchment was raked by twenty-four pound shot from every quarter of the compass. Now became patent to the most inexperienced eye the fatal and irremediable defects of the site which our general had selected for the fortification. The Dragoon Hospital was entirely surrounded by large and solid buildings, at distances varying from three to eight hundred yards: buildings from which the assailants derived protection at least as effectual as that afforded to the garrison by their improvised defences. From roof and window poured a shower of bullets during the hours of daylight, while after dusk troops of sepoys hovered about within pistol-shot, and made night hideous with incessant volleys of musketry. Henceforward, there was but little sleep for our countrymen.

The annals of warfare contain no episode so painful as the story of this melancholy conflict. It is a story which needs not comment or embellishment. Whether related in the inornate language of official correspondence, or in the childish phraseology of Hindoo evidence, it moves to tears as surely as the pages in which the greatest of all historians tells, as only he can tell, the last agony of the Athenian host in Sicily. The sun never before looked on such a sight as a crowd of women and children cooped within a small space, and exposed during twenty days and nights to the concentrated fire of thousands of muskets and a score of heavy cannon. At first every projectile which struck the barracks was the signal for heartrending shrieks, and low wailing more heartrending yet: but, ere long, time and habit taught them to suffer and to fear in silence. Before the third evening every window and door had been beaten in. Next went the screens, the piled-up furniture, and the internal partitions: and soon shell and ball ranged at will through and through the naked rooms. Some ladies were slain outright by grape or round-shot. Others were struck down by bullets. Many were crushed beneath falling brickwork, or mutilated by the splinters which flew from shattered sash and panel. Happy were they whose age and sex called them to the front of the battle, and dispensed them from the spectacle of this passive carnage. Better to hear more distinctly the crackle of the sepoy musketry, and the groans of wounded wife and sister more faintly. If die they both must, such was the thought of more than one husband, it was well that duty bade them die apart.

Never did men fight with more signal determination against more fearful odds. Not at Fontenoy, not at Arcot, not at Albuera was British endurance so stubborn, or British valour so conspicuous. For, while the besiegers worked their guns under cover, the artillerymen of the besieged stood erect upon the bare plain. While the besiegers possessed unbounded store of huge mortars and battering-guns, the besieged had a few cannon too small for efficacious service in the field. While disease and the accidents of combat hourly diminished the numbers of those within, the ranks without were daily swollen by regiments of recent mutineers and fresh clans of rebels. But circumstances such as these are best adapted to exhibit the strange humour of the English warrior. With all that was most dear at their backs, and in front all that was most hateful, and, in their view, most contemptible, undaunted and not uncheerful our countrymen bore up the fray. From the very earliest days of the attack it became apparent that old Sir Hugh was unequal to the exposure and fatigue involved in the conduct of the struggle, and in the inspection and re-distribution of the posts, a labour rendered only too severe by the deadly fire of the enemy. In such a strait men act as acted those ten thousand Greeks, whose memory will never fade, when by the banks of far Euphrates their chief had been slain and their allies scattered to the winds. "Then," says Xenophon, "Clearchus "took the command, and the rest obeyed; not as "having chosen him by formal election, but because "they saw that he, and he alone, had the temper "of a general." The Clearchus of Cawnpore was Captain Moore, an officer in charge of the invalids of the thirty-second foot. He was a tall, fair, blue-eyed man, glowing with animation and easy Irish intrepidity. Wheresoever there was most pressing risk, and wheresoever there was direst wretchedness, his pleasant presence was seldom long wanting. Under the rampart; at the batteries; in some out-picket, where men were dropping like pheasants under a fearful cross-fire; in some corner of the hospital, to a brave heart more fearful still, where lay the mangled forms of those young and delicate beings whom war should always spare:—ever and everywhere was heard his sprightly voice speaking words of encouragement, of exhortation, of sympathy, and even of courteous gallantry. Wherever Moore had passed he left men something more courageous, and women something less unhappy. It is well when such leaders are at hand. It is ill when they are discovered and promoted too late to undo the evil that has been already done.

Across the south-western angle of the intrenchment ran a line of barracks which were still in course of erection. They each measured some two hundred feet in length, and were constructed of red brick, which had not as yet received that coat of white plaster that reduces all Anglo-Indian house decoration to a uniformity of colour diversified only by the various degrees of age and shabbiness. Of these, the buildings marked in the plan by the numbers 2, 3, and 4 were in close proximity to the corner of our fortification, the entire extent of which they commanded, inasmuch as their walls had been already completed to an elevation of forty feet. None of the others had been raised to a height of more than two or three yards from the level of the ground. The floors had not been laid, nor the bamboo poles removed, which, rudely spliced together, form the cheap but frail scaffolding of Hindoo architecture: and the ground both within and without, along the whole row, was thickly covered with piles of the materials used in the progress of the works. From the very first the sepoys possessed the northern half of the range: but they never succeeded in obtaining a hold on Barrack Number Four, which was defended by a party of civil engineers who had been employed upon the East Indian railroad. These gentlemen, over and above that indigenous aptitude for conflict common to all Englishmen of the upper classes, had acquired, during years spent in surveying, a trained sharpness of vision and a correct judgment of distance which rendered them peculiarly dangerous when placed behind the sights of an Enfield rifle. For three days these amateurs baffled every attempt of the enemy: but at the end of that period the assaults of the enemy became so fierce and frequent that they were not sorry to accept the services of a fighting man by profession. And so there came across to them from the redan Captain Jenkins, a valiant soldier, foredoomed to a death of anguish extraordinary even at such a time.

Whether the mutineers were aware of this introduction of the military element, or whether they already had learned to respect civilian skill and bravery, from this time forth they desisted from their efforts in that quarter, and turned their attention to the southernmost of the unfinished erections, which they proceeded to occupy in great force. Hereupon Lieutenant Glanville was posted with a small detachment in the adjoining barrack, which thenceforward was recognised by both parties as the key of our position. What the farm of Hougoumont was at Waterloo,—what the sand-bag battery was at Inkerman,—that was Barrack Number Two in the death-wrestle of Cawnpore. How furious was the strife,—how desperate the case of the little garrison, may be gathered from the fact that, though only sixteen in number, they had a surgeon to themselves, who never lacked ample employment. Glanville came under his hands, desperately wounded: and the vacancy thus caused was soon after supplied by Lieutenant Mowbray Thomson of the Fifty-sixth Native Infantry. This officer did his best to lose a life which destiny seemed determined to preserve in order that England might know how, in their exceeding distress, her sons had not been unmindful of her ancient honour. "My sixteen men," he writes, "consisted in the first instance of Ensign Henderson "of the Fifty-sixth Native Infantry, five or six of the "Madras fusiliers, two plate-layers from the railway "works, and some men of the Eighty-fourth Regi-"ment. The first instalment was soon disabled. "The Madras fusiliers were armed with the Enfield "rifle, and consequently they had to bear the brunt "of the attack. They were all shot at their posts. "Several of the Eighty-fourth also fell: but, in con-"sequence of the importance of the position, as soon "as a loss in my little corps was reported, Captain "Moore sent us over a reinforcement from the in-"trenchment. Sometimes a civilian, sometimes a "soldier came. The orders given us were, not to "surrender with our lives, and we did our best to "obey them."

Nothing contributed so much to check the spread of the rebellion of 1857 as the individual courage and pugnacity of our countrymen resident in the East. Civil and military alike, they were all skilled in the use of weapons, and cool in the presence of personal danger. Such a habit of body and mind they acquired both for policy and for pleasure. Every Anglo-Indian is well aware that he is one of an imperial race, holding its own in the midst of a subject population by dint of foresight and martial prowess. There were villages of evil reputation which on the day of assessment the collector preferred to visit on the back of the steadiest Arab in his stables, with a favourite hog spear carelessly balanced beside his right stirrup. There were notorious bits of road where the traveller felt more comfortable if he heard from time to time the lock of his revolver clanking against the soda-water bottles in the pocket of his palanquin. Never was there a better training-school for warfare than the Indian hunting-field. A man who has heard unmoved above his head the scream of a crippled elephant;—who behind his trusty Westley Richards has awaited, calm and collected, the last rush of a wounded tiger;—need not doubt what his behaviour may be in any possible emergency. He who, like more than one true sportsman, has hardly crawled away, bloody knife in hand, from the embrace of a dying bear:—who has kept at bay a forty-inch boar with the butt of his shivered lance;—will not be at a loss how to meet the charge of a mutinous trooper. The rebels found to their cost that the

Sahibs, like old stalkers of large game, were seldom foolhardy and never remiss :—that they were neither fluttered by peril nor over-excited by success :—that they rarely failed to make the most of what cover they could get, and still more rarely wasted a cartridge. Lieutenant Thomson contrived a sort of perch half-way up the wall of his barrack, in which he stationed a young officer, named Stirling, of high repute as a marksman, who soon proved that a rebel running home to his dinner was at least as easy to hit as an ibex bounding down the crags in an Himalayan valley, or a blue cow dodging in and out amidst the trunks of an Oude forest.

The whole of this range of buildings not included within our posts was literally alive with sepoys. They could distinctly be heard scampering along in troops, like rats behind an antique wainscot, chattering, yelling, or screaming under the emotion of the moment. From door, and window, and drain, and loophole they fired away at our stronghold, accompanying each shot with a taunt, conveying, in Oriental fashion, a random but painful statement concerning a remote ancestress of the person addressed. Ever and anon a fanatic, inspired by some vile drug, would issue forth into the open, brandishing his sword, in order to indulge himself in a dance of defiance; on all which occasions Lieutenant Stirling took good care that the performance should not meet with an encore. When the enemy became more than usually troublesome, the picket which was most hardly pressed would invite their neighbours to come over and assist them: and then the combined force of some thirty bayonets sallied forth to sweep the line of barracks, chasing the foe before them; killing the boldest and slowest of foot; knocking on the head such as were drunk or asleep; shooting down those who, in their anxiety to get a good aim, had ensconced themselves too high up to be able to climb down on so short a notice; and driving the rest out, and across the plain: at which point the gunners of the intrenchment took up the work, and plied the flying multitude with grape and canister. During one of the earliest of these sorties eleven mutineers were captured, and brought into the intrenchment. As no sentry could just then be spared from the front, they were placed under the charge of Bridget Widdowson, a stalwart dame, wife of a private of the Thirty-second Regiment. Secured by the very insufficient contrivance of a single rope, passed from wrist to wrist, they sat quietly on the ground like good school-children, while the matron walked up and down in front of the row, drawn sword in hand. After she had been relieved by a warder of the other sex, they all managed to slip off: and from that time forward it was generally understood that prisoners were to be left on the spot where they had been caught, with the jackal and the vulture as their jailers. A captive, as long as he remained in custody, was a consumer of precious food; and at once became the most dangerous of spies, if he succeeded in making his escape to the rebel lines with a report of our destitute condition.

On Friday, the twelfth, the insurgents made their first general assault upon our position. The cavalry, who on that day week had been the first in the career of sedition, were now with some difficulty prevailed upon to dismount and lead the way to glory; but after the loss of two of their number they concluded that enough had been done to sustain the credit of their branch of the service, and retired to console themselves for their repulse in the opium shops of the suburbs. The sepoy infantry next advanced to try their fortune, followed by all the rabble of the bazaars. They came on like men, but they went thither where there were men likewise. It was not thus that our rampart was to be won. Every English soldier had ready to his hand from three to ten muskets loaded with ball and slug: for there was a plentiful stock of small-arms within the fortification. The civilian held his thumb pressed tight upon the hammer of a pet smoothbore, with a charge of Number Four shot for close quarters snugly packed in the left-hand barrel. The officer in command of the battery was feeling for the leaden tip in each chamber of his revolver, as he gave his final order to take time and aim below the cross-belts. Our people were composed and confident. Sending quiet shots from behind a wall into the middle of a crowd was child's play compared with the daylong hazard of the crashing cannonade. After a short but bitter engagement the assailants withdrew, leaving on the field many of their comrades. Profiting by this harsh lesson they returned henceforward to their old tactics, and applied themselves to pound out the life of our garrison by an unremitting storm of ball, and bomb, and bullet.

Few, and ever fewer, in number; overmatched in weight of metal; ill-provided with ammunition, and protected by not an inch of cover, our artillerymen still sustained the hot debate. Lieutenant Ashe went through his work with a display of professional interest that would not have disgraced Sir William Armstrong during a trial match at Shoeburyness. After each round the besiegers saw with astonishment the zealous young Sahib leap on the heel of the discharged gun, spy-glass in hand, heedless of the missiles which were chirping round his ears. Unfortunately eight out of our ten pieces were nine-pounders, and the supply of nine-pound balls was soon expended. Reduced to load with shot a size too small, our officers could not secure accuracy in their practice. The gunners in our south-eastern battery had suffered much from a small piece which the sepoys had contrived to hoist into position amidst the *débris* of one among the half-built barracks. Lieutenant Delafosse, after despatching a number of six-pound balls in the direction of the embrasure without any perceptible result, at length resolved to bring the matter to a conclusion in one way or another. He rammed down three cannon-balls, filled up the chinks with grape, bade his men stand back, and fired off this portentous charge. To his surprise and delight his own gun did not burst, and nothing more was ever heard of the tiresome little antagonist. The same officer, somewhat later in the siege, was in the north-eastern battery when the carriage of a cannon was ignited by an unlucky accident. The situation was most critical, for the woodwork, which had stood beneath the June sun until it was dry as tinder, blazed furiously, and there was imminent risk of a general explosion of all the powder in the battery. The rebels discerned the opportunity, and concentrated their fire upon the spot where Delafosse, stretched at length on his back beneath the gun, was pulling down the burning splinters and scattering earth upon the flames. By the aid of two private soldiers he extinguished the conflagration, though eighteen pound and twenty-four pound shot were flying past at the rate of six a minute. With such examples before them, people of no class or calling were behindhand in acts of daring when the common safety was at stake. One Jacobi, a coachmaker by trade, and, to judge from his appellation, a person of mixed parentage, descried on the roof of the magazine a fire-ball, which he mistook for a live shell. Under this impression he clambered up, secured the object of his apprehension, and heaved it over the breastwork with a sigh of relief. There was many a Cross of Victoria earned in that camp, where victory was not, nor any reasonable chance of victory.

But the contest was too unequal to last long. By the end of the first week our fifty-nine artillerymen had all been killed and wounded at their posts. Of the officers to whom the charge of the guns had originally been entrusted, few had escaped unhurt from the hail of lead and iron, or the hardly less deadly rays of the Indian noon. Sunstroke had killed Major Prout. Captain Kempland was stretched on the floor of the barrack, dazed and powerless. His next in command, Lieutenant Eckford, a soldier of high promise and an accomplished gentleman, while snatching half an hour's repose under the roof of the verandah, was struck full on the heart by a cannon-ball. In the west quarter Dempster had been shot dead, and from the same battery Martin had been carried into the hospital with a bullet in his lungs. For a while volunteers endeavoured to supply the place of the trained gunners; and all was done that could be expected from bandsmen, and opium agents, and telegraph clerks firing six-pound balls out of damaged nine-pounders, while exposed without protection to a murderous discharge from siege guns and heavy mortars. There could be only one termination to such a business. Our only howitzer was knocked clean off its carriage. One cannon lost the entire muzzle. Some had their sides beaten in, some their vents blown out. At length our park of artillery was reduced to a couple of pieces, which were withdrawn under cover, loaded with grape, and reserved for the purpose of repelling an assault. And even of these the bore had been injured to such an extent that the canister could not be driven home. Our poor ladies, accordingly, in rivalry of those somewhat apocryphal Carthaginian dames who twisted their hair into bowstrings, gave up their stockings to supply the case for a novel but not unserviceable cartridge. Since the days when the shopmen of Londonderry loaded their quaint old ordnance with brick-bats wrapped in strips of gutter-piping, necessity has, perhaps, never been brought to bed of a more singular offspring.

As our reply waned more faint and ever fainter, the fire of the enemy continued to augment in volume, in rapidity, and in precision. The list of individual casualties mounted up in increasing ratio, and before long our misfortunes culminated in a wholesale disaster. Grave fears had been entertained for the security of the thatched barrack by every man who had the common sense to see that fire would burn straw. There were found some who, with admirable self-devotion, had scrambled on to that lead-bespattered slope, and essayed to cover with tiles and rubbish the inflammable material of the roof. On the eighth evening of the bombardment a lighted carcase settled among the rafters, and the whole building was speedily in a blaze. It happened most unfortunately that this barrack, as affording the better shelter and the less confined space, had been selected for the accommodation of our wounded and our sick. No effort was spared, no hazard shunned to rescue those who could not help themselves: but in spite of everything which could be tried two brave men perished a little sooner than their fellows, and by a rather more distressing fate. That was indeed a night of horror. The roar of the flames, lost every ten seconds in the peal of the rebel artillery; the whistle of the great shot; the shrieks of the sufferers, who forgot their pain in the helpless anticipation of a sudden and agonizing death; the groups of crying women and children huddled together in the ditch; the stream of men running to and fro between the houses, laden with sacks of provisions and kegs of ammunition, and private property of value, and living burdens more precious still; the guards crouching silent and watchful, finger on trigger, each at his station along the external wall; the forms of countless foes, revealed now and again by the fitful glare, prowling around through the outer gloom;—these sights and sounds combined to form a scene and a chorus which will be ever memorable to the trio of actors who lived through the catastrophe of that awful drama.

Captain Moore thought it well to give the enemy an early and a convincing proof that the spirit of our people was not broken by this great calamity. At the dead of the ensuing night he stole out from the intrenchment with fifty picked men at his heels in the direction of the chapel and the racket-court. Beginning from this point, the party hurried down the rebel lines under favour of the darkness, doing whatever rapid mischief was practicable. They surprised in untimely slumber some native gunners, who never waked again; spiked and rolled over several twenty-four pounders; gratified their feelings by blowing up a piece which had given them especial annoyance; and got back, carrying in their arms four of their number, and leaving another behind:—a service brilliant indeed, but barren of results: for the sepoys had only to resolve on the calibre that they preferred, and the number of cannon which they could conveniently work, and then take at will from the arsenal so inconsiderately placed at their disposal. This chivalrous act, one among many such, at that time passed without reward or public approval. When in a water-logged vessel men are toiling for their lives, who observes whether his neighbour does more or less at the pumps than he, provided all do their utmost? And when they have betaken themselves to the boats, and are rowing against time and famine, who cares which of the crew feathers most neatly, and which reaches forward with the straightest back? This was no set duel of civilized nations: no stately tournament, wherein the champions fight beneath the eyes of a friendly people, ready with their praise and sympathy; where wounds are bandaged with a ribbon, and self-sacrifice entitles the hero to a corner in our modern Walhalla, the columns of the daily press.

Rare were those who here had leisure or heart to take note, and they who survived to make report were rarer still. As during the ages before Atrides came on earth countless chieftains, unwept, unknown, sank into eternal oblivion because they lacked a sacred bard: so at Cawnpore many a soldier brave as Hodson of Hodson's Horse, nobly prodigal of himself as William Peel of the Shannon, dared, and fell, and was forgotten for want of a special correspondent. Correspondence there was, containing much earnest entreaty for a rescue and some unconscious eloquence; but too important matter had to be compressed into too small a compass to admit of panegyric or recommendation for honours and advancement. Several urgent missives found their way to Lucknow, rolled tightly into quills, sealed up, and hidden with mysterious art in and about the person of Hindoo messengers;—so curiously stowed away that in some cases it took almost as long to produce as to convey the note: though, if the rebels chanced to intercept the despatch, they generally abridged the operation by cutting in pieces the ill-starred courier. On the middle day of June the Lucknow surgeons extracted the following lines from the nose or ear of a native who had been fortunate and adroit enough to elude the manifold perils which beset those forty miles of road:—

"*From Sir H. M. Wheeler, K.C.B. to Martin Gubbins, Esq.*

"My dear Gubbins,

"We have been besieged since the sixth by the "Nana Sahib, joined by the whole of the native "troops, who broke out on the morning of the fourth. "The enemy have two 24-pounders, and several other "guns. We have only eight 9-pounders. The whole "Christian population is with us in a temporary in-"trenchment, and our defence has been noble and "wonderful, our loss heavy and cruel. We want aid, "aid, aid! Regards to Lawrence.

"Yours, &c.
H. M. Wheeler.

"14th June.
"Quarter-past 8, P.M.

"P.S.—If we had 200 men we could punish the "scoundrels and aid you."

The nature of the reply may be gathered from an acknowledgment which it elicited from Captain Moore. The anniversary seems to have inspired his pen. Brief and manly, cheerful and yet thoughtful, it is such a letter as an English officer should write on the eighteenth of June.

"*From Captain Moore, H.M.* 32*d Foot.*
"18*th June*, 10, P.M.

"Sir,

"By desire of Sir Hugh Wheeler, I have the "honour to acknowledge your letter of the 16th.

"Sir Hugh regrets you cannot send him the 200 "men, as he believes with their assistance we could "drive the insurgents from Cawnpore, and capture "their guns.

"Our troops, officers, and volunteers have acted "most nobly, and on several occasions a handful of "men have driven hundreds before them. Our loss "has been chiefly from the sun, and their heavy "guns. Our rations will last a fortnight, and we "are still well supplied with ammunition. Our guns "are serviceable. Report says that troops are ad- "vancing from Allahabad, and any assistance might "save our garrison. We, of course, are prepared to "hold out to the last. It is needless to mention "the names of those who have been killed, or died. "We trust in God, and if our exertions here assist "your safety, it will be a consolation to know that "our friends appreciate our devotion. Any news of "relief will cheer us.

"Yours, &c.
"J. Moore, Captain,
"32d Regiment.

"By order."

And now commenced to our brethren and sisters a period of unspeakable woe; the ante-chamber of ruin; the penultimate syllable of their dismal story. After the destruction of the thatched barrack, dearth of house-room forced two hundred of our women and children to spend twelve days of twice twelve hours without ceiling over head or flooring under foot. At night they lay on the bare ground, exposed to every noxious influence and exhalation that was abroad in the air; and in the morning they rose, those among them who rose at all, to endure, bare-headed often, and always roofless, the blazing fury of the tropical beams. The men off guard attempted to contrive for them a partial protection, by stretching canvass screens across a framework of muskets and poles; but these canopies were soon fired by the rebel shells, and the poor creatures were reduced to cower beneath the shelter of our earthwork, feebly chasing the shadow thrown by the sun as he rose and set. It is impossible for a home-staying Englishman to realize the true character of the great troubles in 1857, unless he constantly bears in mind that all which he reads was devised, and done, and endured beneath the vertical rays of an Eastern summer, and in a temperature varying from a hundred and twenty to a hundred and thirty-eight degrees in the shade. If there are any whose experience of heat is limited to a field-day at Wimbledon in the month of August, or to a tramp over Norfolk stubbles when the dogs are too thirsty to work, and the boy has carried off the beer to the wrong spinney, they will obtain a more just notion from a sad tale simply told than from pages of unscientific rhetoric.

This is what befell Mrs. M——, the wife of the surgeon at a certain station on the southern confines of the insurrection. "I heard," she says, "a number of shots fired, and, looking out, I saw my husband driving furiously from the mess-house, waving his whip. I ran to him, and, seeing a bearer with my child in his arms, I caught her up, and got into the buggy. At the mess-house we found all the officers assembled, together with sixty sepoys, who had remained faithful. We went off in one large party, amidst a general conflagration of our late homes. We reached the caravanserai at Chattapore the next morning, and thence started for Callinger. At this point our sepoy escort deserted us. We were fired upon by matchlock-men, and one officer was shot dead. We heard, likewise, that the people had risen at Callinger, so we returned, and walked back ten miles that day. M—— and I carried the child alternately. Presently Mrs. Smalley died of sunstroke. We had no food amongst us. An officer kindly lent us a "horse. We were very faint. The major died, and "was buried; also the serjeant-major, and some "women. The bandsmen left us on the nineteenth "of June. We were fired at again by matchlock-"men, and changed direction for Allahabad. Our "party consisted of nine gentlemen, two children, "the serjeant, and his wife. On the morning of "the twentieth, Captain Scott took Lottie on to his "horse. I was riding behind my husband, and she "was so crushed between us. She was two years "old on the first of the month. We were both weak "through want of food and the effect of the sun. "Lottie and I had no head-covering. M—— had "a sepoy's cap I found on the ground. Soon after "sunrise we were followed by villagers armed with "clubs and spears. One of them struck Captain "Scott's horse on the leg. He galloped off with "Lottie, and my poor husband never saw his child "again. We rode on several miles, keeping away "from villages, and then crossed the river. Our "thirst was extreme. M—— had dreadful cramps, "so that I had to hold him on the horse. I was "very uneasy about him. The day before I saw the "drummer's wife eating chupatties, and asked her "to give a piece to the child, which she did. I now "saw water in a ravine. The descent was steep, "and our only drinking-vessel was M——'s cap.

" Our horse got water, and I bathed my neck. I " had no stockings, and my feet were torn and " blistered. Two peasants came in sight, and we " were frightened, and rode off. The serjeant held " our horse, and M—— put me up and mounted. " I think he must have got suddenly faint, for I " fell, and he over me, on the road, when the horse " started off. Some time before he said, and Barber, " too, that he could not live many hours. I felt he " was dying before we came to the ravine. He told " me his wishes about his children and myself, and " took leave. My brain seemed burnt up. No " tears came. As soon as we fell, the serjeant let " go the horse, and it went off; so, that escape was " cut off. We sat down on the ground waiting for " death. Poor fellow! he was very weak; his thirst " was frightful, and I went to get him water. Some " villagers came, and took my rupees and watch. " I took off my wedding-ring, and twisted it in my " hair, and replaced the guard. I tore off the skirt " of my dress to bring water in, but it was no use, " for when I returned, my beloved's eyes were fixed, " and, though I called, and tried to restore him, and " poured water into his mouth, it only rattled in his " throat. He never spoke to me again. I held him " in my arms till he sank gradually down. I felt " frantic, but could not cry. I was alone. I bound "his head and face in my dress, for there was no "earth to bury him. The pain in my hands and "feet was dreadful. I went down to the ravine, "and sat in the water on a stone, hoping to get off "at night, and look for Lottie. When I came back "from the water, I saw that they had not taken "her little watch, chain, and seals, so I tied them "under my petticoat. In an hour, about thirty "villagers came, they dragged me out of the ravine, "and took off my jacket, and found the little chain. "They then dragged me to a village, mocking me "all the way, and wondering whom I was to belong "to. The whole population came to look at me. "I asked for a bedstead, and lay down outside the "door of a hut. They had dozens of cows, and yet "refused me milk. When night came, and the "village was quiet, some old woman brought me a "leaf-full of rice. I was too parched to eat, and "they gave me water. The morning after, a neigh-"bouring Rajah sent a palanquin and a horseman "to fetch me, who told me that a little child and "three sahibs had come to his master's house." And so the poor mother found her lost one, "greatly blistered," poor little darling. It is not for Europeans in India to pray that their flight be not in the winter.

These women had spent their girlhood in the pleasant watering-places and country homes of our island, surrounded by all of English comfort and refinement that Eastern wealth could buy. Their later years had slipped away amidst the secure plenty and languid ease of a European household in India. In spacious saloons, alive with swinging punkahs; where closed and darkened windows excluded the heated atmosphere, and produced a counterfeit night, while through a mat of wetted grass poured a stream of artificial air; with piles of ice, and troops of servants, and the magazines of the preceding month, and the sensation novels of the preceding season, monotonous, but not ungrateful, the even days flew by. Early married life has in Bengal peculiar charms. Planted down in some out-station, with no society save that of a casual road-surveyor or a distant planter, the world forgetting, and by the world remembered only at such times as there is talk concerning the chances of official promotion; the young pair have full leisure and a fair plea for indulging in that delicious habit of mutual selfishness which changes existence into a perpetual honeymoon, until that sorrowful epoch, when the children are too old to be kept any longer in the enervating climate of Hindostan; when the period arrives for writing to mothers-in-law, and sisters, and London bankers, and Brighton schoolmasters; when even the pale pet of four years old, who still answers to the name of baby, must go home at the beginning of next cold season, and ought to have gone before the end of last. Then begin the troubles of an Anglo-Indian family.

But though such ladies are often destined to endure the wearing anxiety of an unnatural separation, they never know what it is to experience a moment of physical privation. The services of menials, who make up by their number and obsequiousness what they lack in energy; the unwearied attention of an affectionate partner and friend shield them from distress and excuse them from exertion. To have slept four in a cabin on board an outward-bound steamer; to have passed a night in a palanquin, or a day at a posting-house where there was no tea, and only milk enough for the little ones; had hitherto appeared to the Cawnpore ladies the last conceivable extremity of destitution and discomfort. Now, the Red Sea in July would have been to them an Elysium, and a luncheon on Peninsular and Oriental ale and cheese a priceless banquet. By a sudden turn of fortune they had been placed beneath the heel of those beings whom they had ever regarded with that unconscious aversion and contempt of race which is never so intense as in a female breast. Those who were to them most dear and trusted, were absent from their side, save when a not unkindly bullet released the husband from his post, and restored him to the wife, if but to die. Accustomed to those frequent ablutions which, in England at least a duty, are in India a necessity, they had not a single spongeful of water for washing from the commencement to the close of the siege. They who, from childhood upwards, in the comprehensive and pretty phrase which ladies love, "had "had everything nice about them," were now herded together in fetid misery, where delicacy and modesty were hourly shocked, though never for a moment impaired. Unshod, unkempt, ragged and squalid, haggard and emaciated, parched with drought and faint with hunger, they sat waiting to hear that they were widows. Each morning deepened the hollow in the youngest cheek, and added a new furrow to the fairest brow. Want, exposure, and depression, speedily decimated that hapless company. In those regions, a hideous train of diseases stand always within call: fever, and apoplexy, and the fell scourge of cholera, and dysentery, plague more ghastly still. It was of fever that Miss Brightman died, worn out with nursing a boy who had been shot through his first red coat. Sir George Parker, the cantonment magistrate, complained of sickness and headache, accompanied by a sensation of drowsiness and oppression, which gradually deepened into insensibility, and thence into death. Such, too, was the fate of Colonel Williams of the Fifty-sixth Native Infantry, and of the Rev. Joseph Rooney, the Catholic priest, in spite of the devoted care of the Irish soldiery. The horrors which all shared and witnessed overset the balance of more than one highly-wrought organization. A missionary of the Propagation Society, as each day drew in, would bring his aged mother into the verandah for a breath of the evening. At length a musket-ball, shot, we may hope, at a venture, struck down the poor old lady with a painful wound. Her sufferings affected the reason of her son, and he died a raving maniac. Woe was it in those days unto them that were with child. There were infants born during the terrible three weeks; infants who had no future. There were women who underwent more than all the anguish of maternity, with less than none of the hope and joy. The medical stores had all been destroyed in the conflagration. There remained no drugs, and cordials, and opiates; no surgical instruments and appliances to cure, to alleviate, or to deaden. Perhaps it was as well that the absence of saws and tourniquets rendered impracticable the more critical operations: for here, as at Lucknow, it was found that, during the months of an Indian summer, within the circuit of a beleagured fortification the consequences of amputation were invariably fatal. Science could not regret that she was powerless, when her most successful effort would hardly have prolonged an agony.

But, besides the Nana, another foe, ruthless and pertinacious as he, had broken ground in front of our bulwarks. If our people had eaten as freely as they had fought, their provisions would have been consumed within the ten days: and human abstinence and endurance could not eke out the slender stock beyond the limit of some three weeks. Already the tins of preserved meats were empty, and the meal had fallen low in the casks; and many barrels had been tapped by the enemy's shot, and the rest were ominously light. The store of luxuries contributed from the regimental mess-rooms had been shared by all ranks alike. A noble equality and fraternity reigned through the little republic.

During that year our countrymen in India often debated, in a spirit by no means of idle speculation, whether a member of a blockaded force had a right to reserve food and drink for the exclusive support of himself, his family, and his intimate associates. That period was fruitful in questions of novel and momentous sophistry: questions to be found in no closet compilation of Ethics and Dialectics. Would a man be justified in shooting his wife if it was evident that she would otherwise fall alive into the power of the mutineers? Would a European flying for his life be guilty of murder if he blew out the brains of an innocent villager who had unwittingly viewed him as he broke cover, and who might therefore give information to the pursuers of blood? Morally guilty, that is to say: for it is difficult to conceive the circumstances under which a European would have been found legally guilty of the murder of a native during the year 1857. Might a colonel call out his men, and then mow them down with grape if it was certain that the regiment was on the eve of a revolt? Might he if it was almost certain? If it was most likely? If it was barely possible? These points were raised and determined off hand by stern casuists, who, with a thrust or a shot, broke off the horns of a dilemma which would have sorely tried the subtlety of a Whately.

Theories differed as to the lawfulness of a private store in time of siege: but the defenders of Cawnpore were right in their practice. For in the last extremity of war his own life is not more important to an individual than the life of his neighbour. A community of warriors striving by a fair and equitable division to extract from their hoard of victual all the collective material of strength and valour which it may contain, presents surely an aspect more philosophical, as well as more elevated, than an association of selfish and suspicious men, comrades only in name, resembling nothing so much as jurymen vying to starve each other out by help of concentrated meat lozenges. During the first few days the private soldiers fared sparingly, but, for them, poor fellows, delicately enough. "Here might "be seen one," says Captain Thompson, "trudging "away from the main-guard laden with a bottle of "champagne, a tin of preserved herrings, and a "pot of jam for his mess allowance. There would "be another with salmon, rum, and sweetmeats for "his inheritance." But very soon the dainties came to an end, and the allowance was scantier than ever. It was a favourite saying among the generation of military men, who in Europe kept unwilling holiday between the day of Waterloo and the day of Alma, that an Englishman fights best when he is full, and an Irishman when he is drunk. And yet nowhere in the chronicles of our army does there exist the record of doughtier deeds than were done in the June of '57 by Englishmen whose daily sustenance was a short gill of flour, and a short handful of split peas; by Irishmen who had no stimulant save their own bravery and a rare sip of putrid water.

Numerous attempts were made by friends without to mend the fare of the garrison, which were for the most part defeated by the vigilance of the sepoys. A baker of the town, who had been footman in an Anglo-Indian family, was detected smuggling a basket of bread into the intrenchment. The culprit perhaps fondly imagined that Azimoolah would have had mercy upon him in consideration of their common antecedents; but, if he entertained such an expectation he was doomed to disappointment. Much credit is due to Zuhooree, an official in the Department of Abkaree, a mysterious branch of the Revenue, the periodical occurrence of which in the Indian budget has vexed the souls of a succession of English financiers. This person put himself into communication with Major Larkins of the Artillery, and sent into the fortification, as opportunity served, most acceptable parcels of bread and eggs, with occasional bottles of milk and liquid butter. At length, on the night of the fourteenth of June, fifteen of his emissaries, among whom were two women, were caught as they endeavoured to glide through the cordon of sentries under cover of the flurry and consternation of our sortie. They were all blown from guns, but not before the captors had elicited from them the name of their employer. It was high time for Zuhooree to look to his safety.

Already his family had been imprisoned and maltreated on an unfounded charge of Christianity, and the rebel camp was a dangerous stage on which to play the part of good Obadiah. He accordingly left by stealth for Allahabad, bearing with him a letter of commendation from Major Larkins, attested by a gold ring set with five diamonds, which belonged to the wife of that officer.

Our people did what they could to help themselves. A fat bull, sacred to Brahma, finding nothing to eat in the streets, inasmuch as the corn-dealers had closed their booths for fear of the sepoys, came grazing along the plain until he arrived within range of our profane rifles. To shoot down this pampered monster, the fakeer of the animal world,* was no considerable feat for marks-

* These Brahminee bulls are the standing nuisance of Indian city life. They saunter along the public way, laying the shops under contribution, frightening the women, and disgusting the equestrians. To strike them is a high crime, social and religious. To kill them involves present death, and future damnation. At every turn may be seen some old fellow with a platterful of grain in his hand, alluring one of these creatures away from his store. The authorities of Calcutta at length took courage, collected all the Brahmin bulls, and put them in the carts of the Government scavengers. When Scindiah paid his last visit to the capital, he was much scandalized at so impious a regulation, and expressed his desire to buy up the animals, and restore them to their former condition of life. But he wisely refrained, when it was represented to him that, the moment his back was turned, the bulls would again find their way into the public service.

men who could hit a black buck running at a distance of a hundred and fifty paces. The difficulty consisted in the retrieving of the game, which lay full three hundred yards from our rampart, on a plain swept by the fire of the insurgents. Inside our place, however, courage was more plentiful than beef; and eight or ten volunteers professed themselves ready to follow Captain Moore, who was first at any feast which partook of the nature of a fray. The party provided themselves with a stout rope, which they fastened round the legs and horns of the beast, and dragged home their prize amidst a storm of cheers and bullets, alive but not unscathed.

In the banquet which ensued the defenders of the outposts had no part. On the other hand, they sometimes enjoyed luxuries of their own. A pariah dog, seduced by blandishments never before lavished upon one of his despised race, was tempted within the walls and thence into the camp-kettle of Barrack Number Two. Towards that building, as towards the lion's den in the fable, pointed the footsteps of every kind of quadruped, and from it none. An aged horse, whose younger days had been spent in the ranks of the Irregular Cavalry, was killed, roasted, and eaten up in two meals by the combined pickets. The head was converted into soup, and sent into the intrenchment for the use of some favoured ladies; no explanations being offered or demanded concerning the nature of the stock. Captain Halliday, of the Fifty-ninth Native Infantry, who had come across on a morning visit, begged a portion for his poor wife, who was lying in the hospital, sick unto death of the small-pox. On his way back, walking, it may be, too slowly for security through dread of spilling one precious drop, he fell never to rise again. In the midst of every action and every movement, during the hours of labour and the minutes of refreshment, unlooked for and unavoidable the mortal stroke descended.

For by day and night the fire never ceased; the round shot crashed and spun through the windows, raked the earthwork, and skipped about the open ground in every corner of our position. The bullets cut the air, and pattered on the wall like hail. The great shells rolled hissing along the floors and down the trenches, and, bursting, spread around them a circle of wrack, and mutilation, and promiscuous destruction. In their blind and merciless career those iron messengers spared neither old nor young, nor combatants nor sufferers, but flew ever onwards, inflicting superfluous wounds and unavailing destruction. A single bomb killed and maimed seven married women, who were seated in the ditch;

killed Jacobi, a watchmaker, namesake of the intrepid coachwright; killed too the cashiered officer whose drunken freak had done something to accelerate the outbreak. There were those who endured in one day a double or a treble bereavement; while in some families none remained to mourn. Colonel Williams died of apoplexy, and his wife, disfigured and tortured by a frightful hurt in the face, would fain have rejoined her husband. On the fifteenth of June Miss Mary Williams was stunned by a fall of the ceiling, and expired in the arms of a wounded sister, unconscious of her loving care. Two daughters survived—for a while. Mistress White was walking with a twin child at either shoulder, and her good man, a private of the Thirty-second, by her side. The same ball slew the father, broke both elbows of the mother, and severely injured one of the orphans. Captain Reynolds lost an arm and his life by a cannon-shot, and Mrs. Reynolds, whose wrist had been pierced by a musket ball, sank under fever and sorrow. A half-caste tradesman and his daughter, crouching behind an empty barrel, too late and together discovered that their shelter was inadequate. A son of Sir Hugh was reclining on a sofa, faint with recent loss of blood; one sister at his feet, and another, with both his parents, busied about his wants in different parts of the room; when an uninvited and a fatal guest entered the doorway, and left the lad a headless corpse. No less than three subalterns attached to the same regiment as young Wheeler lost their heads within the redan. Lieutenant Jervis of the Engineers was walking to his battery through a shower of lead, with a gait of calm grandeur, as if he were pacing the Eden Garden beneath the eye-glasses of Calcutta beauty. In vain his comrades raised their wonted shout of "Run, Jervis! Run!" He never returned to head-quarters. He never reached his post. A grape-shot passed through the body of Mr. Heberden, as he was handing some water to a lady. This gentleman, the most undaunted and unaffected of the brave and simple men of science employed upon the East Indian Railroad, lay on his face for a whole week without a murmur or a sigh, but not, we may well believe, without a tacit prayer for the relief which came at last. Mr. Hillersden, the magistrate of the station, was dashed in pieces by a twenty-four pound ball, while talking in the verandah to his wife, weak from an unseasonable confinement. A few days elapsed, and a shot, less cruel than some, displaced an avalanche of bricks which put an end to her short widowhood. But poverty of language does not permit to continue the list of horrors. In such a catalogue the synonyms of death are soon exhausted, and give place to a grim tautology.

"The frequency of our casualties," writes Captain Thomson, "may be understood by the history of one "hour. Lieutenant Prole had come to the main-"guard to see Armstrong, the adjutant of the Fifty-"third Native Infantry, who was unwell. While "engaged in conversation with the invalid, Prole "was struck by a musket-ball in the thigh, and fell "to the ground. I put his arm upon my shoulder, "and holding him round the waist, endeavoured to "hobble across the open to the barrack, in order that "he might obtain the attention of the surgeons there. "While thus employed a ball hit me under the right "shoulder-blade, and we fell to the ground together, "and were picked up by some privates, who dragged "us both back to the main-guard. While I was "lying on the ground, wofully sick from the wound, "Gilbert Bax, of the Forty-eighth Native Infantry, "came to condole with me, when a bullet pierced "his shoulder-blade, causing a wound from which he "died before the termination of the siege."

The youngest were the least to be pitied. In such a plight, ignorance of happier days was indeed bliss: —ignorance that there was a fair world without, where people laughed merrily, and slept soundly, and lived in the anticipations of enjoyment, not in the terrors of death. To the small children the present was very weary; but, reasoning in their way, they concluded that that present could not last much longer. It must come to an end like the tiresome journey up the great river, when the barge stuck fast in the mud, and mamma cried, and papa called the boatman by that Hindoostanee name which they themselves were always whipped for using. The restraint of our protracted incarceration was to them intolerably irksome. There was neither milk, nor pudding, nor jam, nor mangoes, nor any one to cuddle them, or sing to them, or listen to their romances, and their wishes, and their grievances. The gentleman who once was most kind to them would now come home from shooting all black, and grimy, and with a rough beard, and would stand at the table and eat quickly, and then run out again without taking any notice of them: and some day or other he would be carried in on a shutter, looking so pale and weak: and some day, perhaps, he never came back at all. When they asked a lady to scold the servants for getting them such a nasty breakfast, she only kissed them, and sobbed, and called them poor darlings. They sorely missed the fond and patient bearer, that willing playmate and much-enduring slave, whom Mrs. Sherwood's charming tale has rendered a household word in English schoolrooms. Left to their own tiny discretions, the dear creatures, unconscious of danger, would toddle out of the crowded barrack, and betake themselves to some primitive game which demanded no very elaborate provision of toys. What was it to them that every half minute a big black ball came hopping along amidst puffs of dust, or that little things which they could not see flew about humming louder than cock-chafers or bumble bees? With unexampled barbarity the sepoy sharpshooters forbore to respect these innocent groups. The peril, which some incurred through inexperience, was sought by others under the pressure of despondency. One unhappy woman, unable to support the burden of her existence, ran out from the shelter of the walls leading in each hand a child, and was dragged back, despite of herself, by a private soldier, who freely risked his life to preserve that which she was bent on losing. Not a few native domestics refused to desert their employers. Over-worked and under-thanked, with short-commons, and, if captured by the mutineers, a shorter shrift, they stayed on, not for the sake of their pittance of wages, but actuated solely by the ties of duty, gratitude, and attachment. Most of them were soon dismissed from service, for no fault, and with no warning. Three were killed by the explosion of a shell. Another was shot through the head as he was hurrying to the outposts intent upon serving his master's dinner before it had time to cool. An ayah, while dandling an infant, lost both her legs by the blow of a cannon-ball. That was in truth a dismal nursery.

Want of water was a constant and growing evil. At the best, a single well would have furnished a pitiably insufficient supply for a thousand mouths during an Indian June: and that well was from the first the favourite target of the hostile artillerymen. Guns were trained on to the exact spot; so that the appearance of a man with a pitcher by day, and by night the creaking of the tackle, was the signal for a shower of grape. The framework of beam and brick which protected the drawers was soon shot away. The machinery went next, and the buckets were thencceforward hauled up hand over hand from a depth of more than sixty feet. The Hindoo water-carriers were slain early in the siege, and their place was supplied by English soldiers, who nominally were paid at the rate of half a sovereign for every pail: though the brave fellows knew that, when a few days had gone by, it would matter little in whose hands the silver might happen to lie That water was purchased with blood and not with money. John Mackillop, of the Civil Service, veiling devotion under a jocose pretence of self-depreciation, told his friends that, though no fighting-man, he was willing to make himself useful where he could, and accordingly claimed to be appointed Captain of the Well. His tenure of the office was prolonged beyond his own expectation. It was not till a week had passed that he was laid dying on a bed in the hospital with a grape-shot in the groin. His last words expressed a desire that the lady to whom he had promised a drink should not be disappointed. For some days a few gallons were procured at a frightful hazard from a tank situated on the south-east of the intrenchment. Those who were conscious how dear a price was paid for every draught, thirsted in silence; but the babies kept up a perpetual moan more terrible to some stout souls than a ten minutes' hobble across the plain, a heavy skinful of water round the loins, and an ounce of lead in the ancle. Captain Thomson saw the children of his brother officers "sucking the pieces of old water-bags, "putting scraps of canvass and leather straps into "the mouth to try and get a single drop of moisture "upon their parched lips." The distress of our countrymen was enhanced by the plague of dust to which Cawnpore is subject on account of the character of the soil. A traveller who visited the station ten or twelve years before the mutiny, complains that he got no gratification out of a grand review from which he had promised himself much pleasure, because the show was throughout enveloped in clouds which totally concealed it from his eyes.

There was yet another well, which yielded nothing then: which will yield nothing till the sea, too, gives up her dead. It lay two hundred yards from the rampart, beneath the walls of the unfinished barracks. Thither at an hour varied nightly, for fear lest the rebel shot should swell the funeral, with stealthy step and scant attendance the slain of the previous day were borne. When morning broke the battle raged around that sepulchre. Overhead the cannon roared, and men charged to and fro. But those below rested none the less peacefully; their last cartridge bitten; their last achievement performed: their last pang of hunger and affliction undergone and already forgotten. There were deposited, within the space of three weeks, two hundred and fifty English people, a fourth by tale of the whole garrison. As in a season of trouble and lawlessness men bury away their jewels and their gold against the return of tranquillity and order: so the survivors committed to the faithful mould their dear treasures, trusting that time and the fortune of war would enable our country to honour her lost ones with a more solemn rite, and worthier tomb. Brief was the service whispered on the brink of that sad well in the sultry summer night. It was much, when they came to the grave, while the corpse was being made ready to be laid into the earth, if the priest then said: "In the midst of life we are in death. Of "whom may we seek for succour, but of thee, O "Lord, who for our sins art justly displeased?"

"Yet, O Lord God most holy, O Lord most "mighty, O holy and most merciful Saviour, deliver "us not into the bitter pains of eternal death."

And again, while the earth was being cast upon the body by some standing by, the priest might with the assent of all declare that it was of His great mercy that it had pleased Almighty God to take unto Himself the soul of the dear brother there departed.

Throughout the siege public worship, at stated hours, and of prescribed length and form, neither did nor could take place: but the spirit and the essential power of religion were not wanting. The station chaplain, Mr. Moncrieff, made it his concern that no one should die or suffer without the consolations of Christianity. And whenever he could be spared from the hospital, this shepherd of a pest-stricken flock, he would go the round of the batteries, and read a few Prayers and Psalms to the fighting-folk. With heads bent, and hands folded over the muzzles of their rifles; soothed, some by genuine piety, some by the associations of gladsome Christmas mornings and drowsy Sunday afternoons spent in the aisle of their village church; they listened calmly to the familiar words, those melancholy and resolute men. Each congregation was more thin than the last. There were always present some two or three to whom never again would grace be given to join with accord in the common supplication. The people of Cawnpore might say in the language used in a like strait by a brave and God-fearing soldier, the Greatheart of English History:—"Indeed we are at this time a very crazy company; "yet we live in His sight, and shall work the time "that is appointed us, and shall rest after that in "peace."

The condition of the besieged presented a complete contrast to the state of things on the other side of the wall. The numbers and the hopes of the insurgents mounted daily. Every morning some new Rajah or Nawab paraded through the suburbs in his palanquin bright with silver poles and silken hangings, preceded by drums, and standards, and led chargers, and followed by a stream of lances and matchlocks. Every evening a fresh eruption of scoundrelism surged up from the narrow crooked alleys and foul bazaars of the black city. Nor were the Hindoos and Mahomedans of the revolted battalions left without the satisfaction and encouragement of learning what great deeds had been wrought elsewhere by the champions of the united faiths. In the month of June the following document found its way from Delhi to Cawnpore:—

"*To all Hindoos and Mussulmans, Citizens and "Servants of Hindostan, the Officers of the "Army now at Delhi and Meerut send Greet- "ing.*

"It is well known that in these days all the Eng- "lish have entertained these evil designs—first to "destroy the religion of the whole Hindostani army, "and then to make the people Christians by com- "pulsion. Therefore we, solely on account of our "religion, have combined with the people, and have "not spared alive one infidel, and have re-established "the Delhi dynasty on these terms, and thus act in "obedience to orders and receive double pay. Hun- "dreds of guns and a large amount of treasure have "fallen into our hands; therefore it is fitting that "whoever of the soldiers and the people dislike "turning Christians should unite with one heart and "act courageously, not leaving the seed of these "infidels remaining. For any quantity of supplies "delivered to the army the owners are to take "the receipts of the officers; and they will receive "double payment from the Imperial Government. "Whoever shall in these times exhibit cowardice, or "credulously believe the promises of those impos- "tors, the English, shall very shortly be put to "shame for such a deed; and, rubbing the hands "of sorrow, shall receive for their fidelity the reward "the ruler of Lucknow got. It is further necessary "that all Hindoos and Mussulmans unite in this "struggle, and, following the instructions of some "respectable people, keep themselves secure, so that "good order may be maintained, the poorer classes "kept contented, and they themselves be exalted to "rank and dignity; also, that all, so far as it is "possible, copy this proclamation, and despatch it "everywhere, so that all true Hindoos and Mussul- "mans may be alive and watchful, and fix it in some "conspicuous place (but prudently, to avoid detec- "tion), and strike a blow with a sword before giving "circulation to it. The first pay of the soldiers of "Delhi will be thirty rupees per month for a trooper, "and ten rupees for a foot-man. Nearly one hundred "thousand men are ready; and there are thirteen "flags of the English regiments, and about fourteen "standards from different parts now raised aloft for "our religion, for God, and the conqueror; and it is "the intention of Cawnpore to root out the seed of "the Devil. This is what we of the army here wish."

This message was succeeded by a proclamation issued from the peacock throne, in which the Mogul promised a monthly wage of twelve rupees and a respectable estate to every sepoy who would rally to the banner of the ancient dynasty. He likewise ordained that no cows should thenceforward be killed throughout the land, and finished by denouncing a malediction upon the head of any one who should intercept the imperial courier. The wretch was doomed to eat pork and beef: and, as the messenger was eventually hanged by an officer of the Seventieth Infantry, it may be presumed that the curse has by this time been fulfilled to the letter.

The rebel cause was soon strengthened by a more valuable reinforcement than either the posse comitatus of the province, or the sympathy of the Delhi mutineers. At the village of Chowbeypore, on the Great North Road, had been stationed a detachment from the garrison of Lucknow, comprising a squadron of native cavalry, and two companies of sepoys, commanded by Captain Staples, four subalterns, and a European serjeant-major. At about two o'clock on the afternoon of Tuesday, the ninth of June, these gentlemen were roused from their luncheon by the sound of a bugle playing the "Assembly." Rushing forth, they demanded why so strange a liberty had been taken, and were told that it was by the orders of the Nana. At the mention of this ill-omened name our officers flung themselves on horseback, and rode for dear life, with all the disadvantages resulting from ignorance of the country and a bad start. That was a run in which the game was allowed no law. The Captain was shot down from his saddle, and cut in pieces where he lay. Two Englishmen took to the water like hunted stags, and there miserably perished. Two others were headed by a mob of villagers, and driven back among the sabres and pistols of their pursuers. Lieutenant Bolton alone, by dint of hard riding, escaped to Cawnpore with a bullet-hole in his cheek, if escape it may be called, which was only the postponement of death. After a chase of sixteen miles he reached the neighbourhood of the town at nightfall; passed unobserved through the lines of the mutineers; and camped out on the plain, waiting until dawn should disclose to him the outline of the intrenchment. Our sentries, astonished by the apparition of a cavalier riding at the earthwork through the twilight like a mounted Remus, fired, and struck his horse. No one, however, was surprised to find that even a crippled steed could clear those defences at a leap. The fugitive was heartily greeted by his countrymen, and entertained with such hospitality as their situation would admit. Wounded and exhausted as he was, he proved well worth his keep.

The troops who had revolted at Chowbeypore marched into Cawnpore, bringing with them three English heads in a basket, and taking up on their way a toll-keeper named Joseph Carter, and his wife; a young person, who was daily expecting her first baby. This offering, combined agreeably to his taste of the dead and the living, was mightily acceptable to the Nana. With fraternal kindness he made a present of the grisly trophies to Bala Rao, who exposed them in his saloon, and gave a sort of conversazione at which they formed the leading attraction. Mr. Carter was shot, as a matter of course; and his little widow would have shared his fate, had not the relicts of the late Peishwa, the step-mothers by adoption of the Maharaja, felt a womanly commiseration for one so tender and so afflicted. The good ladies begged hard for this single example of clemency, and begged in vain. At length their pride of sex was roused against such determined brutality towards a woman who had so lately been a wife, and was so soon to be a mother, and they threatened to commit suicide unless their petition was granted. The Nana then gave way, and permitted his relatives to carry off their protégee to the apartments appropriated to the females in the palace at Bithoor, where they placed her under the charge of an experienced Mahomedan nurse. He insisted, however, that she should be considered as under custody, and appointed a squad of troopers to see that she was forthcoming whenever it might suit his will and pleasure. He never lost sight of a victim. He boasted the worst half of, at any rate, one kingly quality,—an unerrring memory.

On next Friday the remnant of the native force which had mutinied at Benares made their appearance on the opposite side of the river. The exit of these gentlemen from the Holy City had not been of a nature to gratify their conceit, and their entry into Cawnpore was the reverse of triumphant. They straggled up, jaded and dispirited, without any semblance of martial order, some on horseback, and others perched up in the uncomfortable country-carts of Hindostan, which seem to have been devised with the express object of conveying the least possible amount of freight with the greatest expenditure of traction power. Their condition excited the contempt and cupidity of the officials appointed to superintend the river traffic in the interest of the Nana; who accordingly refused to ferry across these shabby auxiliaries for less than a rupee per head. Considering that the majority of the passengers were of pure Sikh blood, their spirit must indeed have been broken before they could have endured such insolence and extortion.

On the fifteenth of June, a welcome message was brought to the Maharaja from the Meer Nawab, a Mussulman of rank, who sent word that he was coming up from the eastward with a couple of thousand regular infantry, and a full complement of artillery. Azimoolah resolved that his subordinates should not have an opportunity of repeating their conduct of the previous week. Every mark of respect was to be displayed towards so august and puissant a chieftain. The bridge contractors were commissioned to collect barges for the transit of the expected allies, and the confectioners of the town received instructions to prepare for their refreshment a ménu, containing all those dishes of sweetened animal food so nauseous to a European palate. On the morrow the Nawab arrived at the head of two fine regiments, which had been raised on the occasion of Lord Dalhousie's annexation, amidst the deep but suppressed uneasiness of all who gave the native mind credit for the human qualities of ambition, shame, and patriotism; of all who believed the Hindoo capable of any loftier sentiment than the desire to curry favour with an English magistrate, touch a hundred rupees per mensem from an English treasury, talk broken Addison, and read the

"Deserted Village" in the original. On the rolls of our army these battalions were styled the Fourth and Fifth Oude Locals: but sepoys have invariably some pet title for their own corps, in most cases a corruption of the name of its first colonel, more suited to the Indian tongue than our complicated military nomenclature. Thus the First, the Fifty-third, and the Fifty-sixth Bengal Native Infantry, were spoken of familiarly as "Gillises," "Lamboorn's," and "Garsteen's." The Oude soldiers under the Meer Nawab were known to themselves and their compatriots as the men of the Nadiree and the Akhtaree Regiments.

When the new-comers caught sight of the fortress which had hitherto baffled the ingenuity and courage of their associates, they expressed no small contempt for the generalship of the Nana, but bade him be at his ease, for that they would engage to put him in possession of the intrenchment after they had enjoyed a day's rest and surfeit. And so, on the eighteenth of June, at the hour when, exactly two and forty years before, the French tirailleurs were swarming through the woods of Hougoumont up to the loopholes of the wall which they never passed, the Oude mutineers charged in a mass across the plain, and over our rampart; bore down the defenders; overturned a gun; and seemed for a moment in a fair way of justifying their vaunt. A moment only: for, without waiting for orders, angry Sahibs came running from all sides to the rescue. Our people slewed round a nine-pounder; gave them first some stockingfuls of grape, and then an English rush; and sent them back to their master fewer and wiser than they came.

The rebel position presented an aspect animating and picturesque in a high degree. To the north of our fortification, between the Racket-court and the Chapel of Ease, was planted a battery well armed with mortars and twenty-four pounder cannon. In this region the command was taken by the Nunhey Nawab, the Mahomedan grandee, who, with Bakur Ali, and others, had been plundered and imprisoned by the Brahmins during their first outbreak of religious spite. The high-spirited Moslem soldiery at once refused to brook this outrage, and began to talk of setting up the Nawab's claim to royalty against that of the Maharaja: upon which the latter released his prisoners, and thenceforward behaved towards them rather as an equal than as a master. The Nana's rival showed both judgment and vigour. He beat up all the pensioned veterans of the neighbourhood who had formerly served in the artillery, and employed work-people of both sexes in keeping him supplied with red-hot shot. On one occasion an apprentice to the trade took it into his head to try the experiment of heating a loaded shell, and succeeded in blowing up a woman and five men, including, we may presume, himself. The Nawab passed most of his time in the gallery of the Racket-court, where, in the late afternoon of more quiet days, had lolled a cluster of chatty Englishmen; opening bottles of soda-water; chaffing the players with the threadbare raillery that suffices for the simple taste of a limited community; descending in parties of four, cheroot in mouth, when the cry of "game-ball all," warned them that their turn was come. Occasionally he would issue forth to see how his gunners were getting on, and to watch the effect of their practice through a telescope. A half-caste Christian, who had disguised himself as a Mahomedan with admirable skill, gives an interesting account of what passed in this quarter. He says, "I saw Nunhey Nawab coming to the "batteries accompanied by a number of troopers, "and sepoys, and his own attendants also; and "I was told by the people that the Nawab had received a post of great dignity, and was in command of a battery. About one o'clock I came "close to Major-general Wheeler's bungalow, and, "finding a piece of mat in the compound, lay down "on it, and saw several troopers going about, "forcing people to carry water to the batteries. "Hearing an uproar I rose from the place where "I was, when a trooper, seeing me, told me that it "was a great shame for a young Mussulman like me "to be thus idling away my time, and that I should "assist at the batteries. He also told me that "a young man, the son of Kurrum Ali, the one-"eyed, a pensioned soubahdar, was sent for by the "Nawab, and had laid a gun so precisely that the "shot carried away a portion of one of the barracks "within the intrenchment, for which he received "a reward of ninety rupees, and a shawl. I replied "to this that I possessed no arms, and had never "been a soldier." It was no wonder that a battery where the service was conducted on so open-handed a system soon became the popular resort. The lovely Azeezun made this spot her head-quarters. She appears to have exercised a strange fascination over our good friend Nanukchund, so frequently does she appear in the course of his narrative. Whether he cherished towards her a sneaking kindness; or a grudge for some past incivility; or, as is most probable, both the one and the other, he certainly never leaves her alone for many pages together. In his quaint way he writes:—"It shows "great daring in Azeezun, that she is always armed "and present in the batteries, owing to her attach-

"ment to the cavalry; and she takes her favourites "among them aside, and entertains them with "milk, &c. on the public road." It is to be hoped that the et cetera did not include kisses.

The Meer Nawab planted the cannon, which he had brought with him across the river, on the south-east of our position, near the Artillery Mess House. This manœuvre forthwith debarred the garrison from obtaining occasional and perilous access to the tank; a privation the more severely felt, because the Oude men, bent on avenging their repulse, worked their pieces with a will, and kept up at point-blank range so hot a fire upon the mouth of our well that the drawing of water was a deed of heroism by night, and in daylight an act of insanity. In the west, Bakur Ali, who had shared with the Nunhey Nawab his disgrace and his restoration to favour, bombarded our outposts from among the stables of the Second Cavalry; while in and about the lines of the First Native Infantry stood a number of heavy guns, known by the collective appellation of "the Sepoy Battery," under cover of which a Jemmadar, who fancied himself gifted with a turn for engineering, was sinking a mine by the aid of some invalid sappers and miners, whom he had persuaded to place themselves at his disposal. In the south-west direction was a stately mansion, which formerly held rank as a charitable institution, under the title of the "Salvador," a name which the effeminate articulation of the native had long before this converted into the "Savada." As the Mahomedan faction mustered strong in the vicinity of the Racket Court, so the Savada soon became the centre of Hindoo influence. It was the special haunt of the Nana. Here were his ministers, his diviners, his courtiers, and the prisoners from whom he purposed to extort something besides their breath. Here was the battery which went by his name. Here was the tent of his most able and ardent partizan, Teeka Sing, the generalissimo. Here too, in an agreeable corner of the grounds, under the shade of a conspicuous grove, conveniently remote alike from the camp of the Moslem and the muzzles of the English artillery, was pitched his own pavilion; for he seems to have inherited the Mahratta preference for canvass over brick and mortar. The chiefs of that hardy and unquiet race seldom had a tight roof over their heads until they were laid beneath some mausoleum of fair white marble, sparkling with cornelian and jasper and lapis lazuli, constructed out of the spoils and the tribute of nations.

The mutineers showed every intention of enjoying their spell of liberty and domination. These revolted regiments were rapidly turning into mobs. The work of the batteries was left to the retainers of ambitious Rajahs; to pensioned gunners; and to such amateurs as had a stomach for fighting, and a taste for the shawls and cash lavished by the Nunhey Nawab. The sepoys, meanwhile, lounged in the shops which fringed the canal, eating sweetstuff with schoolboy avidity, and drinking sherbet to their hearts' content; or swaggered along the streets with a nonchalance copied from their reminiscences of the fashionable frequenters of the band-stand, criticizing the driving of those among their comrades who had been fortunate enough to lay their hands upon a buggy belonging to a British officer. No decent people were to be seen in the public places. No business was done in the main thoroughfares. The tradesmen in piteous trepidation, eyed the passing scamps from behind their shutters, consoling their enforced idleness by recollecting in what angle of the garden their money was interred, and framing excuses against the probable visit of the Nana's tax-collector, or the possible return of the English authorities. The opium-sellers and the innkeepers, who in these days anterior to Mr. Wilson's budget had not attained to the dignity of licensed victuallers, alone drove a thriving trade. The warriors of the Religions smoked, and chewed, and snored supine, clad in cotton drawers and a pair of clumsy shoes; their necks encircled by the Brahminical thread, token of their privileged and sacred extraction. To this costume they superadded a red coat, at such times as the stings of conscience, or the reproaches of priest and paramour, drove them out to get a lazy shot at the infidels and an appetite for their curry.

The earliest care of the Nana had been to set on foot a respectable municipal organization. With this object in view, he appointed to the chief magistracy in the city one Hoolass Sing, who may have been a traitor, but was, apparently, only a time-server. This person was chosen by the advice of a deputation composed of the leading townsmen; a tent-maker, a jeweller, and a dealer in opiates. Hoolass Sing had no sinecure. It was only by the exercise of judicious firmness, alternating with seasonable pliability, that he contrived to protect Cawnpore from the rapacity of the soldiery, and the wrath of those rural nobles whose paternal acres had been sold by the English Government to recover arrears of land-tax, and purchased by moneyed cits, who wished to cut a figure in country society. The duty of victualling the troops was committed to a blind gentleman of the name of Moolla, who, doubtless, saw quite well enough to water the rice and omit to sift the meal. A burlesque judicial court was formed of Azimoolah, Jwala Pershad, and other creatures of the Maharaja; and presided over by Baba Bhut, who delivered his decisions seated on a billiard-table in Mr. Duncan's hotel. This tribunal passed a variety of sentences without establishing any very valuable precedent. Once, in an unaccountable fit of morality, it sentenced a luckless rogue to lose his hand for theft; but, for obvious and selfish reasons, the judges appear to have refrained from again taking cognizance of this crime. A Mahomedan butcher was condemned to mutilation for having killed a cow; and certain individuals were paraded through the town on donkeys, "for disreputable livelihood:" a punishment which, when the charge was made known, must have excited very general sympathy and indignation. Gradually this body, like the Committee of Public Safety in the French Revolution, assumed to itself a supervision over every department of the administration. When the powder ran short, the principal dealer in saltpetre was thrown into prison, until he produced the requisite quantity of that article. A native merchant was required to provide cloaks for half a battalion, at the rate of two and threepence apiece; a scale of payment which must have inspired him with an unaffected regret for the liberal contracts of the old Company. With a keener relish, Baba Bhut undertook to account for the Englishmen who still lurked about, watching for an opportunity of slipping away to Allahabad or Agra. On the eleventh of June, Mr. Williams, a writer in one of the public offices, was traced out and slaughtered. Two days subsequently, the head of young Mr. Duncan was brought into his own father's house. The murderer was rewarded with the present of a pound, and the porter got a couple of rupees.

At the expiration of a fortnight, an event occurred which, for a while, afforded to the besieged people a more suggestive and agreeable matter of conversation than the rise of the mercury in the tube, and the sinking of the flour in the barrels. A native water-carrier skulked over from the opposite lines, and gave out that, on account of his love and respect for the Sahibs, he had set his heart upon being the first to bring them the good news; that there were two companies of white soldiers on the other side of the Ganges, who were supposed to have marched down from Lucknow; that they had guns with them, and were making as if they would cross the river on the morrow; that the rebel camp was in panic, and that everybody was saying how much he had all along intended to do for the Sahibs, had he only dared. Next day he turned up again with the intelligence that the Europeans had been detained on the opposite bank by an unexpected flood, but that they were busily engaged in knocking together rafts, and might be looked for within the forty-eight hours. Those hours passed, and twice and thrice those hours, and there came not the aspect of help, nor the renewal of confidence, nor the welcome sight of light faces, nor the welcome sound of approaching artillery. The soi-disant water-carrier made no third appearance. His two first visits had taught him all that Azimoolah desired to know of our impoverished and defenceless plight.

Our spies were less lucky; or, it may be, that the sturdy and straightforward British nature cannot promptly adapt itself to those frauds which are proverbially fair in war. There was in the garrison a soldier named Blenman, an Eurasian by birth, astute, and singularly courageous, but in temper uncertain, and impatient of control. There, and at that time, such a man was worth his weight in meal or powder, and his superiors did well to humour him. Cool, observant, and bold to temerity, the most delicate and hazardous of services had for him an innate attraction. After trying his wings in some partial flights, he prepared for a great and final enterprise, and volunteered to penetrate as far as Allahabad with a report of our calamities, and an appeal for instant succour. He disguised himself as a native cook, an easy task, for his complexion showed that he had far more than the due share of maternal blood; and sallied forth with a pistol and fifteen rupees stuffed into his cotton drawers. He passed unnoticed or unsuspected no less than seven horse pickets. The eighth stopped, and searched him, in spite of his asseverations that he was a poor leather-dresser, taking a walk through the night air, after working all day in a close alley, over the saddles and holsters of the gentlemen troopers of the Second Cavalry. Too plausible to be killed off-hand, and too questionable to be neglected, he was stripped and sent back whence he came, with no other information than that the investment of our position was even more strict and complete than had been apprehended.

A half-caste government official offered to make an attempt to obtain intelligence, and to bribe over some of the influential citizens of Cawnpore, on condition that Sir Hugh would permit his family to leave the intrenchment. His terms were accepted. He set forth, but was at once detected, and taken before the Maharaja, who sentenced him to three years' imprisonment with hard labour; a unique example of leniency, curious, as proving how firmly that usurper was persuaded that his rule would now be permanent. Ghouse Mahomed, a faithful sepoy of the Fifty-sixth, succeeded in getting farther than his predecessors. He crept along the ground in the darkness, until he met two or three men with four yoke of oxen taking supplies to the Savada house. He told them that he was going to the city to buy some grave-clothes for his brother, a brave who had died that day for the good cause in one of the advanced batteries. He was allowed to proceed upon his pious errand; but, when he reached the native town, it was as much as he could do to conceal himself from the inquisition of the rebel police. Many emissaries were despatched from our fortification, but Blenman alone returned. The others, through the months subsequent to our re-occupation of the district, came straggling in, as they could effect their escape from the camp of the fugitive Nana; with noses slit, and hands or ears chopped off by an ignorant and inhuman operator.

The remaining contents of the Cawnpore budget derive their principal interest from a consideration of the circumstances under which they were produced. Not even at such a season would Englishmen put their deeper feelings within an envelope; and the gossip of the station in that June was hardly calculated to enliven a correspondence. On the night of Sunday, the twenty-first, Major Vibart transmitted these lines to Lucknow:—

"We have been cannonaded for six hours a day "by twelve guns. This evening, in three hours, up- "wards of thirty shells [mortars] were thrown into "the intrenchment. This has occurred daily for the "last eight days; *an idea may be formed of our "casualties*, and how little protection the barracks "afford to the women. Any aid, to be effective, "must be immediate. In event of rain falling, our "position would be untenable.

"According to telegraphic despatches received "previous to the outbreak, a thousand Europeans "were to have been here on the fourteenth instant. "This force may be on its way up. Any assistance "you can send might co-operate with it. Nine- "pounder ammunition, chiefly cartridges, is required. "Should the above force arrive, we can, in return, "insure the safety of Lucknow. Being simply a "military man, General Wheeler has no power to "offer bribes in land and money to the insurgents, "*nor any means whatever* of communicating with "them. You can ascertain the best means of "crossing the river. Nujuffgurh Ghaut is sug- "gested. It is earnestly requested that whatever "is done may be effected without a moment's delay. "We have lost about a third of our original num- "ber. The enemy are strongest in artillery. They "appear not to have more than four hundred or

" five hundred infantry. They move their guns with " difficulty, by means of unbroken bullocks. The " infantry are great cowards, and easily repulsed.

" By order,

" G. V. VIBART, Major."

In the following letter there is one sad touch: the widower writing over his elbow "on the floor," "in the " midst of the greatest dirt, noise, and confusion."

" I was agreeably surprised to receive your most " welcome letter of the twenty-first, the messenger " of which managed cleverly to find his way here; " but that surprise was exceeded by the astonish- " ment felt by us all, at the total want of knowledge " you seem to be in regarding our position and " prospects; while we have been, since the sixth of " the month, equally in the dark respecting the " doings of the world around us. Your loss at " Lucknow is frightful, in common with that of us " all; for, since the date referred to, every one here " has been reduced to ruin. On that date they " commenced their attack, and fearfully have they " continued now for eighteen days and nights; " while the condition of misery experienced by all " is utterly beyond description in this place. Death " and mutilation, in all their forms of horror, have " been daily before us. The numerical amount of

" casualties has been frightful, caused both by sickness and the implements of war, the latter having been fully employed against our devoted garrison by the villainous insurgents, who have, unluckily, been enabled to furnish themselves therewith from the repository which contained them. We await the arrival of succour with the most anxious expectation, after all our endurance and sufferings; for that, Sir Henry Lawrence has been applied to by Sir Hugh, and we hope earnestly it will be afforded, and that *immediately*, to avert further evil. If he will answer that appeal with 'deux cents soldats Britanniques,' we shall be doubtless at once enabled to improve our position in a vital manner: and *we deserve* that the appeal should be so answered forthwith. You will be grieved to learn that among our casualties from sickness, my poor dear wife and infant have been numbered. The former sank on the twelfth, and the latter on the nineteenth. I am writing this on the floor, and in the midst of the greatest dirt, noise, and confusion. Pray urge our reinforcement to the Chief Commissioner.

" Yours,

" L. M. WIGGENS."

The employment of the French sentence is worthy of remark. During these troubled times, every modern language was pressed into our service, and more than one old field-officer mustered up his school reminiscences of the Anabasis and the Iliad, to compose a bulletin, curiously blended of Attic, Æolic, and Aldershot, which would have puzzled Grote or Hermann at least as much as it could possibly perplex any mutineer or highwayman who might chance to intercept the messenger.

Things had got to a terrible pass on our side of the wall. All the present sweetness of existence was long since vanished, and the last flicker of future hope had now died away. But, moved by a generous despair and an invincible self-respect, our people still fought on. By daring and vigilance, by countless shifts and unremitting labour, they staved off ruin for another day, and yet another. At rare intervals behind the earthwork, they stood—gaunt and feeble likenesses of men,—clutching with muffled fingers the barrels of their muskets, which glowed with heat intolerable to the naked hand, so fierce was the blaze of the summer sun. Straining their ears to catch any fancied sounds of distant cannonading, they gazed across the plain to where the horizon faded into a fantastic mirage, which mocked their fevered eyes with fair scenes of forest, and mountain, and with infinite expanses of glassy water broken by golden islets; while in the foreground the jackals prowled about the debated space, and the pariah dogs snarled at the grey crows, and slunk away from the spots where the great vultures sat in obscene and sulky conclave. Dim must have been the thoughts, confused the images, which flitted through their wearied intellect; indistinct memories of home and youth; faint regrets, and fainter resolutions; fitful yearnings for dear beings whom they would never again behold. One would surmise how his mother in far-off England would bear her sorrow, and who would be selected to break the news. Another would calculate dates, and try to convince himself that his boy at Rugby should have got the scholarship examination off his mind before the receipt of the fatal tidings. But, whatever might be the subject of contemplation, no smile relieved the stolid apathy of their careworn features, save when dejection was for an instant charmed away by the buoyant audacity of Moore. "He was a "strong man. In the dark perils of war, in the high "places of the field, hope shone in him like a pillar "of fire, when it had gone out in all the others." Brave and vivacious himself, he was the cause that bravery and vivacity were in other men. It was not that he had less at stake than those around him, for his wife and children were in the intrenchment. When the vicissitudes of battle called her husband to the outposts, Mrs. Moore would step across with her work, and spend the day beneath a little hut of bamboos covered with canvas, which the garrison of Barrack Number Two had raised for her in their most sheltered corner. Seldom had fair lady a less appropriate bower.

The twenty-third of June, 1757, was the date of the great rout that placed Bengal beneath the sway of the foreigner. In 1857 the ringleaders of the mutiny had fixed on the dawning of that day as the signal for a general rebellion over the entire north of India; but the outbreak at Meerut and the massacre of Delhi precipitated and weakened the blow. In that dread year those awful events were to us as saving mercies. At Cawnpore, however, the Nana and his crew, actuated by a partiality for the celebration of centenaries not altogether confined to Asiatics, were bent upon effecting something worthy of the occasion. All through the night of the twenty-second the defenders of the outlying barracks were kept on the alert by sounds which betokened that the sepoys in the adjacent buildings were more than usually numerous and restless. Lieutenant Thomson sent to head-quarters for a reinforcement; but Moore replied that he could spare nobody except himself and Lieutenant Delafosse. In the course of a few minutes the pair arrived, and at once sallied forth armed, one with a sword, and the other with an empty musket. Moore shouted out, "Number one to the front!" and the enemy, taking it for granted that the well-known word of command would bring upon them a full company of Sahibs with fixed bayonets and cocked revolvers, broke cover and ran like rabbits. But towards morning they returned in force, and attacked with such determined ferocity that there remained more dead Hindoos outside the doorway than there were living Europeans within. At the same moment the main fortification was assaulted by the whole strength of the insurrection. Field guns, pulled along by horses and bullocks, were brought up within a few hundred yards, unlimbered, and pointed at our wall. The troopers, who had bound themselves by the most solemn oath of their religion to conquer or to perish, charged at a gallop in one quarter, while in another advanced the dense array of infantry, preceded by a host of skirmishers, who rolled before them great bundles of cotton, proof against our bullets. It was all in vain. Our countrymen, too, had their anniversary to keep. They shot down the teams which tugged the artillery. They fired the bales, drove the sharpshooters back upon the columns, and sent the columns to the right-about in unseemly haste.

They taught the men of the Second Cavalry that broken vows, and angered gods, and the waters of Ganges poured fruitlessly on the perjured head were less terrible than British valour in the last extremity. The contest was short but sharp. The defeated combatants retired to brag and to carouse; the victors to brood, to sicken, and to starve. That evening a party of sepoys drew near our lines, made obeisance after their fashion, and requested leave to bury the slain. This acknowledgment of an empty triumph, which would have spread a lively joy throughout the ranks of an old Spartan army even in the most desperate strait, was but a poor consolation to these Englishmen under the shadow of their impending doom.

CHAPTER IV.

THE TREACHERY.

THE event of this conflict produced a sudden change in the projects of the Nana. He forthwith began to despair of carrying our fortress by storm, and the circumstances of his position were so critical that he dared not await the unfailing but tardy process of starvation. The clearing out of the intrenchment proved to be a more serious undertaking than he had anticipated. From forty to fifty score of his stoutest warriors had bitten the dust in front of our rampart, and he appeared to be as far as ever from the object which he had in view. Every day the English fought with increased gallantry and firmness, while in his own camp disaffection and disgust gained ground from hour to hour. An Oriental army which has turned its back on the foe can seldom, in the language of the prize-ring, be induced once more to toe the scratch; and every section of the rebel force had by this time been well beaten. The sepoys were already grumbling, and it was to be feared that another repulse would set them conspiring. Even the Oude men preferred the toddy-shops to the batteries; and the mutineers of the Cawnpore brigade swore that no power in heaven or earth should prevail on them again to look the Sahibs in the face. Meanwhile the Mahomedans, whom the Maharaja dreaded only less than the British, gathered strength and impunity from the popular discontent. Teeka Sing, the soul of the Hindoo faction and the right hand of the Nana, was imprisoned in his tent on the charge of amassing a private treasure by a party of Moslem troopers, who were growing hungry for the largess so long deferred. Delay was perilous, and defeat would be fatal. By fair means, or, if need was, by the very foulest, it behoved the usurper to bring the matter to a speedy termination. One method remained; swifter than famine; more sure than open force. It might be possible to cajole where he could not frighten; to ensnare those whom he might not vanquish; to lure our countrymen from the shelter of that wall, within which no intruder had set his foot and lived.

In one of the rooms in the Savada House the Greenway family, of whom mention has been made above, had now been shut up for about a fortnight, in strict confinement, diversified by an occasional conversation with an underling of the Maharaja. He had fixed their ransom at forty thousand pounds, and was at present discussing the terms of a bill of exchange on a Calcutta bank, for which they were never to receive any consideration. In the same apartment lived an elderly person, named Mrs. Jacobi, who had been taken while endeavouring to escape towards Lucknow, disguised in native clothes. On the evening of Tuesday, the twenty-third, these unhappy people were surprised at receiving a call from Azimoolah and Jwala Pershad, who seemed in very low spirits on account of the collapse of their centenary. These gentlemen informed Mrs. Jacobi * that she had been designated as the bearer of a message to Sir Hugh Wheeler. She readily undertook the office, and in the course of the next day was favoured by an interview with the Nana, who gave her a letter and her instructions. At nine o'clock on the following morning, she proceeded to the intrenchments in a palanquin, and was admitted as soon as the sentries had ascertained that she was an envoy, and not a spy. She delivered

* On the important point of the identity of the messenger a strange discrepancy exists between the best informed authorities. Captain Thomson "recognised her as Mrs. Greenway." On the other hand, the confidential servant of Mr. Greenway affirms that the choice of the Nana fell upon Mrs. Jacobi, and his statement is supported by the great majority of the depositions.

the document which had been entrusted to her charge; a note in the handwriting of Azimoolah, attested by no signature, of which the superscription was "To the subjects of Her Most Gracious Majesty "Queen Victoria;" and the contents ran as follows, in caricature of a proclamation issued from the Government House at Calcutta:—

"All those who are in no way connected with "the acts of Lord Dalhousie, and are willing to "lay down their arms, shall receive a safe passage "to Allahabad."

This protocol, unique for brevity and impudence, was laid before a council, consisting of General Wheeler, and Captains Moore and Whiting. The debate was prolonged and earnest. Poor Sir Hugh could not bear to abandon the position that he had chosen so ill, and in the defence of which he had been so little able to participate. It seemed a miserable conclusion of a not discreditable career to stipulate with his own sepoys for the liberty of slinking away after the loss of all his men and half his officers. Such was indeed an exorbitant price to pay for the sad remnants of a broken life. Better to lie within that well not far above his brave boy than to bargain for the privilege of being interred a few months later beneath one of the unsightly masses of brickwork which encumber the European graveyards of India. But the scruples of the old man at length yielded to the arguments produced by Moore and Whiting—and they were no drawing-room soldiers; for the one throughout those three weeks had never left a corner on which converged the fire of two powerful batteries, and the other had so borne himself that it might well be doubted whether he knew what fear was. They represented that, if the garrison had consisted exclusively of fighting people, no one would ever dream of surrender as long as they had swords wherewith to cut their way to Allahabad. But what could be done with a mixed multitude, in which there was a woman and a child to each man, while every other man was incapacitated by wounds and disease? The setting in of the wet weather (so they urged,) long dreaded as an overwhelming calamity, and delayed hitherto by what resembled the special mercy of Providence, could not now be distant. When the heavens were once opened, when the rain of the East descended in all its first violence, their fortification would straightway cease to be habitable and secure. The walls of the barracks, shakened and riddled by the cannonade, would sink and crumble beneath the fury of a tropical tempest. The holes in which our ladies sought refuge from the glare and the shot would be filled ere many inches had fallen. The marksmen who, provided with weapons worthy of their skill, could hardly guarantee those paltry bulwarks, would be helpless when damp powder and dirty gun-barrels had reduced them to their bayonets and hog-spears. In another week they must expect to be washed out of their defences; but, before that week had elapsed, the state of the barometer would concern them little; for the provisions were fast coming to an end. Their stores had dwindled to less than a quart per head of almost uneatable native food. The choice lay between death and capitulation: and, if the latter were resolved on, it was well that the offer came from the enemy. Loth and late Sir Hugh gave way. In order to avoid the appearance of a suspicious eagerness to accept the advances of the Nana, Mrs. Jacobi was dismissed with an announcement that our commander was in deliberation as to the answer that should be sent. That the intention to treat was generally known among our officers is evident from a note addressed by Lieutenant Master, of the Fifty-third, to his father, a colonel of cavalry, dated at half-past eight in the evening of June the twenty-fifth.

"We have now held out for twenty-one days "under a tremendous fire. The Raja of Bithoor "has offered to forward us in safety to Allahabad, "and the General has accepted his terms. I am "all right, though twice wounded. Charlotte "Newnham and Bella Blair are dead. I'll write "from Allahabad. God bless you.

"Your affectionate son,

"G. A. MASTER."

The old lady returned to the rebel lines early in the afternoon, but somewhat cheered by her short visit. While the summons was under consideration, she had made the most of such an excellent opportunity for pouring out her troubles and terrors to a friendly audience. Her escort conducted her to the Maharaja, who listened to what she had to say, and then sent her back into captivity. He had no further need of her services. A pacific intercourse had been established between the camps, and thenceforward his ambassadors might traverse the intervening ground without apprehension lest a conical bullet from Lieutenant Stirling's rifle should put an abrupt end to the negotiations. That evening there was assembled in the Nana's tent a council of war, to which repaired five or six congenial advisers, who, in their inmost hearts, were conscious that they had been bidden to a council of murder. One hour after dusk was the time appointed for that accursed colloquy. A subject was to be broached on which few would dare to enter until the kindly sun had veiled his face. History will never cease to shudder at the deeds which thence resulted; but of the words that there were spoken she will be content to abide for ever ignorant.

The morrow was a busy day. The first thing in the morning, at our invitation, Azimoolah walked up to within half a quarter of a mile of our outposts, accompanied by Jwala Pershad, a myrmidon of Bithoor Palace, who, by zeal and servility, had risen to the dignity of a brigadier. To them went forth Moore and Whiting, together with Mr. Roche, the postmaster. These gentlemen, whom Sir Hugh had invested with full powers, undertook to deliver up the fortification, the treasure, and the artillery, on condition that our force should march out under arms, with sixty rounds of ammunition to every man; that carriages should be provided for the conveyance of the wounded, the women, and the children; and that boats victualled with a sufficiency of flour should be in readiness at the neighbouring landing-place. These stipulations appeared to meet the approval of the native commissioners; one of whom volunteered the remark, "We will give you "sheep and goats also."

The terms were committed to paper, and handed

to Azimoolah, who broke up the conference with a promise to do what he could towards persuading his master to accede to our proposals. That same afternoon a trooper brought back a document, with a verbal message to the effect that the Nana had no alteration to suggest, and desired that the barrack should be evacuated that very night. This extravagant demand produced a remonstrance on our part, to which the response was an insolent assurance that the Peishwa must have his will, and that disobedience or even hesitation would bring upon the delinquents the fire of all his batteries; that he was not so blind as to give us credit for having abundance of food or serviceable cannon; and that another week's bombardment would leave nobody alive to haggle with his behest. To this flourish of Oriental vanity Whiting replied in good English style, that, if Seereek Dhoondoo Punth wanted the intrenchment, he had only to come and take it; that his soldiers knew the way thither and the way back again; and that, if the worst came to the worst, there was powder enough in our magazine to blow into the Ganges everything south of the Canal. This last allusion closed the controversy. The Maharaja consented that we should delay the embarkation till morning, and accorded a most gracious reception to Mr. Todd, who formerly had been his English tutor, and who now prevailed upon him, without difficulty, to sign his worthless name on the margin of the treaty. Men give easily what costs them nothing. The Nana informed his old acquaintance that arrangements should be made to enable our countrymen to breakfast and dine on board, and start comfortably in the cool of the evening. The servants, he said, had better stay behind, as ladies could look to their own wants on the voyage. Which was true, God knows.

There was much to be done that night. On the one side preparations were on foot for a departure; on the other, measures were being taken that the departure should never be. Hoolass Singh, the magistrate of the city, sent for the principal persons who gained their living by letting boats on hire, and ordered them to provide conveyance for five hundred passengers. They declared themselves unable to fulfil his injunctions, a refusal on which, after the re-establishment of British rule, they insisted as an irrefragable proof of loyalty. It is more likely that they were influenced by a rational doubt as to whether they would ever see the colour of the Nana's money. Hoolass Sing, however, knew what he was about, as appears from the pathetic language of one of the sufferers. "I told him," says Buddhoo, aged forty years, "that, when I received orders from the

"Europeans to procure boats, I was advanced "money, and allowed a month or fifteen days to "collect the same, and that it was impossible to "procure boats on so short a notice. On this he "was much annoyed, and said I was only putting "him off, and ordered his attendants to take me, "give me a good beating, and make me get boats. "They did as ordered, kept me there the whole "night, beating me, and threatened to blow me "from guns if I did not comply with their request. "They continued threatening me till 12 A.M.: but "I did not get them any boats." Buddhoo's companions had more regard for their skins; and, being not unaccustomed to this mode of carrying on a commercial transaction, after a due modicum of vapulation discovered that they could muster two dozen barges between them. These were punted down the river, and moored at the appointed spot. Presently a committee of English officers, riding upon elephants, and guarded by native troopers, arrived for the purpose of inspecting the proceedings and reporting progress. These gentlemen expressed great vexation at the dilapidated state of the little fleet. Four hundred workmen were at once engaged, and set to repair the thatch of the roofs, and construct a temporary flooring of bamboo. During the presence of our countrymen some provisions were brought along and placed on board, with a considerable show of assiduity: but they were not satisfied with all that they saw, and still less with what they seemed to hear. Some sepoys, idling on the bank, interspersed their talk with frequent repetitions of the word "kuttle," which, being interpreted, is "massacre."

And so the stage had been selected whereon to enact the tragedy. Hoolass Sing had furnished the properties; Azimoolah had composed the plot; and there lacked only a skilful manager, who should distribute the parts, instruct the actors, and dispose the supernumaries. The Nana could discover many a one among his pimps and parasites suited to such a job as far as moral constitution was concerned. In his familiar circle there was no dearth of fellows by the hand of nature marked, quoted, and signed to do a deed of shame. But in that degenerate circle there was only a single courtier who had retained something of the old Mahratta dash and martial craft. Tantia Topee was destined ere long to demonstrate that he could run away every whit as successfully as those chieftains who more than half a century before wearied out the hot pursuit of Lake and Wellesley; and on this particular occasion he evinced qualities which might have secured to him a share of fame in a cause less detestable to God and man. Laurels were not to be reaped in that contest. The due meed for such victors was a wreath of cypress and a necklace of hemp. But the bad deed was right cleverly done. Among all the feats of arms performed by the rebel forces during the eighteen months which succeeded the explosion at Meerut, no operation was so perfect in all its parts, so able in design, and so prosperous in execution, as the memorable treachery of Cawnpore.

The Suttee Chowra Ghaut, or landing-place, lay a short mile to the north-west of our intrenchment. At this point a ravine runs into the Ganges, after crossing at a right angle the main road, which is distant three hundred yards from the river. During summer the bed of the stream is dry, and presents the appearance of a sandy lane of irregular width, uneven with frequent lumps of broken soil, and inclosed on either side within high banks crowned by decaying fences. Standing half way down this passage the tourist sees behind him a bridge which carries the highway across the defile, the rails of which, then as now coated with white paint, have little of an Oriental aspect, and remind him for an instant of a bit in a Surrey common. On reaching the shore he finds himself in an open space, some hundred and fifty yards long and a hundred deep, bounded in the rear by a precipitous rising ground surmounted with prickly pear, in front by the Ganges, and to the left by the ruins of what in 1857 was the village from which the Ghaut takes a name. On his right hand rises a picturesque temple, dedicated to the patron deity of fishermen, small but in good repair, resembling nothing so much as those summer-houses of a century back which at the corners of old gardens overhang Dutch canals and suburban English byways. Passing down the wall of this edifice a steep flight of steps terminates in the very water of the river, so that a man cannot round the corner without wading. This is the scene where the traveller experiences to the full the sentiment of the spirit of Cawnpore. In other quarters of the station there are objects which evoke no light and transient feelings. It is painful to trace the faint line of the fortifications, and recognise the site of the barrack which contained so much sorrow and agony. It is interesting to observe the neat garden that strives to beguile away the associations which haunt the well of evil fame, and to peruse the inscription indited by a vice-regal hand. It may gratify some minds, beneath the roof of a memorial church that is now building, to listen while Christian worship is performed above a spot which once resounded with ineffectual prayers and vain ejaculations addressed to quite other ears. But it is beside that little shrine on the brink of the yellow flood that none save they who live in the present alone can speak with unaltered voice, and gaze with undimmed eye. For that is the very place itself where the act was accomplished, not yet transformed by votive stone and marble. There, at least, in the November evening, an Englishman may stand with bare head, and, under the canopy of heaven, breathe a silent petition for grace to do in his generation some small thing towards the conciliation of races estranged by a terrible memory.

In the course of the Friday evening Tantia Topee was closeted with the Nana, and, on leaving, gave orders that five guns and as many hundred picked musketeers should be mustered at the landing-place two hours before daybreak. He likewise enjoined certain among the rebel nobles to be in attendance with their followers at the same rendezvous. The cavalry soldiers, to whom the design was imparted, exclaimed against such a dastardly breach of faith, and would not be convinced until the Maharaja himself took the trouble to assure them, on the authority of a royal Brahmin, that according to his creed it was permissible to forswear at such a juncture; and that, for his own part, when the object was to annihilate an enemy, he would not hesitate to take a false oath on burning oil or holy water.

At the prescribed time, Tantia Topee found his power assembled on the bank, and straightway proceeded to make his dispositions. One gun, under the charge of a detachment, was placed among the ruins of Mr. Christie's house, which, from a considerable height above the stream, commanded the whole line of boats. A strong body of sepoys took cover behind the village of Suttee Chowra. A squadron of troopers concealed themselves to the south of the Fisherman's Temple. A couple of sections were secreted in and about some timber, which lay ready to be shipped away; while a mixed party of horse and foot were told off to follow our garrison, with directions to form up on the wooden bridge as soon as the English rear-guard had entered the ravine, and thus cut off the single avenue of escape. A fieldpiece, protected by a company of infantry, was posted a quarter of a mile down the river: and at a somewhat wider interval was stationed a third gun and another company. On the opposite shore, directly facing the mouth of the lane, stood two cannon, guarded by an entire battalion of infantry and a regiment of cavalry, who had recently attached themselves to the insurrection.

The boats, some few excepted, had been hauled into the shallows, and were literally resting on the sand. They were of the ordinary country build, thirty feet from stem to stern, and twelve feet in the beam. They were covered in by a heavy roof of straw, with a space at either end left open for the steersman and the rowers. At a distance they had the air of floating haystacks, rather than of vessels; and, indeed, were not unlike the Noah's ark of our nurseries, both in their outlines and in the number of their crew. Tantia called the boatmen together, and bade them hold themselves prepared, at a given signal, to fire the thatch, and make for the shore; and then, secure of the issue, mounted the stairs of the little temple, there to await, amidst a crowd of armed retainers, the outcome of his able combinations. The men in ambush chattered, and shivered, and munched their cold rice, and shared the alternate pipe; and the Mussulmans in the various groups performed a leisurely obeisance towards the rising sun, not sorry when his rays broke through the chill mist of the morning; and the bargemen gathered round fires heaped with a larger supply of charcoal than the economic Hindoo is wont to expend upon the preparation of his frugal breakfast.

All was quiet in the intrenchment. Brigadier Jwala Pershad, with two companions, came overnight to Sir Hugh Wheeler, and announced that the trio were to remain until the embarkation as hostages for the good faith of the Peishwa. The plausible Hindoo made himself exceedingly agreeable to his host; condoled with the General upon the privations which he had undergone, so trying at that advanced age; and intimated his disapprobation of those ungrateful soldiers who had turned their arms against an old and indulgent commander. He promised that, as far as in him lay, he would take care that no harm should befall us; and he soon had occasion to submit to a test of his good intentions, for a rebel sentry in the outlying barracks dropped his musket, which exploded in the fall, an accident that called forth a rapid and wild discharge from all the hostile batteries. Jwala at once despatched to the head-quarters of the enemy a message explaining the cause of the commotion, and procured an immediate cessation of the bombardment. In spite of this interruption, the garrison, rendered by long suspense and wretchedness careless rather than unsuspicious of the future, held high festival upon a double ration of boiled lentils and meal-cake, washed down by copious draughts of water clouded with brick-dust and powdered cement. Though many a wish was uttered for bread, and eggs, and milk-porridge, and curried fowls, no one dare beg or buy of the native sutlers. And so our people filled themselves with such food as they could get, and rested as men rest who have not slept for a great while, and know not when they may sleep again. There were those at hand who knew right well. Meanwhile, as an earnest of our defeat, a squad of mutineers stood guard over the shattered remains of the glorious guns which had done all that English iron could effect for the conservation of English honour and English lives.

On the morrow, at a very early hour, all Cawnpore was astir. The townspeople poured down to the landing-place by thousands; some desirous to catch one more glimpse of the kind-hearted strangers who had so long sojourned in their midst, and unfeignedly sorry to see the last of such easy customers and such open-handed masters; others, curious to observe whether the Sahibs were much changed by their hardships; others, again, drawn thither by a dim expectation that something might happen, which it would be a pity to have missed. And the mutineers, and the matchlockmen, and the rabble of the revolt, swarmed forth from the various dens of debauchery, and slouched off, yawning and half-armed, to bear their part in whatever might be going on. And Azimoolah and the brothers of the Peishwa, accompanied by a host of nobles, mounted their horses, and joined Tantia Topee on the platform of the temple. And the Nana did not sleep late, if, indeed, he slept at all. When his courtiers had departed, he dismissed his attendants, and listened in solitude for the sounds which should announce that the supreme moment had arrived. His mind was not in tune for company.

And our countrymen awoke for the last time. There was a great deal to be thought and talked of, but not much to be done. The packing did not take long. Little had been brought into those hateful walls, and less yet remained worth removal when they came to break up their melancholy establishment. Some hid about their persons money, or jewellery, or fragments of plate. Others seemed to think that a bible or a book of prayers was a treasure more likely to be of service in the coming emergency than turquoises, and silver spoons, and gold sovereigns. The able-bodied folk, intent on the common safety, stuffed their hats and pockets with ball-cartridge; while a few, over whose hearts, softened by the influence of the occasion, affection and regret held exclusive sway, bestowed all their care upon tokens which the dying had put aside as a legacy for the bereaved in England. Many and strange were the relics that crossed the Indian Ocean in the homeward-bound packets of that autumn; locks of hair, and stained sleeves or collars, and notes scribbled on the fly-leaf of an orderly-book, and pistols, of which some of the barrels were still loaded, and others had been fired in vain. It was then much as it had been in the days of Troy, throughout the villages of ancient Achaia. "The household knew those whom "it sent forth to the war; but, instead of the "men, an urn and a poor handful of ashes alone "returned."

And now began to make itself felt a strong disinclination to quit for ever the place where so much had been done and suffered; a frame of mind which afterwards was remarked among the besieged at Lucknow who outlived the relief of the Presidency. Death, in one of the forms with which all had lately grown so conversant, and among associations that, if not dear, were at any rate familiar, seemed preferable to novel exertions and untried perils. More than one young subaltern who, a month previously, would have been ashamed to confess to an emotion, stole ten minutes to pay a farewell visit to the loophole at which, on the morning of the great assault, he had fought till his shoulder was blue, and his rifle clogged with lead; or to stand with wet cheeks in a nook of the hospital, sacred to his first great grief. Not a few peered down the well that lay outside the breastwork, with a tacit adieu to those whom they left behind, and a wish that it had pleased God to unite them, even there.

If a start was to be made before the advancing day had dispelled the freshness of dawn, there was no time to be lost. A crowd of carriages and beasts of burden had gradually assembled outside the north-western corner of the intrenchment. Some of the women and children disposed themselves in the bullock-carts, while others climbed up to an insecure seat on the padded back of an elephant. A fine animal, equipped with a state howdah, and steered by the Peishwa's own driver, had been sent for the accommodation of Sir Hugh Wheeler. The General was touched by the attention; but (unwilling, it may be, to form a conspicuous object in a *cortège* so far from triumphal) after seeing his wife and daughters safely mounted in the place of honour, he ensconced himself in a palânquin, which he never left alive. Our soldiers bestowed their disabled comrades in the litters, without receiving the slightest assistance from the native bystanders. It was cruel work, the loading of this mournful train. The inexperienced good-will of that amateur ambulance corps occasioned grievous agony to some who ought not to have left their beds for months, and to some who should never have been moved again.

A number of sepoys mingled with the throng of

English people, and entered into conversation with the gentlemen under whom they had formerly served. One and all, they expressed lively admiration for the unaccountable obstinacy of our defence. Many spoke with commiseration of the distressing condition to which those had been reduced for whom they entertained so deep a respect; inquired eagerly after their missing officers; and learned their fate with tears: conduct which none who have studied the Hindoo character can attribute to sheer dissimulation. Less equivocal were the demonstrations displayed towards their employers by certain among the better class of domestics. The head bearer of Colonel Williams, who commanded the Fifty-sixth before the mutiny, deserves to tell his own simple story. He says, "Even after the cessation of hos-" tilities, we were not allowed to go and see our " masters. On the morning of the twenty-sixth of " June, three officers of the Fifty-sixth, Goad, " Fagan, and Warde, mounted on elephants, and " two Europeans, whose names and regiments I don't " know, mounted on another elephant, came out " of the intrenchments and went to the river, to " inspect the boats. The gardener and I, taking " some grapes, went up to the officers, and told them " that we were in a starving condition, and wanted " to come to our masters in the intrenchment.

"They said, 'No, you can't come with us, but we "'shall come out to-morrow, and you shall accom-"'pany us to Allahabad in boats.' Goad Sahib "and Warde Sahib gave me each two rupees. They "told me that my master had died a natural death; "that my mistress was well, but slightly wounded; "and that Miss Mary was dead. Her death was "caused by fright at the cannonade, and that she "was not wounded. On the twenty-seventh of June, "a little before six A.M. as many as could walk came "out; some of the wounded in doolies, others of "whom were left behind. The party from the in-"trenchment was surrounded by sepoys. I had "great difficulty in reaching my mistress. I applied "to Annundeedeen, the Havildar-Major of the Fifty-"sixth, who said the thing was impossible. I ap-"pealed to him, and begged him to remember the "kindness he had received from the Colonel. After "persuasion, he said that he could not show his face "before the Colonel's lady, but directed four sepoys "to take me to my mistress, and prevent my being "disturbed. I was then taken to my mistress, with "whom were her two daughters, Miss Georgiana, "and Miss Fanny. They were in wretched plight; "scorched and blistered by the sun. My mistress "had a slight bullet-wound on the upper lip. She "said that my master had died on the eighth of

"June. My mistress then asked about the property "left in the house, and inquired about all the ser- "vants, and especially after the cook. She then told "me to go and fetch him, as she wanted him to go "down to Allahabad with her; and told me to go to "her son in the Hills, and inform him of all that had "occurred. She told me to make every endeavour "to join her son as soon as the roads should be "open, and to show him the spot where the Colonel "was buried. I told her I did not know the spot. "She said the groom who had remained with them "in the intrenchment would show it to me." To judge from the attachment of her servants, Mrs. Williams must have ruled her household like a true lady of the kindly old Anglo-Indian school.

No prayer was said, no blessing invoked, no pass-over eaten before that inauspicious exodus. Moore went about from group to group, and impressed upon his colleagues that it would be idle to attempt to preserve order in the embarkation. His instructions were to push off as soon as all had been got on board, and make for the opposite shore, where further arrangements might be completed at leisure and in comparative safety. And then a drink of water was handed in at the door of each palanquin, and the expedition set forth. A mob of peasants at once rushed upon the deserted premises, and spread themselves about in quest of plunder. They might have spared their pains. A camel-rider, who entered among the first, saw nothing except "three "useless brass guns that had been split, two leathern "bottles of liquid butter, a sack of fine flour, and "the bodies of eleven Europeans. They were on "quilts on the floor, some of them still breathing, "though dying from severe gunshot wounds."

The show was not such as would dazzle a vulgar eye: but in the soul of those with whom glory is not skin-deep, the retinue of an imperial coronation would fail to inspire the reverence excited by that ragged and spiritless cavalcade. First came the men of the Thirty-second regiment, their dauntless captain at the head;—thinking little, as ever, of the past, but much of the future;—and so marching unconscious towards the death which he had often courted. Then moved on the throng of naked bearers, groaning in monotonous cadence beneath the weight of palanquins, through whose sliding panels might be discerned the pallid forms of the wounded;—their limbs rudely bandaged with shirt-sleeves, and old stockings, and strips of gown and petticoat. Mayhap, as they jolted along, they fed their sickly fancies with a listless anticipation that the hour was not remote when they might forget the miserable present amidst the joys of ice, and lemonade, and clean sheets, and nourishment more appetising than parched grain and bad pease-porridge. Behind these creaked a caravan of carts, dragged by bullocks, on which were huddled ladies used to a very different equipage; while here and there paced a stately elephant, his tusks adorned with rings of brass, and his forehead painted in grotesque patterns, who, perchance, a century back, was tugging a gun across the field of Plassey, and who now bore a cluster of English women and children clinging nervously to the ropes which encircled his huge girth. And next, musket on shoulder and revolver in belt, followed they who could still walk and fight. Step was not kept in those ranks. Little was there of martial array, or soldier-like gait and attitude. Lace might not be seen, nor embroidery, nor facings, nor uniforms which could be recognised at the Horseguards or smiled on in county ballrooms. In discoloured flannel and tattered nankeen, mute and in pensive mood, tramped by the remnant of the immortal garrison. These men had finished their toil and had fought their battle: and now, if hope was all but dead within them, there survived, at least, no residue of fear.

The last to quit the intrenchment was Major Vibart, of the Second Cavalry. He brought up the rear of our column alone, amidst a numerous escort of mutineers belonging to his late regiment, who insisted on conveying his luggage down to the landing place;—a marked instance of complaisance on the part of these gentlemen troopers. There were many, however, among the rebels, who no longer thought it worth while to dissemble. Lady Wheeler's Ayah, a few minutes before, had been presented by her mistress with a bag of rupees as an acknowledgment of her fidelity. She now was forced to exchange her treasure for a slash with a sabre. Some sepoys, who had stood by us to the last, were seized and carried off in spite of the urgent expostulations of their adjutant: and the hour approached when a brave woman was to meet that face to face, the bitterness of which, to repeat her own language, had already been tasted many, many times. Colonel and Mrs. Ewart had started late; she on foot; he on a bed, carried by four native porters. From one cause and another they made slow progress. The bearers were lazy; and paid no attention to a Mem Sahib, whose husband, prostrate with wounds, was unable to enforce her orders with his cane. Gradually the main body drew farther and farther ahead of the helpless pair; who, at length, like a sick child dreaming that he is kidnapped by gipsies, saw the backs of the English rear-guard disappear round a distant corner. As the litter came abreast of

St. John's Church, seven or eight rascals belonging to the Colonel's own battalion stepped up; bade the porters set down their load and stand back; and began to mock their victim, saying: "Is not this a "fine parade, and is it not well dressed up?" They then hewed him in pieces with their swords, and afterwards turned to Mrs. Ewart, and desired her to throw down whatever she had about her, and go her ways, for that she was a woman, and they would not kill her. She took out of her dress a piece of stuff, with something tied up in it, and delivered it to one of the gang, who thereupon cut her down dead. Those who loved her, and they were many, could not have wished it otherwise.

Presently the van reached the white rails of the wooden bridge, and, leaving them on the left hand, turned aside into the fatal ravine. A vast multitude, speechless and motionless as spectres, watched their descent into that valley of the shadow of death. Only some sepoys, gazing on the trappings of the elephants, said one to another: "They are taken out "of their fortress grandly. They go gladly. They "know not what is before them. Now let them "repent of their misdeeds, and ask pardon of God." Soon Tantia Topee, who for some while past had been anxiously glancing towards the west, saw the white faces and gleaming bayonets; saw the dark tops of thė palanquins dancing up and down; saw the howdahs swaying from right to left above the sea of heads. Then he called to a bandsman who was in attendance, and directed him to proceed up the lane, and sound his bugle when once the Europeans were well within the trap. Slowly, very slowly, with many a halt and many an entanglement, the unwieldy mass of men and brutes wound along the bed of the torrent.

And now the last Englishman walked down into the lane; and immediately the troops who had been appointed to that duty formed a double line across the mouth of the gorge, and told all who were not concerned to retire and keep aloof, for that within that passage there was no admittance save on one baleful business. Meantime the embarkation was progressing under serious difficulties. No temporary pier had been provided, nor even a plank to serve as gangway. None of the Hindoo boatmen or bearers spoke a word or lent a hand, while, standing knee-deep in the stream, our officers hoisted in the wounded and the women. Already they were themselves preparing to scramble on board;—already the children were rejoicing over the sight of some boiled rice which they had discovered in the corner of a barge;—when, amidst the sinister silence which prevailed, the blast of a bugle came pealing down the defile. Thereupon the native rowers leaped into the water, and splashed towards dry ground; while those very troopers who had conducted Major Vibart from the barrack with such professions of esteem discharged their carbines at the nearest vessel. The Englishmen, whose rifles were handy, at once opened fire, some on the traitorous crews, others on the hypocritical scoundrels who had commenced the attack. But of a sudden several of the straw roofs burst into a flame, and almost the entire fleet was blazing in the twinkling of an eye. The red-hot charcoal had done its work. At the same moment from either shore broke forth a storm of grape and musketry. To the imagination of our countrymen, oppressed and bewildered by the infernal tumult, it seemed that the land was alive with a hundred cannon and a myriad of sharpshooters. The wounded perished under the burning thatch, while all who could shift for themselves dropped into the river. Of the ladies, some crouching beneath the overhanging prows, some wading up to their chins along the shelving bottom, sought shelter from the bullets, which sprinkled the surface like falling rain. The men set their shoulders against the planking, and tried to launch off into the mid-current. But he who had chosen those moorings never intended that the keels should leave the sand-bank on which they lay.

All the boats stuck fast, save a poor three, of which two drifted across to the Oude bank into the jaws of the perdition which in that quarter also awaited their inmates. The third got clear away from the shallows, and floated steadily down the main channel. Whether fortuitously, or by the attraction of like to like, it so befell that the flower of the defence was congregated between those bulwarks. There were Vibart; and Whiting, good at need; and Ashe, bereaved of his beloved nine-pounder; and Delafosse of the burning gun; and Bolton, snatched once more from present destruction. There was Moore, with his arm slung in a handkerchief; and Blenman, the bold spy; and Glanville of Barrack Number Two; and Burney of the south-east battery. Fate seemed willing to defer the hour which should extinguish those noble lives.

When, after the lapse of some twenty minutes, the dead began to outnumber the living;—when the fire slackened, as the marks grew few and far between;—then the troopers who had been drawn up to the right of the temple plunged into the river, sabre between teeth, and pistol in hand. Thereupon two half-caste Christian women, the wives of musicians in the band of the Fifty-sixth, witnessed a scene which should not be related at second-hand. "In the boat where I was to have gone," says Mrs

Bradshaw, confirmed throughout by Mrs. Setts, "was the schoolmistress and twenty-two missies. "General Wheeler came last, in a palkee. They "carried him into the water near the boat. I stood "close by. He said 'Carry me a little further "'towards the boat.' But a trooper said: 'No; "'get out here.' As the general got out of the "palkee, head foremost, the trooper gave him a cut "with his sword into the neck, and he fell into the "water. My son was killed near him. I saw it: "alas! alas! Some were stabbed with bayonets; "others cut down. Little infants were torn in "pieces. We saw it; we did; and tell you only "what we saw. Other children were stabbed and "thrown into the river. The school girls were burnt "to death. I saw their clothes and hair catch "fire. In the water, a few paces off, by the next "boat, we saw the youngest daughter of Colonel "Williams. A sepoy was going to kill her with his "bayonet. She said, 'My father was always kind "'to sepoys.' He turned away, and just then a "villager struck her on the head with his club, "and she fell into the water." These people likewise saw good Mr. Moncrieff, the clergyman, take a book from his pocket that he never had leisure to open, and heard him commence a prayer for mercy which he was not permitted to conclude. Another deponent observed a European making for a drain like a scared water-rat, when some boatmen, armed with cudgels, cut off his retreat, and beat him down dead into the mud.

At this point those Englishmen who had learned to use their limbs in the water, perceiving that all was lost, with a hurried last look and a parting shudder, stripped, and made for Vibart's boat, which just then was aground not far from the opposite shore. Thomson swam, and Private Murphy, neither for the last time. Three cavalry soldiers chased Lieutenant Harrison on to a small island two hundred yards from the land. One only waded back again, quicker than he came; while Harrison made the best of his way to the stranded vessel, and clambered over the side, satisfied at having taught his pursuers that it was never safe to trifle with a Sahib, as long as he had breath in his body and a charge in a single chamber. Few were vigorous or fortunate as he. Their strength failed some; while more than one stout swimmer, shot dead in the middle of his stroke, rolled over and sank amidst the reddening tide. Of the two Hendersons, the younger went down in his brother's sight, while the elder hardly struggled in with a shattered hand through the pattering mitraillade. At length all were on board who had not disappeared below the waves; and, by dint of hard shoving, the boat scraped herself off the shoal, and continued her sluggish and devious course:—that hapless Argo with her freight of heroes.

"At nine, or half-past nine in the morning," writes Nanukchund, who was in hiding at a neighbouring village, "I heard the report of cannon, "and immediately despatched my servant for news, "and to learn why guns were being fired. At about "noon, more or less, he returned, and reported that "the people who came to bathe in the Ganges "informed him that the intrenchment had been "taken by the rebels, and the corpses of Europeans "were floating down the river. The villagers ex-"claim, in their village dialect, that the Ganges has "turned crimson, and it is impossible to look upon "it. The terror and alarm that now seizes me "baffles description. It seems sacrilege to take "any sort of food or drink. I can think of nothing "but moving about from side to side with terror." Besides Nanukchund, there was another, whose agitation, arising from very different passions, displayed itself by the same noticeable symptom. A rich Hindoo, even though he be not of such gross habit as was the Nana, never walks a step unless under dire compulsion: and yet, during the early forenoon, Dhoondoo Punth seldom rested quiet in his chair, but paced to and fro in front of his tent, straining his ears to catch the noise of horse-hoofs. At last a trooper galloped down with the tidings that all was going well, and the Peishwa would soon obtain ample compensation for his ancient wrong. The Maharaja bade the courier return to the field of action, bearing a verbal order to keep the women alive, but kill all the males. By the time Tantia's aide-de-camp returned to his chief, the latter injunction appeared all but superfluous: though there was still something to be done. The sepoys posted on the Oude bank had excepted certain Englishmen from the slaughter of the two boatfuls which had fallen into their hands. These, to the sum of seventeen, they now sent over as their contribution. On reference being made to the Maharaja, he graciously acknowledged the present, and desired a firing-party to be told off; suggesting, however, that powder should not be wasted on the wounded. His directions were obeyed to the letter. A couple of files were likewise detached to see that the sufferers who still lingered in the intrenchment did not take too long to die.

Meanwhile the women and children, whom the shot had missed and the flames spared, had been collected and brought to land in evil case. Many were pulled out from under the charred woodwork of boats, and others were driven up from four feet depth of water. Before they emerged from the river, some of the ladies were roughly handled by the troopers, who tore away such ornaments as caught their fancy with little regard for ear or finger. But, when all had been assembled on the landing-place, sentries were posted around, with a strict charge to suffer no one to molest the prisoners. There they sat, a hundred and twenty and five by count, some on logs of timber, and others in the trodden sand, a very feeble company in sore distress. Their destitution aroused the compassion of a party of water-carriers, who gave them drink out of the skin's mouth, as they cowered beneath the pitiless sun. On the shore of the Ganges, in the midst of that devilish horde, those English girls and matrons abode till the morning was almost spent. And then they were led back along the road which they had traversed a few hours before; not as they came, for nothing was left them now, save a new grief and a sharper terror. In front, behind, and on either side, surged along a crowd of sepoys, exulting with an unholy joy, and rich with inglorious spoils. This one carried a girdleful of rupees and broken jewellery. That had secured a double-barrelled fowling-piece, marked with a name illustrious in the London trade. Another dragged a fine setter or Skye terrier, the pride of some cadet who, in too harsh a school, had taken his first and last lesson of war. They started beside the Fisherman's Temple. They threaded the winding lane. They plodded wearily past the white railing and the European bazaar; past the chapel, and the racket-court, and the ruinous intrenchment. Through the disputed line of outposts, and across the plain they went, until the procession halted before the pavilion of the Maharaja; who, after reviewing his captives, ordered them to be transported to the Savada House, and there confined until further notice. Two large rooms, where a number of native soldiers had slept nightly during the previous month, were cleared out for their reception; and a guard placed over them from the ranks of the Sixth regiment, which had lately marched in from Allahabad.

"I saw that many of the ladies were wounded," says one who watched them go by. "Their clothes "had blood on them. Two were badly hurt, and had "their heads bound up with handkerchiefs. Some "were wet, covered with mud and blood; and some "had their dresses torn, but all had clothes. I saw "one or two children without clothes. There were "no men in the party, but only some boys of twelve "or thirteen years of age." Another eye-witness remarks: "The ladies' clothing was wet and soiled, "and some of them were barefoot. Many were "wounded. Two of them I observed well, as "being wounded in the leg and under the arm." To such a plight had come the bloom which once, fresh from the breezes of home, charmed and puzzled Calcutta; and the toilettes whose importation and inspection supplied matter for a month's conjecture, and a week's happy occupation. Where were now the tact, the cultivation, and all the indefinable graces of refined womanhood? Simplicity and affectation amiability and pride, coquetry and reserve, discretion and sweet susceptibility, were here confounded in a dull uniformity of woe.

Four Englishwomen, and three others of mixed parentage, were appropriated and carried off by the soldiers of the Second Cavalry: a corps which, now that the fighting was over, never lost an opportunity of distinguishing itself. These men were summoned into the presence of the Nana, who remonstrated with them at some length, and insisted that the whole seven should be restored without delay. It may be that he regarded his prisoners as hostages, and was unwilling that they should be scattered about in places where he could not lay his hand upon them at the precise moment when his life or power might be at stake. All obeyed promptly, with the exception of Ali Khan, a young trooper, described as of "a fair complexion; height about "five feet seven inches; long nose; dark eyes; wears "a beard and small moustache." This fellow had selected, as his share of the booty, the youngest daughter of Sir Hugh. He must have been one of a pair who were observed "leading away from the "boats a lady on horseback. She wore a green "chintz gown, which appeared to be wet. She "seemed to be eighteen or nineteen years of age." Ali Khan now contrived to spread a report that his victim flung herself down a well, after killing her captor, his wife, and his three children. His device met with extraordinary success. In Hindostan it is never a very difficult matter to find witnesses who will swear to anything; and, before long, a private in the Second began to remember that he had been passing his comrade's door when Miss Wheeler came out, with a sword in her hand, and said: "Go in and see how nicely I have rubbed "the Corporal's feet." Another individual, blessed with an elastic memory, had been present at the dragging of the well, and had seen "Missy Baba "taken out, dead and swollen." The impudent fabrication was generally accepted in the city and the cantonments; and met with ready credence in England, where the imaginations of men were excited by a series of prurient and ghastly fictions.

Under one shape or another the incident long went the round of provincial theatres, and sensation magazines, and popular lectures illustrated with dissolving views. Meanwhile the poor girl was living quietly in the family of her master under a Mahomedan name. Our police made diligent inquiries, which resulted in a strong conviction that she had accompanied the flight of the rebels, and, after being hurried about from camping-ground to camping-ground, had met a natural death in a corner of Nepaul. She was by no means of pure English blood. To some the very statement of the fact may appear heartless, but truth demands that it should be made.

The ladies on board the surviving vessel had no reason to congratulate themselves on their fortune: for they were embarked on a voyage which, for concentrated misery, has no parallel even among the narratives of famous shipwrecks so dear to the taste of our forefathers. Soon after leaving the shore, Major Vibart had taken a large party off a sinking boat; so that more than five-score persons were crowded into a space which could barely accommodate fifty. It was difficult to propel the craft, and impossible to guide her. A shot from the southern bank sent her spinning round in the current, with a broken rudder; and the native boatmen had taken good care to leave behind neither oar nor punt-pole. Alternately stranding and drifting; paddling with planks torn from the bulwarks, and trying to steer with a spare stretcher; our countrymen tended down towards Allahabad at the rate of half a mile an hour, under a shower of canister and shells from either bank. "We were often," says Thomson, "within a hundred yards of the guns on "the Oude side of the river, and saw them load, "prime, and fire into our midst." Presently the bullocks which drew the sepoy artillery broke down in the deep sand of the Ganges; but incessant volleys of musketry, at point blank range, allowed our countrymen little leisure to rejoice over the intermission of the cannonade.

That day dismissed to Hades many valiant souls of warriors, and left their bodies a prize for dogs and every kind of fowl. But the will of God was accomplished. Ashe and Bolton leaped out to help haul the boat off a sunken bank: and a few minutes later she proceeded on her way without those two young Sahibs whom a thousand bullets had spared to perish here. Moore, regardless of an ill-set collar-bone, was pushing with might and main, when a musket-ball pierced his gallant heart. One and the same round shot at length killed Burney, and at length Glanville; and so maltreated a third officer that it would have been well had he died likewise. The wounded and the slain lay entangled together amidst the broken flooring. It was a matter of extreme difficulty to extricate the corpses from the bottom of the vessel: but the desire of decreasing her draft, and the intense heat of what proved to be the last day of that year's dry weather, obliged the crew to cast overboard the dear but useless cargo.

About five o'clock that evening the boat settled down deep in the sand. Our countrymen waited patiently till the sunset allowed them to disembark the women under the screen of darkness. Having thus lightened their unwieldy ark they set to with a will, and succeeded eventually in getting her adrift. The rebels did what they could to impede the operation. They launched a fire-ship down the current, which came within a few feet of its mark; and, when this contrivance had miscarried, they shot off a flight of arrows tipped with lighted charcoal. Though no very skilful archers, they could not well help hitting the thatched roof which loomed through the dusk like the top of a great barn: so that our people thought it better to cut away and tumble into the flood the entire framework of straw and bamboo. No one slept that night, and no one ate: for food there was none on board. They had abundance of water: for Ganges flowed beneath; and from overhead descended a light and refreshing shower, the unfailing precursor of the annual deluge.

When the day broke, those of our officers who had learned the bearings of the locality during many a hot tramp after snipe and wild-fowl saw with chagrin that they had hardly gained ten miles in twice as many hours. And yet that dawn brought one last glimmer of hope. The wet weather had arrived: the river would soon be mounting fast: and nothing was to be seen of the enemy. Presently some natives walked down the bank for their morning wash; and Vibart sent on shore a native drummer, with five rupees in his hand, and directions to obtain information, and, if possible, some provisions. He accosted a peasant, who desisted from the occupation of cleaning his mouth with a bit of stick chewed into a tooth-brush, and listened very civilly to what our envoy had to say. This man undertook to procure some rice and flour, but assured the drummer that our people would have no further need of victuals, as Baboo Ram Bux, a powerful noble whose estates lay a little further down on the Oude side, had engaged that not an Englishman should pass his territory alive. He, however, showed no objection to take our money, and went inland, leaving behind his brass drinking-vessel to guarantee his fidelity: a pledge which he never came back to redeem. On hearing the report of their messenger the fugitives agreed to despair. After the manner of becalmed and starving mariners, Whiting pencilled some lines on a scrap of paper, which he enclosed in a bottle, and committed to the stream: the faithless stream, that has never rendered up the sad deposit.

At two in the afternoon the barge struck off a village called Nuzzufgur, which was within the boundary of Ram Bux. Straightway the shore was covered with a multitude of feudal militia, intermingled with sepoys and mounted troopers. A gun was brought forward, and unlimbered; but, while the artillerymen were taking their aim, there came down from heaven that unbroken sheet of water for which men had been looking during the past fortnight. The rains had begun in earnest. The piece could only be discharged once; but the storm did not protect our people from a keen fusillade. Whiting fell dead; and Harrison's trusty revolver here availed him nothing; and dark Blenman, sorely hurt, implored a comrade to put an end to his wayward existence. Vibart was shot through the arm, and his subordinates, Quin and Seppings; while Mrs. Seppings and Captain Turner of the First Infantry were badly wounded in the leg. After five hours of this bitter work there hove in sight a boat manned by fifty or sixty mutineers, armed to the teeth, who had been deputed by the Nana to follow and destroy the relics of our force. This vessel, likewise, ran on a sand-bank; not altogether against the inclination of the crew, who did not relish the notion of forming themselves into a boarding-party. They liked the idea still less when a score of Englishmen came dashing at them through the shallows. The half-dozen ablest swimmers alone escaped to tell their master that, after all they had gone through, those extraordinary Sahibs were the same as ever.

Amidst pelting rain and freshening wind the second night closed in. Faint and hungry they sank asleep, those men who would only yield to death. At midnight some of their number awoke, and became conscious that they were again afloat. It was blowing a hurricane; the stream had risen; and there were found those who hoped. But daylight told another story, for it revealed that they had turned aside out of the navigable channel into a back water, from which egress was none. And then their vessel grounded, and the musketry recommenced. Vibart, who was already dying with a ball through either arm, desired Thomson and Delafosse to land and beat away the enemy, while those who remained attempted to ease off the boat. The two officers selected a sergeant and eleven rank and file of various regiments ; and the party sallied forth, fortunate in that it was appointed for some to tread once more on English soil, and for the rest at least to die sword in hand. They had not departed many minutes when a host of insurgents poured down upon the helpless troop of women and wounded men, like wolves upon a flock of sheep deserted by their dogs. The boat was captured after a short but murderous conflict, and escorted back to Cawnpore by a strong body of horse and foot.

Thomson and Delafosse had enough on their hands already, and could do little or nothing towards a rescue. On gaining the shore they drove the foe in style over a considerable space ; but were imperceptibly surrounded in flank and rear by fresh swarms of rebels. Then they faced about, and cut their way back to the place whence they started, bleeding, but undiminished in number. They recognised the spot, but the boat was gone, and so the little troop, reduced henceforward to travel afoot, followed the course of the stream ; partly on the slender chance of catching up their lost companions ; partly from an instinctive feeling which drew them in the direction of Allahabad, as the wounded rabbit makes for its burrow, or the winged partridge scurries to the nearest hedge. With an interval of twenty paces between man and man, to lessen the hazard of the hostile musketry, they retreated step by step, loading and firing as best they might upon the horde of pursuers, who pressed nearer and even nearer. Shoeless on rugged ground, bare-headed beneath the burning sun, they fought over three weary miles of alternate rock and sand, until all but one got safe into a little temple, or "Sammy-house," as it is called in the jargon spoken by the British private in India; a jargon which he himself denominates "Moors." This rustic shrine, situated about a hundred yards from the river-brink, was just large enough to contain the thirteen as they stood erect. The mob of natives charged helter-skelter at the doorway, which was raised three feet above the surrounding earth; but there was no room for any of them inside, and they presently retired to a distance, except the eight or ten who had managed to squeeze themselves to the front. Clio cannot repress a smile as she records that among those who learned by experience that the rust of the rainy season had not yet blunted the British bayonets was a brother of Baboo Ram Bux; the inhospitable chieftain who knew no reverence for suppliants who had sought sanctuary in the precincts of his local gods, and who now sent an express to the Nana to the effect that the Nazarenes were still invincible.

Our countrymen after this enjoyed a short respite, during which they shared a pint or two of putrid water which had collected at the bottom of a hole in the stone altar. Unfortunately the piety of the neighbourhood had of late failed to contribute any oblations of fruit or cakes, which would certainly not have been respected by the famished Christians. But the insurgents soon returned to the attack; made an unsuccessful attempt to dig up the foundations; and finally, with the view of smoking the besieged out of their citadel, constructed and set alight a large pile of faggots. It was not till the enemy showed signs of an intention to mend the fire with some bags of gunpowder that the garrison began to be seriously alarmed. Then they rushed out, scattering the embers with their bare feet, and leaped the parapet which enclosed the plot of dedicated ground. Six, who could not swim, ran full into the middle of the crowd, carrying their lives for sale to the best market. Seven reached the bank, and flung in their firelocks, and then themselves. The lead in their pouches dragged them so far down that the first flight of bullets splashed harmless on the troubled surface. By the time the sepoys had reloaded their pieces, a score of rapid strokes had rendered our countrymen by no means easy targets for an excited Hindoo marksman. Two were shot through the head. Another, overcome with exhaustion, turned over on his back, and yielded to the stream, which impelled him towards a shoal where his murderers were awaiting him with uplifted bludgeons. The others resisted the blandishments of the wily foe, who endeavoured to coax them within push of lance by offers of food and life, and, ducking like coots at the flash of musketry, swam, and floated, and swam again; while Ganges, as if resenting the desecration of its holy waves by such an Iliad of bloodshed, bare bravely up the chin of these fugitives who had confided themselves to his protection. One by one the hunters desisted from the chase. A trooper on horseback kept the game in view for some miles; but in the end he too fell behind, and was no more seen.

The four Englishmen were sitting up to their necks in water, two good leagues below the point where they first plunged, when the sound of approaching voices again sent them diving after the manner of otters surprised by the throng of hounds and spearmen. As they rose to the upper air, they were greeted with a shout of, "Sahib! Sahib! "Why keep away? We are friends." The newcomers, however, were so formidable in aspect and equipment that Thomson refused to come to land until, after a short parley, they volunteered to throw their weapons into the river as a proof of their sincerity. Their assurances of amity afforded our countrymen a passable excuse for giving in, without inspiring any great amount of confidence. At the very worst, a blow on the head or a thrust in the chest killed more expeditiously than drowning or inanition. It was better to die and have done with it, than to endure all the torment of death without the repose, as of late had seemed to be their apportioned lot. And so they turned, and swam in, and were helped ashore naked as Ulysses when he was washed up on the Phœnician coast after his wrestle with the Adriatic surf. Like him, their knees and wrists gave way beneath them: for their vigour was subdued by long toil among the billows: and their bodies were livid and swollen; and much water oozed from mouth and nostril; and they lay without breath, and speech, and well nigh without life, stricken by an exceeding weariness. They had between them a flannel shirt, a strip of linen cloth, and five severe wounds. Exposure to the heat had puffed the skin of their shoulders with huge blisters, as if their clothes had been burned off their backs by fire. But they found an Alcinöus in the person of Dirigbijah Sing, a loyal gentleman of Oude; the landlord of that district, and the chieftain to whom their captors owed feudal allegiance. Good-natured as they proved to be, these fellows could not resist the temptation of plundering the Englishmen who had been so unaccountably delivered into their hands. They abstracted a cap-pouchful of rupees which poor Murphy had tied under his right knee, the nominal price, it may be, of some buckets drawn at a risk which could not be valued in money. After lying for a while wrapped in blankets, the refugees recovered strength sufficient to allow of their being supported to the nearest village, over a distance which appeared to them more miles than it was furlongs in reality. They were taken to the hut of the headman, who received them kindly, and set before them lentil porridge, wheat cakes, and preserves, of which they eat like men who had fed little and badly during a month past, and for seventy hours had not fed at all.

After a long meal and a short nap the Englishmen set out for the fort where Dirigbijah Singh resided; Thomson clad with the solitary shirt, and Delafosse in a borrowed rug. Private Murphy and Gunner Sullivan were suffering too much from recent wounds to care about appearances. The officers resigned to them an elephant which had been despatched for their conveyance, and bestrode a pony, like a pair of needy and valiant knights belonging to a primitive order. As they passed through the villages, peasants came forth with milk and sweetmeats, and discovered that the Sahibs had changed their opinion as to the acceptability of "dollies;" those presents of Oriental dainties which collectors and commissioners contemptuously make over to their servants, reserving a handful of pistachio nuts for the children, and a box of Cabul grapes to improve the dessert of their next dinner-party. Darkness set in ere the cavalcade rode up to the fort of Moorar Mhow. The rajah, an old man of venerable presence, was seated in the open air encircled by his sons, his body-guard, his tenants, and his torch-bearers, to the number of some hundred and fifty persons. He requested our countrymen to alight; inquired minutely into the story of the siege; evinced warm approbation of their courage, and wonder at their escape; and after promising his countenance and hospitality, sent them indoors to an abundant repast washed down with native wine. Tired of everything save eating, they supped right well, and then, stretched on horse-litter and covered with a bit of carpet, the wanderers rested at last. Soundly they slumbered that night; and soundly, too, slumbered their six comrades, on whom the moon looked down through her watery veil as they lay around the little temple amidst the trampled brushwood, on their brow the frown of battle, and in their breast the wound that doth not shame.

Here the four Englishmen remained for three weeks unmolested and tolerably happy. They had spent at least one equal period of time in far less comfortable quarters. They wore coats and trousers cut by a native tailor. Their hurts were poulticed by a native doctor. They sat down thrice a day with British appetites to a meal of native food; and, whenever there was nothing else to be done, they slept. Heedless of the flies, which clustered about their bandaged limbs; careless of the future, and willingly oblivious of the past,—they dreamed, and woke, and yawned, and shifted their straw, and settled themselves down for another fit of drowsiness. Azimoolah might have his eye upon them: the Nana might have spoken the word of doom: up to Delhi and down to Patna every pass might be blockaded by a rebel post: but for the present they could doze, morning, noon, and eve. Their principal diversion consisted in viewing the performance by the Rajah and his priests of some quaint and pretty domestic rites. The master of the house paid them a daily and very pleasant visit; and his good lady sent constantly to ask after the welfare of the strangers, whose fearless deportment under their abject and precarious circumstances she had noted with womanly interest, as she gazed, herself invisible, from behind the fretted stone-work which fenced her verandah.

Thomson and his companions were forbidden by their host to set foot outside the circuit of the walls: as the vicinity was infested with rebels, who already regarded the country as their own, and appeared to imagine themselves welcome anywhere. There were generally some of them inside the fort, vapouring about sword on thigh and matchlock in hand, and pestering the domestics to get them a sight of the Sahibs. The soldiers of the Cawnpore brigade were indulged in frequent interviews with their former officers, always in the presence of a detachment from the Rajah's body-guard. These mutineers were full of the great things that were going to be done in the course of the next year by the armies of the religion. A trooper had been despatched to Moscow on a camel, and was to return with a host of Russian Mussulmans. Such Englishmen as had not yet been knocked on the head were to be secured and shipped off at Calcutta; and afterwards the Nana would embark for Europe, conquer our island, and make it over to Hindoo shareholders constituted into a joint-stock Kumpani. That magic word would conjure up a fresh train of ideas, and they would descant upon the flagrant iniquity of Lord Dalhousie, and maintain that, had it not been for the annexation of Oude, the empire of John Kumpani might have endured for all time: but that it was not so ordained; inasmuch as the ancient oracles, which could not lie, had allotted to that empire a duration of a hundred years, and no more. This prediction came true, but not in the sense anticipated by the leaders of the insurrection. The honour of justifying this prophecy was reserved for Sir Charles Wood and Lord Stanley; not for Azimoolah and the Maharaja of Bithoor. That potentate repeatedly summoned Dirigbijah Singh to deliver up the refugees to his regal arbitrement: but the stout old fellow answered that he held of His Majesty the King of Oude, and knew nothing of Seereek Dhoondoo Punth and his pretensions to royalty. Havelock and Neill soon provided the Nana with more pressing business than the pursuit of his vengeance, or the assertion of his supremacy.

The Rajah came to the conclusion that a change of domicile was essential to the security of our countrymen, about the time that they were growing sated of laughing at sepoy bluster, and watching the Brahmins of the household ring bells and sprinkle flowers with holy water. They accordingly retired to the seclusion of a hamlet bordering on the river, where they amused themselves as best they could with a volume bearing the inscription "53rd Regiment "Native Infantry Book Club;" which had been picked out of the stream by one among their attendants, as it floated by amidst a quantity of torn papers and smashed furniture: so many indications of the minute and searching character of the mischief that was being wrought above. After the lapse of a week, the Rajah sent them across to a landholder of his acquaintance, who lived on the south bank, and who undertook to hand them on to the nearest European encampment. They took leave of their chivalrous preserver with many expressions of unaffected regret, and a silent resolution never to rest until he had received some tangible mark of their gratitude and regard. On reaching the other shore their new patron packed them off towards Allahabad by a cross-road, in a bullock-cart without springs, preceded by an escort of four armed retainers. After bumping along for an hour the driver stopped, and informed them, in low and agitated tones, that there were guns ahead, planted athwart their path. And so they alighted, those way-worn fugitives, solicitous to learn whether they should again have to run, and swim, and lurk, and starve; and they crept stealthily along the edge of the road; and, turning the corner, found themselves within a few yards of the white and freckled face of an English sentry.

Five years subsequently Murphy left his old regiment, and volunteered for India in another corps. Presently it began to be rumoured at mess that there was a man in the ranks who had gone through the siege and the slaughter of Cawnpore. The Colonel made all necessary inquiries, and reported the matter to the Commander-in-chief: who at once appointed Murphy custodian of the Memorial Gardens. Here he may be seen, in the balmy forenoons of the cold weather, sauntering about in a pith helmet and linen jacket; a decent little Irishman, very ready to give a feeling and intelligent account of what took place under his immediate observation, and insisting much on the fact that he and the gunner, unable to speak a syllable of "Moors," would have been helpless but for the knowledge of Hindoostanee possessed by the sepoy officers. He retains a lively impression of the eagerness with which the English privates whom they encountered on the Allahabad highway contributed their allowances of liquor to treat the men who had not tasted beer for eight summer weeks. He points out the stone beneath which reposes poor Sullivan, who died of fatigue and debility, taking the form of cholera, within a fortnight of his restoration to safety. Delafosse lived once more to play the man, fighting under Chamberlain, in the passes of the

Hindoo Koosh: and Thomson to compose the story of what he had seen and undergone, so told that it may be read by a Christian without horror, and by an educated person without disgust. He was of opinion that a soldier who had performed his duty should not stoop to the vocabulary of a hangman. This man, scarred from head to heel with sepoy bullets,—who had carried his life in his hand for months together,—who had lost friends, possessions, and health in the frightful mêlée,—could still write like a modest and tolerant gentleman: while officers, to whom the rebellion had brought nothing except promotion and an opportunity for distinction, were declaiming and printing about battues, and fine bags, and tucking up niggers, and polishing off twenty brace of Pandies. He made it his care that the worthy Rajáh of Moorar Mhow should be rewarded with a handsome pension; that the faithful sepoys of his own battalion should obtain credit for their loyalty; that a fitting monument should be erected to the memory of his dead comrades; and that the services of his living companions in arms should not pass unrecorded. He left it for others to exult when shopkeepers and bankers, whose property had been confiscated by the Nana, and plundered by our own mutinous troops, were condemned and executed for having acknowledged a *de facto* monarch; when pedlars and bazaar-porters were strung up by scores to a gallows planted across the mouth of the funereal well: truly a graceful tribute to the manes of gentle English women.*

At five in the evening on the twenty-eighth of June, the Nana held a state review in honour of his victory of the preceding day. His force looked well on paper, and made a very respectable show in the field. There turned out six entire regiments of foot, and two of horse; besides strong detach-

* A single specimen will suffice of the style which, during those days, a British officer, a Colonel and Companion of the Bath, allowed himself to adopt in a published work. The page is headed "Major Ouvry's Battue."

"Major Ouvry had made his dispositions for 'a bag.' Unlike a "true member of the chase, who loves to see his fox take well to "the open, he had headed his game; spreading his cavalry right "and left of the road, to beat back the high crops into which the "enemy had skulked. Forming his line precisely as he would "have beaten a field of turnips for game, a scene commenced which "baffles all description."

Unhappily it does not baffle the description of Colonel George Bouchier, C.B. who proceeds as follows:—

"Peafowl, partridges, and Pandies rose together. The latter gave "the best sport. Here might be seen a Lancer running a-tilt at a "wretch who had unfortunately taken to the open; there a Pun-"jaub trooper cutting right and left as his victims rose before him; "while the enemy, who were Goojahs, and armed with swords and "hatchets, started up as the line approached, and dashed at their "nearest opponent.

"Two troopers and a horse were our only casualties, while about "one hundred brace of Goojahs bit the dust."

ments from battalions which had been disbanded at a distance from Cawnpore. The ranks of the artillery were perceptibly thinned by three weeks of desperate fighting. To them was especially due the success of the cause: and they now bore the brunt of the rejoicing. Few but zealous, they worked their pieces with a will, and fired away their ammunition as if henceforward there was no occasion for keeping any against the day of battle; as if the clubs of villagers and the daggers of banditti might safely be trusted to gather up the leavings of the sepoys. Bala Rao was welcomed on to the ground with seventeen discharges. The Maharaja himself at length enjoyed the compliment of the royal reception which had been so ardently coveted and so strenuously denied. He was greeted on his appearance by the full sum of twenty-one explosions, each bought with a day of carnage. His ears tingling at the unaccustomed sensation, he congratulated the mutineers on their common triumph, and promised to distribute a hundred thousand rupees as an instalment of the debt which he owed to the army: an announcement that produced a repetition of the salute. Then he took his departure: but the enthusiasm which he left behind could evaporate only in a wholesale expenditure of Government powder. The nephew of the Nana, and his brother

Baba Bhut, were each honoured with seventeen reports. Bala, who was deservedly a favourite with that gang of disciplined assassins, came in for a second bout of eleven guns: while Jwala Pershad and Tantia Topee got the same number a-piece. This closed the proceedings: during which Tantia, whose mind had decidedly a practical cast, was better employed than in listening to an idle cannonade. He was closeted with a man of business named Dabeedeen, liquidating accounts with the owners of the flotilla which had been sunk or burned. Between four and five thousand rupees were paid over as compensation for the boats; and fifty pounds were put aside to remunerate the bargemen for their share in the operations. It was afterwards asserted that Dabeedeen took undue precautions to avoid cheating himself in the transaction.

On the morrow, some boys loitering about on the Oude side of the river came upon an English officer skulking in a ravine. He was of tall stature, and about forty years old, with a bit of sacking twisted round his waist, but otherwise naked. The children imparted their discovery to the peasants of an adjoining hamlet, who took the fugitive to their headman. The unhappy gentleman did not speak any native language, and could only point towards the East with an imploring gesture, and pronounce the word "Lucknow." They gave him sugar, which he eat up greedily with both hands, and so afforded a bystander an opportunity for observing that he bore the mark of a ring fresh on his finger. Touched by the contrast of his fallen state, these good people showed a disposition to do what they could for his preservation; but just then some landholders of the neighbourhood arrived at the head of a numerous array, and prevailed over these benevolent intentions by threats of present violence and future punishment. A short while afterwards, an ex-clerk of the commissariat department met fifty or sixty fellows "with drawn sabres and lighted matches, bringing "along a Sahib bound." They halted under a grove which stood near the chapel of ease, and sent one of their party to fetch the Nana. In his stead came Baba Bhut, and, in the name of his brother, bade them kill their prisoner. To this they answered: "Put weapons into his hand, and let him strike us, "and then we will strike in return: but we will not "slay him thus." Some troopers of the Second Cavalry, who happened to be in attendance, had a less nice theory of honour. Three-quarters of an hour subsequently, while the clerk was performing his ablutions, the corpse was thrown into the Ganges, gashed all over with sword-cuts.

All the night of the twenty-ninth our people who

had been captured at Nuzzufgur by Baboo Ram Bux were slowly remounting the stream. As it grew light they began to recognise objects and places which they had trusted never again to behold: and, two hours before noon, the doomed boatload lay to at the landing-place whence they had set forth, to return thus after three such days as had not repaid them for the trouble of making their escape. What ensued an Englishman would willingly tell in phrases not his own. The following account was taken from the lips of a native spy, and is supported by a mass of evidence. The mention of General Wheeler is, of course, inaccurate.

"There were brought back," says the man, "sixty "Sahibs, twenty-five Mem Sahibs, and four children. "The Nana ordered the Sahibs to be separated from "the Mem Sahibs, and shot by the First Bengal "Native Infantry. But they said, 'We will not "'shoot Wheeler Sahib, who has made our regiment's "'name great, and whose son is own Quarter-master. "'Neither will we kill the Sahib people. Put them "'in prison.' Then said the Nadiree regiment: "'What word is this? Put them in prison? We "'will kill the males.' So the Sahibs were seated "on the ground: and two companies of the Nadiree "regiment stood with their muskets, ready to fire. "Then said one of the Mem Sahibs, the doctor's "wife: (What doctor? How should I know?) 'I "'will not leave my husband. If he must die, I "'will die with him.' So she ran, and sat down "behind her husband, clasping him round the waist. "Directly she said this, the other Mem Sahibs said: "'We also will die with our husbands.' And they "all sat down, each by her husband. Then their "husbands said: 'Go back;' but they would not. "Whereupon the Nana ordered his soldiers; and "they, going in, pulled them away forcibly. But "they could not pull away the doctor's wife, who "there remained. Then the Padre called out to "the Nana, and requested leave to read prayers "before they died." (This Padre was Captain Seppings, with his broken arm. The doctor's wife, good soul, is known to have been Mrs. Boyes.) "The "Nana granted it, and the Padre's hands were "loosened so far as to enable him to take a small "book from his pocket, with which he read. But "all this time one of the Sahibs, who was shot in the "arm, kept crying out to the sepoys: 'If you mean "'to kill us, why don't you set about it quickly and "'have the work done?'" Poor impatient Sahib! Making the responses in his passionate way! "After "the Padre had read a few prayers, he shut the "book, and the Sahibs shook hands all round. Then "the sepoys fired. One Sahib rolled one way, one

"another, as they sat. But they were not dead:
"only wounded. So they went in, and finished them
"off with swords."

Here is a thing which was actually done on the last Tuesday of June, eight years back from the present date. Three months before, these Sahibs and Mem Sahibs were passing an existence no more eventful, and apparently no less secure than the career of a county-court judge, or a military man quartered at Sheffield or Colchester. They laid their plans for the Meerut race-meeting and the biennial trip to an Himalayan station in a confidence of fruition equal to that with which a home-staying public servant anticipates the cup-day at Ascot, and the pass which he is going to discover in September. In April, Cawnpore society was lamenting the departure of one period of cold weather, and looking forward to the arrival of another; but, ere the rains had well set in, it had come to this, that the last batch of English officers were lying stiff and stark on the parade-ground, in front of the building where their widows and orphans were enduring a brief imprisonment for life.

The number of captives had yet to receive a final addition. At the station of Futtehgur, which was situated about seventy miles up the river from Cawnpore, some hundred and eighty English people of every age and profession were alive when the month of June commenced. The cantonments were occupied by the Tenth Native Infantry, under the command of Colonel Smith, a man distinguished by courage so closely allied with rashness, and firmness so nearly akin to obstinacy, that the European residents could not have fared worse had they been under the charge of a waverer or a coward. He was a zealous adherent of that sect among the Bengal officers which worshipped the sepoy. A willing martyr to the creed that he professed, his devotion would have excused his fanaticism, had he been the only victim: but no personal calamity can atone for pedantry which staked and lost nine score English souls on the truth of the axiom that a mutineer was still docile and affectionate until he could be proved a murderer.

During the latter half of May successive tidings of massacre, insurrection, and, finally, of an approaching rebel force, excited the fears of our countrymen, and the impious hopes of the soldiery: as turbulent a set of scamps as any in Northern India. At length Mr. Probyn, the magistrate of that district, whose acute discernment, if left to itself, would have saved a large asset of life from the wreck of our fortunes, took measures for evacuating Futtehgur before the extreme crisis. He put himself into communication with Hurdeo Bux, a loyal noble whose estates lay on the left bank, and obtained an escort of fifty picked men and the offer of an asylum. At midnight, between the third and fourth of June, more than a hundred of the English inhabitants started down the river in a fleet of twelve or thirteen boats, laden with baggage, merchandise, furniture, and an ample store of provisions. Colonel Smith was not a little disgusted that so many people should combine to put a slight upon his pet battalion; but consoled himself with the reflection that time and the issue would judge between the sepoys and their defamers. The fugitives comprised the merchants of the place, and the planters of the vicinity; the civilians, missionaries, clerks, craftsmen, and pensioners; together with at least forty women, several nurseries of children, and a multitude of native domestics. They anchored for refreshment after accomplishing a stage of four leagues, and, before breakfast was finished, were joined by certain officers of the Tenth, who announced that the regiment had mutinied on parade, and that all was over at Futtehgur. The expedition proceeded on its way, under a desultory fire of musketry from the country people, who were for the most part hostile to our cause. Next morning arrived the bailiff of Hurdeo Bux, who brought Probyn an invitation from his master to take refuge in his fort of Dhurrumpore. It was resolved to split the party. The magistrate, with forty others, accepted the proffered hospitality: while three of the most roomy vessels, containing nineteen men, twenty-three women, and twenty-six children, pushed forwards in the direction of Cawnpore.

And they reached their destination. On the evening of the ninth of June the little squadron was brought to on a sand-bank a few furlongs above Nawabgunge, the north-west suburb of Cawnpore. Here they abode forty-eight hours, listening to the ceaseless cannonade which pealed along the stream from the south. Then they sent a messenger bearing a request for permission to pass on their way: the answer to which was brought by a horde of mutineers, who had no sooner appeared in view than the boatmen set the thatch a-light, and fell with bludgeons and sabres upon the passengers, who were taking their afternoon tea, and who now threw themselves over the bulwarks, and sought concealment in a patch of high grass. But their cover was fired by the rebel guns; two ladies and a child were scorched or suffocated to death; and the rest of the company fell into the hands of the troopers of the Second Cavalry, to whose *esprit-de-corps* this one-sided work was more suited than the dubious contest which was raging around our intrenchment. The captives were made fast to a long rope, and marched as far as ladies with bare and bleeding feet could carry the babies and drag along the children: for by this time all their servants had fled, with the exception of two Ayahs and a few menials of the very lowest order. Here, as elsewhere, fortitude and fidelity were in inverse proportion to dignity of caste. Our people spent the night supperless, on the spot where they had halted; and at daybreak, after breakfasting on a mouthful of water a-piece, were distributed among sixteen bullock carts, and conveyed into the presence of the Nana: to whom they pointed out the folly of which he would be guilty if he indulged himself in wanton and indiscriminate murder. It was no easy task, they bade him reflect, to empty Europe of Europeans. He is said to have been inclined to mercy: but Bala Rao, who, if there was a choice between the brothers, seems to have been the blackest villain of the three, made such an outcry that the Nana stifled his nascent humanity in order to prevent the scandal of a family quarrel. The ladies and the little ones received orders to seat themselves on the ground; and the gentlemen, with their hands tied behind them, were drawn up as a rear rank. The Second Cavalry had soon another victory to inscribe upon their standards. "I witnessed all this with my own eyes," says a Hindoo nurse, who, while they were both above the soil, would not lose sight of her dear young charge: "for I was sitting about thirty paces "on one side. Two pits were dug, and all the bodies "thrown in. The Nana was not present. May God "take vengeance on him, and on these wicked "men."

Nanukchund notes in his diary that "reports of "guns were heard from the direction of Nawabgunge. "A little after twelve A.M. two dead bodies of Euro-"peans were seen floating down the Ganges; and "sepoys were seen in a boat coming down behind "these corpses and firing off their muskets as they "came." Next day he found occasion to seek a retreat in a village which lay at some distance up the river. "I perceived," he writes, "bodies of "ladies and gentlemen lying along the banks of the "Ganges. I cannot describe the grief I felt at this "sight. The corpses could not float down from the "shallowness of the river. I saw three boats and a "barge which had been burnt by the rebels. I ques-"tioned the people of the place, and learned that "wine and other articles of merchandise were in the "boats, but the boatmen had plundered the liquors, "and, when drunk, cut down the gentlemen."

Soon after, "a body of troopers from the Nana "came to seize me, and surrounded the house where

"I was. But I was saved from the hands of these "ruffians, and kept in concealment in a garden. At "nightfall the gardener sent four men with me, and "thus I managed to reach the shore. It was not, "however, my fate to find a boat, and I resolved to "drown myself in the river, as I thought it better to "die than to fall into the hands of so cruel a foe. "After midnight I left the garden. The first ford I "came to had water up to the waist only, and it was "moonlight: so I waded across, and reached the "next channel. There I saw the corpses of the "Europeans whom the boatmen had slain when "drunk: I cannot tell the exact number of bodies, "but they extended here and there about a mile. "I saw three dead young ladies. They all were "dressed, but the low caste people had commenced "to take off their clothes; and some had been torn "by animals. Portions of property, books, and "papers, belonging to the plundered boats, were "also strewn about the shores. These drunken "boatmen were armed, some with clubs, some with "weapons; and they were running about the woods "like wild men. I cannot describe the terror which "seized me at that moment. How I sighed for the "British rule! I was trembling with fear, and knew "not where I was going. On reaching the opposite "bank I was senseless for four hours."

Meanwhile at Futtehgur was being played an unique tragi-comedy. On the fourth of June, during morning parade, twenty thousand pounds' worth of Government silver was in course of removal from the treasury to the fort. This mark of distrust, coming close upon the departure of the flotilla, proved too much for the sensibility of these military Brahmins; a number of whom stepped out from the ranks, surrounded the carts, and insisted that the money should be taken to their own quarters. Colonel Smith and the adjutant came forward and expostulated with the insurgents; but they were pushed up against the wall, and kept within a semicircle of levelled bayonets until the cash was safely deposited in the middle of the sepoy lines. These proceedings caused a slight unpleasantness, which did not wholly disappear until the troops had been gratified with an advance of two months' pay, a promise of six months' extra allowances, and an assurance that the treasure should henceforward be kept on the parade-ground under their exclusive custody: inasmuch as the Company's property could be nowhere so secure as in the guardianship of the Company's soldiers. That evening Smith harangued as many of the battalion as chose to attend; told them that their conduct had been disgraceful, but threw the blame on the shoulders of the recruits; and entreated them to believe that he could forgive and forget. He then pronounced the regiment faithful and staunch. And so the first little difficulty between the colonel and his men had been patched up, and both parties were living together on terms of contemptuous acquiescence on the one side, and doting credulity on the other.

Such was the state of things which Probyn found when, after an interval of four days, he rode into the cantonment accompanied by a lieutenant and ensign of the Tenth. Immediately upon their arrival the colonel informed the magistrate that his services were no longer required, as the district was entirely under martial law, and put the two subalterns in arrest for having deserted their posts. The poor lads represented that they had been driven from Futtehgur by the fire of their own companies: but this man, whom sepoy steel pointed at his chest would not convince of sepoy disaffection, refused to accept the word of his officers when it clashed with a darling theory. Probyn, who foresaw the result, wrote to the Europeans then residing under the roof of Hurdeo Bux, stating that in his opinion the battalion could not possibly be kept together; and recommending that their host should put his fort into a defensible condition, and engage five hundred matchlockmen on the credit of the English Government. Feeling that he was useless while in the same locality with the colonel, he shook from his feet the dust of the devoted station, and made his way back to Dhurrumpore.

He was followed by a letter from Smith earnestly inviting the refugees to leave their new ally, and throw themselves into the arms of their natural protectors, the native soldiers of the Tenth regiment. He affirmed that there were at least a hundred and fifty men upon whom he absolutely relied; and that, if the worst should come to the worst, he could with their aid fight his way down to Allahabad. The poor creatures, who were very uncomfortably lodged, and who regretted the punkahs and musquito-curtains, the soda-water and bottled beer of their abandoned homes, jumped at the proposition in spite of all the logic and eloquence which Probyn could bring to bear upon their infatuation. He persuaded no one except his own family, and a solitary civilian, who had escaped from a slaughter and tumult in Rohilcund too narrowly and recently for him to care to move again. The rest of the party returned to Futtehgur, and re-instated themselves in the good graces of the deluded veteran. Before very long, they were treated with a specimen of sepoy loyalty. On the sixteenth of June the colonel took measures to carry out a capital sentence of the civil courts. The soldiery, however, considered that at such a time there might be something awkward in the precedent of an execution, and intimated that the criminal had better be released. Their intimation met with prompt obedience.

The Seetapore mutineers, laden with English booty, and reeking with English blood, were now close at hand. Their ringleaders despatched a letter to the men of the Tenth, calling upon them to murder their officers: to which the reply was: "Come. We will "not oppose you. We have sworn not to do so: but "our vows do not bind you." So little reciprocity of affection existed in that indecorous dalliance between authority and sedition. On the eighteenth of June the troops, eager to fling aside even the pretence of submission and the semblance of discipline, broke forth into open rebellion; sacked the public chest; and set up a pretender, whom the event showed to be better than a mere puppet. The Europeans shut themselves up in the fort, in company with one Kalay Khan, the sole representative of the colonel's hundred and fifty faithful sepoys. That evening the Seetapore mutineers marched into the station, hungry for pillage; and, on discovering an empty treasury, vented their rage by killing every man of the Tenth on whom they could lay hands. In the course of a week, however, stimulated by the prospect of a liberal bounty, and the co-operation of some powerful Rohilla chieftains, the regiments made up their differences, and united to exterminate the common enemy. For ten days and nights five and thirty of our countrymen maintained against as many hundred assailants a rambling tumbledown old earthwork extending over a space of twenty acres. They fired bags of screws and scrap-iron for grape, and the heads of sledge-hammers for round-shot. They repulsed three general assaults. They lived amidst an atmosphere alive with bullets and flying splinters, and dim with the smoke of blazing houses and exploding mines. At length, when the besiegers were gradually but surely blowing their way through the rampart, the defenders took to their boats, and dropped down the current, encumbered by thrice their own number of women, children, and invalids.

The rest is soon told. The river was low: the pursuit hot and persistent. The barges grounded; and were got off; and grounded for the last time. The crews waded ashore to drive away the hostile sharpshooters: and some were borne back dying; and some never stirred from the spot where they fell. Vessels hove in view, unwarlike in their external aspect; but which, as they ran alongside, proved to be crammed with swordsmen and musketeers. And then ensued mad confusion, and promiscuous butchery, and suicide that did not merit the name. On the tenth evening of July, after losing a life for every mile of the voyage, the expedition got as far as Nawabgunge, but no farther. The ladies helped to swell the throng of prisoners, and their husbands were sent whither the men of the Cawnpore garrison had gone before. Three only were spared upon their engaging to bring about that the citadel of Allahabad should be made over to the rebellion. The Nana had reason for his self-denial. It was worth his while to forego any gratification to purchase security in the southern quarter. That was the direction in which was brewing the storm of retribution and reconquest.

CHAPTER V.

THE MASSACRE.

AND now Seereek Dhoondoo Punth purposed in the face of all India to invest himself with the ensigns and the titles of royalty. The contest had been fought out. The prize lay ready to his grasp. But it was no light matter to fix upon the auspicious hour when the Mahratta might take possession of the kingdom that he had carved out with his blade from the very heart of the dominions held by the alien race which had despoiled his sire. The soothsayers were consulted on this momentous point: but they were forestalled in their office by Dabeedeen, the individual who acted as agent for Tantia Topee in his dealings with the boatmen; and who now, stimulated by his success in that transaction, aspired to try his hand at divination. With the audacity of an amateur he at once named five in the evening of the thirtieth June as the season when, in accordance with the will of heaven, the Maharaja should proceed to Bithoor for the purpose of assuming his kingly functions. There must have been considerable discontent among the members of the Sacred College when they learned that this volunteer augur had been rewarded with a fee of five hundred rupees, and a horse on which to attend the ceremony. The Nana set forth, accompanied by Bala Rao, and in the course of the next day took his seat as Peishwa on the paternal throne. The consecrated mark was affixed to his forehead amidst the roar of guns, and the acclamations of a crowd composed chiefly of townsmen who had repaired thither to surrender in the shape of an honorary gift such of their valuables as had not already passed by a more direct channel into the coffers of the usurper.

Some there were, however, who on this august occasion might rejoice with unfeigned rapture. The sepoys were gladdened by an announcement that a large quantity of gold had been sent to the Magazine, and would there be fashioned into decorations for the ankles of those warriors who had borne the burden and heat of the great struggle. The Ganges Canal was bestowed as a perquisite upon Azimoolah. It is difficult to conceive what would have been the indignation of the Directors who sat in Leadenhall Street during the years of the Crimean war, had they been told that the very equivocal native prince who was for ever hanging about the India House, would one day become sole proprietor of the gigantic concern which grew dearer to their hearts the more it cost and the less it yielded.

That night the city of Cawnpore was illuminated, and the following proclamations were posted in all places of general resort:

"As by the kindness of God and the good fortune "of the Emperor all the Christians who were at "Delhi, Poonah, Sattara, and other places, and even "those five thousand European soldiers who went in "disguise into the former city and were discovered, "are destroyed and sent to hell by the pious and "sagacious troops, who are firm to their religion; "and as they have been all conquered by the present "Government, and as no trace of them is left in "these places, it is the duty of all the subjects and "servants of the Government to rejoice at the de- "lightful intelligence, and carry on their respective "work with comfort and ease."

"As by the bounty of the glorious Almighty and "the enemy-destroying fortune of the Emperor the "yellow-faced and narrow-minded people have been "sent to hell, and Cawnpore has been conquered, it "is necessary that all the subjects and landowners "should be as obedient to the present Government "as they have been to the former one; that all the "Government servants should promptly and cheer-

"fully engage their whole mind in executing the "orders of the Government; that it is the incumbent "duty of all the peasants and landed proprietors of "every district to rejoice at the thought that the "Christians have been sent to hell, and both the "Hindoo and Mahomedan religions have been con-"firmed; and that they should as usual be obedient "to the authorities of the Government, and never "suffer any complaint against themselves to reach "to the ears of the higher authority."

There is something quaint in the notion of a paternal Government setting the national mind at ease as to the damnation of the enemy, and ordaining a public rejoicing over "the delightful intelli-"gence." Our authorities never went so far as to imitate the example: but Calcutta journalism did its best to supply the deficiency. "Fas est et ab "hoste doceri" was the motto of that remarkable department of ephemeral literature. Among other gems which in 1857 adorned the poetry corner of the "Englishman," one stands conspicuous both for sentiment and expression:

> "Barring Humanity pretenders
> "To hell of none are we the willing senders:
> "But, if to sepoys mercy must be given,
> "Locate them, Lord, in the back slums of heaven."

Be it observed that Lord Canning, Sir John Peter

Grant, Mr. Charles Buxton, and Sir Henry Rich are here esteemed unworthy even of the partial and secondary felicity dealt out to Teeka Singh and Mungul Pandy. A critic who takes into account the creeds held by the respective writers will of the two productions regard with less aversion the performance of the Nana. That year of sin and horror afforded what was in truth an ill commentary upon the injunction to practise the mercy which rejoiceth against judgment, and on the oft-repeated assurance that in forgiveness and forbearance, if in nothing else, the disciple may emulate his master. And we wonder, forsooth, that our missionaries labour in vain to exalt the effective power of our faith in the eyes of those very heathen who are conscious how in the day of temptation talked and acted men calling themselves after the name of Him whose last miracle was the healing of his captor, and whose last prayer was for the pardon of his murderers!

On the first of July the prisoners were removed from the Savada Hall to a small building north of the canal, situated between the black city and the Ganges. It was their final change of lodgings. To this day they occupy those premises on a lease which no man may dispute. This humble dwelling, the residence of some poor quill-driver, Hindoo or half-caste, as the case may be, had long stood amidst a group of sightly villas and edifices of social resort, unnoticed except by a casual sanitary commissioner, and distinguished only by a numeral in the map of the Ordnance Survey. It has since been known in India as the Beebeegur, or House of the Ladies; in England as the House of the Massacre. It comprised two principal rooms, each twenty feet by ten, certain windowless closets intended for the use of native domestics, and an open court some fifteen yards square. Here, during a fortnight of the Eastern summer, were penned two hundred and six persons of European extraction: for the most part women and children of gentle birth. The grown men were but five in number: the three gentlemen of Futtehgur, who are supposed to have been Mr. Thornhill, the judge, and Colonels Smith and Goldie: together with Mr. Edward Greenway, and his son Thomas.

If the various degrees of wretchedness are to be estimated by the faculty for suffering contained in the victim, then were these ladies of all women the most miserable. Few or none amongst them had been aware that in some corner of the mansion beneath whose roof their happier days were passed, there existed such foul holes as those in which they now lay panting by the score. It was much if they had cared to hazard a supposition that "the servants "slept somewhere about the compound." They had neither furniture, nor bedding, nor straw; nothing but coarse and hard bamboo matting, unless they preferred a smoother couch upon the bare floor. They fed sparely on cakes of unleavened dough, and lentil-porridge dished up in earthen pans without spoon or plate. There was some talk of meat on Sundays, but it never came to anything. Once the children got a little milk. The same day the head-bearer of Colonel Williams came to pay his respects to the daughter who was the sole survivor of the officer's household. "I could not," he says, "get "near the ladies on account of the sentries, but saw "that food was being distributed to them. It con-"sisted of native bread and milk. I remonstrated "with a soldier who had formerly served under my "master, and begged of him to supply with better "food people who had lived in a very different way. "He gave me eight annas" (twelvepence) "to go "to the bazaar and buy some sweetmeats. I did "so; and on my return Miss Georgiana and a "married lady came into the verandah to meet me. "Miss Georgiana repeated to me her mother's in-"junctions about my going to her brother. I gave "them the sweetmeats, and had little time to speak "to them, for, seeing me, the other ladies came out "into the verandah: on which the sentries turned "me out."

The matron of these female prisoners, whom it took so little to keep in order, was a woman described as tall; of a fair complexion; twenty-eight or thirty years in age; but with a few grey hairs. She went by the nickname of "the Begum," and her character was no better than could be looked for in a waiting-maid of the courtezan who then ruled the circle of the Nana. She superintended a staff of sweepers, who furnished the captives with their food. The attendance of such debased menials was in itself the most ignominious affront which Oriental malice could invent: and even these were provided exclusively for the humiliation of our countrywomen, and might do nothing for their comfort. A young Brahmin, who chanced to look over the fence of the enclosure, saw some ladies washing their own dirty linen. With the irrepressible loquacity of an Hindoo he began asking some strangers who were standing by whether there was no washerman who would undertake to do for the Mem Sahibs: an ill-timed curiosity which procured him a slap on the face and a night in the guard-room.

Seventy-five paces from the abode where our people were confined stood an hotel owned by a Mahomedan proprietor: an erection of considerable size, daubed with bright yellow paint. Allured, probably, by the gaudiness of colour, an attraction which no genuine native can resist, the Nana had selected this building as his head-quarters. A couple of guns were planted at the entrance of the compound, and a strong detachment of his retainers kept guard under the portico. Two spacious centre rooms were reserved for the Maharaja's public receptions. One of the wings was set apart for the duties of the kitchen and the altar: and, side by side with religion, cooking went merrily on through every hour of the twenty-four. In the other Dhoondoo Punth lived from day to day in a perpetual round of sensuality, amidst a choice coterie of priests, pandars, ministers, and minions. The reigning beauty of the fortnight was one Oula or Adala. She was the Thais on whose breast sunk the vanquished victor, oppressed with brandy and such love as animates a middle-aged Eastern debauchee. She is said to have counted by hundreds of thousands the rupees which were lavished on her by the affection and vanity of her Alexander: and could well afford to spare one of her suite to look after the prisoners for the fraction of time during which they were likely to need her services. Every night there was an entertainment of music, dancing, and pantomime. The hit of the evening was made by a buffoon who took off amidst shouts of laughter the stiff carriage of an English officer.

The noise of this unhallowed revelry was plainly audible to the captives in the adjoining house ; and, as they crowded round the windows to catch the breeze which sprang up at sunset, the glare of torches and the strains of barbarous melody might remind them of the period when he who was now arbiter of their existence thought himself privileged if he could induce them to honour with a half-disdainful acceptance the hospitality of Bithoor. They sometimes got a nearer view of the festivities. The Begum daily took across two ladies to the Nana's stables, where they were set down to grind corn at a hand-mill for the space of several hours. They generally contrived to bring back a pocketful of flour for the children.

Hardship, heat, wounds, and want of space and proper nourishment released many from their bondage before the season marked out by Azimoolah for a jail delivery such as the world had seldom witnessed. A native doctor, himself a prisoner, has left a list of deaths which occurred between the seventh and the fifteenth of the month. Within these eight days, of which one was incomplete, as will be seen by those who read on, there succumbed to cholera and dysentery eighteen women, seven children, and an Hindoo nurse. There is a touching little entry which deserves notice. In the column headed "Names" appear the words "eck beebee" (one baby): under that marked "disease" is written "ap se" (of itself).

Dying by threes and fours of frightful maladies, the designations of which they hardly knew; trying to eat nauseous and unwonted food, and to sleep upon a bed of boards; tormented by flies, and musquitoes, and dirt, and prickly heat, and all the lesser evils that aggravate and keep for ever fresh the consciousness of a great misfortune: doing for the murderer of their dearest ones that labour which in Asia has always been the distinctive sign and badge of slavery: to such reality of woe had been reduced these beings whose idea of peril had once been derived from romances, and who had been acquainted with destitution only through tracts and the reports of charitable institutions. Alas for the delicate Mem Sahibs, and the pretty Missy Babas, for whom nothing had formerly been too dainty and well-appointed! Alas for the handy and patient soldiers' wives, who had followed their good men into the discomfort of barrack life to be rewarded thus! Alas for sturdy Bridget Widdowson, and tender Mrs. Moore, who bore on her bosom a child destined never to lisp the name of his brave father!

Her perchance one of the victors, whose son or brother had fallen beneath her husband's sword, (for he was no sluggard in the onset), might see weeping like Andromache over her toil at the weary mill, and might say: "This was the wife of him who of all the "English fought the best, whenever the battle waxed "hot around their wall." And, so speaking, he would renew her grief at thought of the man who was no longer there to shield her from the day of bondage. But he, floating on his face past some distant city, or stranded on a bank of sand trodden by none save the vulture and the crocodile, saw not how she was misused, nor heard when she cried for succour.

The number of captives diminished so fast that the Nana began to fear lest he should soon have no hostages wherewith to provide against the consequences of a possible reverse. They were accordingly driven twice a day into the verandah, and forced to sit there until they had inhaled as much fresh air as, in the judgment of the Begum, would support an English constitution for the space of twelve hours. This substitute for the morning gallop and the evening promenade was very distasteful to our ladies, on account of the idlers who came to stare, and remark how odd a Lady Sahib looked when neither on horseback nor in her carriage. The poor creatures were overheard whispering among themselves that the British never used their prisoners thus.

It is probable that from this circumstance originated the rumour concerning European females who had been publicly maltreated in the bazaar. Two or three sentences must here be written upon those fables which it is our misfortune that we once believed, and our shame if we ever stoop to repeat. Delhi, Cawnpore, and Futtehgur were the three stations in which any considerable multitude of our countrywomen were placed under the disposal of the mutineers. With regard to the two latter places, if we except one single case of abduction, it is absolutely certain that our ladies died without mention, and, we may confidently hope without apprehension of dishonour. Those revolting stories which accompanied to Southampton the first tidings of the tumult at Delhi may all be traced to some gossip regarding the fate of Miss Jennings, the daughter of the chaplain, and her friend, Miss Clifford. It is now ascertained beyond all question that these girls were sitting in an upper room of the palace gateway, when they heard on the stairs a rush of footsteps and a clattering of scabbards, and were cut down dead as they rose from their chairs to learn the cause of this strange intrusion.

Some, who love to attribute every event to the special interposition of Providence, have insisted that nothing short of fabricated indignities, and tales of mutilation equally untrue and more easily disproved, could have kindled the explosion of wrath and pity which sent forth by myriads the youth of England again to subdue Hindostan beneath a Christian yoke. Piety, unwilling to pronounce authoritatively on such a matter, will be loth to imagine that God provoked men to utter and to credit lies for the furtherance of any purpose which could conduce to His glory. As must ever be in the order of things by Him determined, the evil seed produced evil fruit. Grapes came not of those thorns, nor figs of those thistles. The murder of a hundred families, the ruin of a thousand homesteads, were incentives capable of exalting our national enthusiasm to the requisite pitch without the aid of exaggeration or invention. Those hateful falsehoods served but to evoke from the depths of our nature the sombre and ferocious instincts which religion and civilization can never wholly eradicate. To their account unhappy India may charge most of the innocent blood that was spilt and the bad blood that remains.

It was not long before the usurper began to experience the proverbial uneasiness of a crowned head. At no time a favourite with the Cawnpore population, he now was cordially detested by all the respectable inhabitants; who, after his downfall, testified their hatred by refusing to pronounce his name without the addition of some disparaging epithet. The majestic appellations of Maharaja and Peishwa were at once cut down to "Nana soor," "that pig of a Nana:" and this was the mildest and the most decent of all his agnomina, with the exception, perhaps of "budmash," which answers as nearly as possible to the French "coquin." "That "great budmash, the Nana," occurs in the peroration of one of Nanukchund's outbursts of Hindoo eloquence. For the present, however, the townspeople evinced their ill-will by a tacit but very effective opposition to the new *régime.* His requisitions of money and supplies met with no response; and he could procure nothing except by open force, which he was not slow to employ. The city had, indeed, little motive to love him or the state of things which he represented. A Mahomedan author describes the aspect of a locality where the rebellion had obtained the ascendancy in these graphic words:—"Since the day of my arrival I never found "the bazaar open, unless it were a few poor shops. "The shop-keepers and the citizens are extremely "sorry for losing their safety, and curse the muti-"neers from morning to evening. The people and "the workmen starve, and widows cry in their "huts."

The class who had most cause to pray for the return of order were the natives of Bengal Proper, then settled in the Upper Provinces for purposes of commerce. Impoverished, suspected, menaced, and outraged, they were conscious that neither life, limb, nor liberty were worth a fortnight's purchase. Many a rich Bengalee within the borders of the insurrection sat all day behind closed blinds, with a pistol in his girdle, a bag of jewels in his turban, and a horse ready saddled at the back door of his garden. And it was not without reason that these men suffered so cruelly: for they were only less loyal than the English themselves. The wealthy, industrious, and effeminate denizens of Lower Bengal had no desire to see the many-headed and irrational despotism of a Prætorian guard substituted for the mild and regular sway of old John Company. The conduct of the soldiery rendered them exceedingly uncomfortable and not a little indignant: and they lost no opportunity of wreaking their spite upon the turbulent mercenaries who would not allow honest folks to go about their business in peace. The sepoys who mutinied at Chittagong and Dacca, both of which stations lie within the limits of Bengal, met with such hostility from the country-people that they gave up all thoughts of moving on Calcutta, and endeavoured to make their way into Assam. Few ever reached the frontier. They literally rotted away in the jungle. Some died of starvation: some of fever and ague. The foragers were knocked on the head by the peasantry, skilled, like all Hindoo villagers, in the play of the quarter-staff. The stragglers were carried off by wild animals which swarm amidst the swamps and forests that fringe the great rivers of eastern India. At length, driven into a corner, they one morning cut the throats of the women who had hitherto accompanied their march, and dispersed into the wilderness, to re-appear not even on the gallows. They could not have fared worse amidst the moors of Yorkshire or Northumberland.

It is painful to remember how we requited the attachment and fidelity of Bengal. At a time when all good citizens, without distinction of birth and creed, should have united in one firm front against the common foe, it was the delight of many among the English residents in the capital to heap insult and accusation on their dark-skinned neighbours. Then, in the presence of that portentous danger, every condition of soul, from the height of magnanimity to incredible baseness, might be observed in striking and instructive contrast. While at one end of Northern India stout Sir John was fighting his province in the interests of the general weal; denuding himself of British soldiers, and committing his existence and reputation to the faith of Sikh allies; doing steadfastly in the hour the work of the hour; remedying the evil which was sufficient unto the day, and, like a good Christian as he was, leaving to God the things of the morrow: at the other end a clique of Englishmen, driven insane by terror and virulence, were plotting how to form themselves into a Committee of Public Safety, depose the viceroy, seize the reins of the state, and have their will upon the native population. While at Arrah a handful of heroes were defending a billiard-room against drought, and hunger, and cannon, and the militia of a warlike region, backed by three regiments of regular infantry: in Calcutta a pack of bullies were moving heaven and earth to eject from the Photographic Society a Bengalee member, who had given vent to some remarks reflecting upon the habits and tone of low European loafers. As if they themselves never sinned against charity with tongue or pen! As if "traitor," and "hypocrite," and "fawning nigger," were not terms all too weak to express their feelings towards those deputations of Hindoo and Mahomedan gentlemen who filled the shelves of Lord's Canning's cabinet with addresses setting forth their devotion to our rule!

July had not well set in before the insurgents of Cawnpore showed symptoms that marked the wilfulness and inconstancy of soldiers who have once forgotten their duty. Idleness bred discontent, and discontent speedily ripened into sedition. The honeymoon had not yet drawn to a close, and already this unnatural connexion between the Nana and the army was distasteful to the stronger of the contracting parties. Regiments which had refused to obey such men as Ewart and Delafosse were not likely to entertain any very profound reverence for an effete Hindoo rake. The Peishwa evinced an inclination to enjoy for a while the contemplation of his recent dignity in the retirement of Bithoor: but the troops had no notion of letting their paymaster out of sight, and brought him back into their midst by violence which they hardly cared to disguise beneath the semblance of respect. On the third of the month a donation was distributed among their ranks, and accepted with anything but gratitude. Few got as much as, in their own opinion, they deserved; and all less than they desired. What they had was not in a portable form. Government silver proved to be an inconvenient burden for the loins; and, if things went ill, it might procure a still more unpleasant girdle round the neck. There were disagreeable anecdotes current regarding certain gentlemen, late of the Company's service, who had been executed at Allahabad on the discovery about their persons of some new copper coins, which had never issued from the Treasury by a regular payment, and which they were suspected of having intended to put into premature circulation. There accordingly was a brisk demand for gold. Azimoolah ordered it to be proclaimed in the bazaar by beat of drum that bankers should supply the mutineers with mohurs at a minimum price of twenty-one rupees. The Cawnpore exchange, however, had so little confidence in the star of the maharaja, that these coins could not be bought for less than twenty-eight rupees, which was an advance of seventy-five per cent. on their ordinary price. The sepoys, who were not more acquainted than European privates with the laws which regulate the money-market, and knew only that they had ended by pocketing little more than half the cash that they expected, were soon talking about a fresh change of masters. The Mussulman faction gained ground rapidly and surely. Men began to recollect how cleverly the Nunhey Nawab had managed his battery without any prior experience in gunnery, and drew the conclusion that he might be equally successful if he could be bribed by an offer of sovereignty to turn his attention towards the rate of discount.

But military greediness, and Moslem ambition, and the jealousy of the nobles, and the enmity of the bourgeoisie ceased ere long to occupy the thoughts of the tyrant. These sources of uneasiness were absorbed in one great and pressing terror, when, at the first doubtful and intermittent, but more frequent ever and clearer, came surging up from the south-west the fame of the advancing vengeance. Couriers mounted on swift camels were sent down the road, and returned with the intelligence that the British were certainly approaching by forced marches, laying down a telegraph as they proceeded, and hanging the inhabitants of the villages within which were found pieces of the old wire. This information naturally produced a strong effect upon men whose crimes were not such as to meet with impunity under the new scale of penalties that seemed to have been adopted by the Sahibs. The consternation was so deep and universal that the Nana had recourse to his customary palliative. On the fifth of July he issued the following proclamation:—

"It has come to our notice that some of the "city people, having heard the rumours of the "arrival of the European troops at Allahabad, are "deserting their houses and going out into the "districts. Be it therefore proclaimed in each lane "and street of the city that regiments of cavalry, "and infantry, and batteries have been despatched "to check the Europeans either at Allahabad or "Futtehpore; that the people should therefore "remain in their houses without any apprehension, "and engage their minds in carrying on their work."

This manifesto was probably considered too tame and brief for such a crisis. Next day there appeared a truly notable state-paper, which, to judge from internal evidence, may be attributed to the pen of the prime-minister. It is regarded as the masterpiece of that author, and may serve for a model to all Governments that undertake to enlighten the public mind by means of an official organ.

"A traveller just arrived at Cawnpore from Allahabad states that before the cartridges were distributed a Council was held for the purpose of "taking away the religion and rites of the people "of Hindostan. The Members of Council came to "the conclusion that, as the matter was one affecting "religion, seven or eight thousand Europeans would "be required, and it would cost the lives of fifty "thousand Hindoos, but that at this price the "natives of Hindostan would become Christians.

"The matter was therefore represented in a despatch "to Queen Victoria, who gave her consent. A second "Council was then held, at which the English mer- "chants were present. It was then resolved to ask "for the assistance of a body of European troops "equal in number to the native army, so as to "insure success when the excitement should be at "the highest. When the despatch containing this "application was read in England, thirty-five thou- "sand Europeans were very rapidly embarked on "ships, and started for Hindostan, and intelligence "of their despatch reached Calcutta. Then the "English in Calcutta issued the order for the dis- "tribution of the cartridges, the object of which was "to make Hindostan Christian; as it was thought "that the people would come over with the army. "The cartridges were smeared with hog and cow's "fat. One man who let out the secret was hung, "and one imprisoned."

"Meantime, while they were occupied in carrying "out their plan, the ambassadors of the Sultan of "Roum" (Turkey) "in London sent word to his "sovereign that thirty-five thousand Europeans had "been despatched to Hindostan to make all the "natives Christians. The Sultan (may Allah per- "petuate his kingdom!) issued a firman to the "Pacha of Egypt, the contents of which are as

" follows: 'You are conspiring with Queen Victoria. " 'If you are guilty of neglect in this matter, what " 'kind of face will you be able to show to God?'"

" When this firman of the Sultan of Roum reached " the Pacha of Egypt, the Lord of Egypt assembled " his army in the city of Alexandria, which is on the " road to India, before the Europeans arrived. As " soon as the European troops arrived the troops of " the Pacha of Egypt began to fire into them with " guns on all sides, and sunk all their ships, so " that not even a single European escaped. The " English in Calcutta, after issuing orders for biting " the cartridges, and when these disturbances had " reached their height, were looking for the assist- " ance of the army from London. But the Almighty " by the exercise of his power made an end of them " at the very outset. When intelligence of the " destruction of the army from London arrived, the " Governor-General was much grieved and distressed, " and beat his head.

> " At eventide he intended murder and plunder.
> " At noon neither had his body a head, nor his head a cover.
> " In one revolution of the blue heavens
> " Neither Nadir remained, nor a follower of Nadir."

" Done by order of his Grace the Peishwa. 1273 of the Hegira."

But the onward march of the English was not to be checked by quotations from Oordoo poets. It behoved that some weapons besides the eloquence of Azimoolah and the sign-manual of Dhoondoo Punth should be found, and found quickly. The rebel chiefs were enjoined to muster their retainers, and Teeka Singh to beat up the bazaars for sepoys. Reluctant and dispirited the truants turned out to fight for a sovereign whom they were scheming to dethrone, and for plunder which had already by some magical process melted away to half the original value. Baba Bhut undertook to provide carriage for the stores and ammunition: and accordingly impounded the conveyances of the town, particularly all vehicles formerly the property of European gentry: a measure which caused no small vexation to the mutineers who had been cutting a dash in the buggies that had belonged to our subalterns. The merchants received extensive indents for tents and water-proof great-coats: a most essential article of equipment during the first weeks of the rainy season. The Ordnance Office reported itself to be short of percussion caps; and the whole staff of the department was at once set to work at converting detonating muskets into matchlocks. These preparations were completed by the ninth of July, on which day Brigadier Jwala Pershad left the station in the direction of Allahabad at the head of detachments from three regiments of cavalry and seven of infantry, together with a strong body of feudal militia: in all some thirty-five hundred sabres, bayonets, and lances. The column was accompanied by twelve guns of various pattern and calibre, which the result of the earliest action enabled General Havelock to describe with minute accuracy.

They did well to hurry: for the avenger was abroad. Late in May there landed at Calcutta a wing of the First Madras Fusileers, under the command of Major Renaud and Lieutenant Colonel Neill: who, after securing an order which enabled them to draw upon the Patna Treasury, proceeded straight to the Terminus situated on the bank of the Hooghly facing the capital, with the intention of performing the first stretch of their journey by rail. A train was on the point of starting; and the stationmaster, jealous, it may be, to obtain his new line a reputation for punctuality, refused to delay until the rear-guard could be embarked in the cars. Hereupon Neill, an Indian veteran, who during a long absence from home had lost what little reverence he ever possessed for the authority of Bradshaw, clapped the official under arrest in his own waiting-room, and gave the guards and stokers to understand that he had constituted himself traffic-manager for the time being. Travelling in this high-handed style he reached

Benares when least expected either by the English residents, who were waiting to have their throats cut, or by the native force, which was looking out for an excuse to mutiny, and which now found a pretext in the arrival of Neill. After a rough and tumble fight he bundled the insurgents out of the place; quieted the fears of the European population; and at once began his arrangements for penetrating to Allahabad, where a feeble garrison, closely invested by an enormous rebel host, was defending a mile and a half of wall with scanty prospect of deliverance.

On the evening of the ninth June he sent on in bullock-carts a hundred and seventeen of his people; despatched thirty-six others in a small steamer; and packed himself, with two officers and forty-four men, into such stage-carriages as had shafts and axles. Posting in the East is never a very expeditious method of locomotion; and at this conjuncture every stable along the Grand Trunk Road had been plundered more or less thoroughly. But the agents of the Dawk Company knew their man; and it may safely be asserted that the grooms were less sleepy than usual, and the drivers less sulky; that the horses jibbed not quite so pertinaciously, and the wheels came off at somewhat wider intervals. No promise of treble gratuities from an embryo member of Parliament, hurrying up country in search of statistics, ever so surely cut short a stoppage or an altercation, as did the rattle of the panels of the foremost van, which betokened that Neill Sahib was awake, and in another moment would be thrusting out his head to ask what the matter was. When the animals broke down, strings of peasants were harnessed to the traces: and by the afternoon of the second day the relieving army, numbering a short four dozen of exhausted men, had found their way into the beleaguered place. On the following morning the struggle began in earnest, and continued for a full week. Successive instalments of Fusileers swarmed in by road and river: while the enemy had soon consumed most of their courage and all their ball-cartridge, and were reduced to load with morsels of telegraph wire: a device whereby, over and above the effect of their fire, they got rid of an article the possession of which came under the chapter of capital offences in the Criminal Code as revised by Colonel Neill. That officer by the nineteenth July had re-conquered the city of Allahabad, and cleared the district of insurgents. He now found leisure to make some inquiries into the past, which resulted in a series of executions: not more than the crisis warranted, (for, though an austere man, he was no savage,) but quite numerous enough, in the expressive dialect of the day, to "establish a great "funk."

Meanwhile the heat was such as no words can adequately describe. The Europeans died of sunstroke at an average rate of two a day. Our troops had outstripped their Commissariat, and could get neither bread, nor coffee, nor drugs, nor fans, nor screens of moistened grass: appliances which, known to an English housekeeper as "luxuries" and "comforts," in the estimation of those who have spent an Indian June in the tented field merit quite another denomination. Unfortunately, though the larder and the medicine-chest were empty, the cellars of Allahabad were only too well furnished. They were pillaged by some Sikhs, who, without applying for a licence, at once opened a lively trade: selling beer, brandy, madeira, and champagne at a uniform charge of sixpence the bottle. Cholera soon broke out among our poor fellows, living as they did on wine and spirits without even a halfpenny-worth of bread in a temperature of a hundred and thirty-five degrees. In the course of seventy-two hours forty deaths occurred in the ranks of the Madras regiment. The Colonel bought up and destroyed the whole stock of liquor; ransacked the neighbourhood in quest of wholesome provisions; removed his patients to the most healthy quarters which he could command; and was repaid by seeing the mysterious disease vanish as suddenly as it had appeared, after carrying off one out of every nine among his soldiers.

As when a slender rill, ominous to an experienced eye, trickles through the crack in an embankment behind which is gathered, not long there to stay, an immense weight of water: so came along the valley of Ganges this little band, the forerunner of a mighty multitude of warriors. Every evening brought into Allahabad a fresh batch of Englishmen, jaded, indeed, and suffering cruelly from the climate, but eager to be led forward to rescue or revenge. Continental authors who descant glibly on the stolidity and insensibility of the British private might have learned a useful lesson could they have overheard the talk of those pale and sickly lads. By the last day of June Neill judged himself strong enough to detach towards Cawnpore two guns and eight hundred men, half of whom were Europeans. The column was placed under the orders of Major Renaud, who pushed up the road; fighting as occasion offered; tranquillizing the country by the very simple expedient of hanging everybody who showed signs of insubordination; and using all endeavours to procure information concerning the fate of the Cawnpore garrison. On the fourth July he was met by a report of the capitulation and the massacre. Corroborated, and contradicted, and qualified, and again confidently affirmed, rumour insensibly matured into undoubted fact: but to this day no man ventures to name the precise hour when he himself became assured that the worst was true.

With July arrived Brigadier-General Havelock, who, after having employed a week in collecting his resources, moved northwards from Allahabad with six cannon and a thousand English soldiers. That was not a joyous expedition. The hearts of all were occupied with forebodings of evil which they dared not shape into words: and the face of creation seemed to reflect the universal gloom. As in that fantastic canvas of old Dürer, whereon the knight is journeying towards an unknown goal in unhallowed company, so to the fancy of those who were not incapable of vivid emotion even inanimate and irrational nature partook that shade of the future that was on every soul. They waded in a sea of slush, knee-deep now, and now breast high, while the flood of tropical rain beat down from overhead. As far to right and left as eye could pierce extended one vast morass: and the desolate scene was enlivened by no human sound. Nothing was heard save the melancholy croaking of the cicalas, mingled with an under hum of countless insects. The air was heavy with the offensive odour of lime-trees. There were no indications that the column was traversing an inhabited country, except the bodies which hung by twos and threes from branch and signpost, and the gaunt swine who by the roadside were holding their loathsome carnival. After three days of steady toil through the mud and the water Havelock was made aware that the enemy were ahead, and that Renaud was advancing unsupported into the teeth of an overwhelming force. Then our troops hastened forward, and made one march of five leagues and another of eight beneath a blazing sun; (for at this point the weather cleared, and they lost the protection of the clouds;) until they caught up the Major and his detachment and finally halted in a state of entire prostration five miles from the town of Fúttehpore, where Jwala Pershad was encamped with all his chivalry.

It was early morning. Our weary people were enjoying their "little breakfast" of tea, that pleasantest of Indian meals, when the rebel vanguard came pouring down the causeway. Havelock, who wished earnestly to give his harassed soldiers rest, resolved to wait until this ebullition should expend itself. But the affair grew serious; and he had soon no choice but to accept the challenge and draw up his army. In front were the guns, protected by a hundred skirmishers armed with that Enfield rifle which, then a rarity, is now a familiar object to every other household in Great Britain. The Fusiliers and the Seventy-eighth Highlanders struggled through the swamps on the right. The Sixty-fourth Regiment went forward in the centre; and the Eighty-fourth on the left, supported by a battalion of Punjabees. The cavalry moved along some firm ground which lay on the extreme flank.

Never was there such a battle. "I might say," writes the General, "that in ten minutes the action "was decided, for in that short space of time the "spirit of the enemy was utterly subdued. The "rifle fire, reaching them at an unexpected distance, "filled them with dismay; and, when Captain Maude "was enabled to push his guns to point-blank range, "his surprisingly accurate fire demolished their little "remaining confidence. In a moment three guns "were abandoned to us on the *chaussée,* and the "force advanced steadily, driving the enemy before "it on every point. Their guns continued to fall "into our hands; and then in succession they were "driven from the garden enclosures; from a strong "barricade on the road; from the town wall; into "and through, out of and beyond the town. Their "fire scarcely reached us. Ours, for four hours, "allowed them no repose."

In fact it was a mere rout: a memorable triumph

of outraged civilization. The Second Cavalry made a flourish which for a while checked our onset: but the troopers of that redoubted corps soon had had enough of English lead, and felt no appetite for a taste of English steel. Accustomed to deal with feebler adversaries, they were spoilt for fighting with grown men. By noon nothing was to be seen of the mutineers within six miles of Futtehpore save their dead, their accoutrements, and their whole park of artillery. Flying in irretrievable disorder they spread everywhere that the Sahibs had come back in strange guise; some draped like women, to remind them what manner of wrong they were sworn to requite; others, conspicuous by tall blue caps, who hit their mark without being seen to fire. Our list of killed and wounded contained not one British name: though a dozen or so of Sowars, Jemadars, and Russeldars made it as incomprehensible to a home reader as an Indian bulletin should ever be. But the bloodless day was not costless: for twelve of our privates were slain outright by the sun. Our irregular horsemen, who recognised some comrades in the hostile ranks, had flatly refused to charge, and were consequently dismounted and disarmed: a precaution that diminished our cavalry to a score of volunteers.

When the Nana learned how his soldiers had conducted themselves he flew into a violent passion, which could be relieved only by vicarious letting of blood. After attending at the execution of eight ill-fated couriers, who had been intercepted from time to time with English despatches in and about their persons, he felt sufficiently composed to face the emergency. Determined to reserve his own sacred self for the supreme venture, he sent into the field a Patroclus in the person of Bala Rao, whose stake in the cause was indeed no light one. Every available mutineer was equipped and marched down the road, and the captured pieces were replaced from the magazine. On the morrow the Peishwa's brother followed his reinforcements, and took up a position round a hamlet named Aoung, twenty-two miles south of Cawnpore. He found the rebel mind in high perturbation. The gossip of the camp-fires ran mainly on the disagreeable sensations produced by strangulation; and the disquisitions of certain among the sepoys who had witnessed that operation were so circumstantial and picturesque that many who had come best off in the partition of the spoil doffed the remains of their uniforms, and stole away with their riches to the seclusion of their native villages. The behaviour of those who remained proved that the army had rather gained than lost in efficiency by the withdrawal of such as had nothing to acquire and something to enjoy.

Their valour was soon to be tested. At nine in the morning of the fifteenth up came the English; Maude and his battery leading the way; with the Fusiliers and the sharpshooters of the Sixty-fourth close at his heels. Shrapnel shells and conical bullets quickly cleared away everything from our front, and strewed the highway with corpses, weapons, and abandoned tents and waggons. The Second Cavalry caught sight of our baggage, which had been left beneath a grove in the care of a slender guard, and fancied that they discerned an occasion for distinguishing themselves after their own fashion. But they were lamentably disappointed. The regiment had to bustle back with empty pockets and not a few empty saddles, and thenceforward was contented to rest on the renown of previous exploits.

Bala Rao withdrew his troops behind a stream which crossed the road a league in rear of the contested village. The water was too deep to be forded. The bridge was strongly fortified, and defended by two twenty-four pounders. Our force proceeded to the attack after a slight tiffin, and a short siesta for all whose nerves were firm enough to allow them a snatch of sleep between two of the rounds in a fight for such a prize. Maude raked the hostile cannon, which stood in a salient bend of the river: while the Fusiliers advanced in skirmishing order, enraged at the fall of gallant Major Renaud, whose thigh had been broken early in the day. After plying their rifles with deadly effect, they suddenly closed up, and flung themselves headlong on the bridge. Bala Rao, to whom cannot be charged the cowardice which a popular maxim associates with cruelty, had purposed to maintain his post to the last: but on this occasion he had not to do with a front-rank of seated ladies and children, and a rear-rank of gentlemen whose hands were strapped behind their backs. With set teeth, and flashing eyes, and firelocks tightly clenched, pelted by grape and musketry our people converged at a run upon the narrow passage. When they came near enough to afford the enemy an opportunity of observing on their countenances that expression which the Sahibs always wear when they do not mean to turn back, the rebel array broke and fled. The fugitives took with them their general, who carried off in his shoulder a lump of Government lead, to which he was most heartily welcome; but did not find time for the removal of their artillery. There passed into our hands four guns; which cannot be said to have been dearly purchased at six casualties a-piece.

Wounded as he was, Bala Rao brought to Cawnpore the tidings of his own defeat. He went straight to the quarters of his brother, which were soon crowded with the leading rebels, who came to hear what had happened, and to impart their apprehensions and suggestions. The deliberations of this improvised council were at first confused and desultory. Some were for retiring to Bithoor ; some for uniting their forces with the mutineers of Futtehgur. At length, by a slender majority of voices, it was decided to make one more stand south of Cawnpore.

When the resolution had been adopted, Teeka Singh asked whether the Nana had made up his mind as to what should be done with the prisoners ; and hinted that, in case things went ill, it might be awkward for some then present should the Sahibs find such a mass of evidence ready to their hands ; nay more, that the chances of a reverse would be considerably lessened if the captives were once put out of the way. The British were approaching solely for the purpose of releasing their compatriots, and would not risk another battle for the satisfaction of burying them. They would be only too glad of an excuse to avoid meeting the Peishwa in the field. Dhoondoo Punth was not hard to convince on such a point. Whenever bloodshed was in question, he showed himself the least impracticable of men. In the present instance he would never have required prompting, but for the importunity of the royal widows, his step-mothers by adoption, who had sent him word that they would throw themselves and their children from the upper windows of the palace if he again murdered any of their sex. As a pledge that this was no vain parade of philanthropy they had abstained from food and drink for many hours together. In order to anticipate their remonstrances, directions were given to set about the work forthwith. In fact, for every reason, 'twas well that it should be done quickly. The assembly broke up; but all who could spare the time stayed for at least the commencement of such a representation as none could hope to behold twice in a life-time.

At four o'clock in the afternoon, or between that and five, some of the Nana's people went across to the house of bondage, and bade the Englishmen who were there to come forth. Forth they came;—the three persons from Futtehgur, and the merchant and his son;—accompanied by the biggest of the children, a youth of fourteen, who, poor boy, was glad perhaps to take this opportunity of classing himself with his elders. Some ladies pressed out to watch the course which the party took, but were pushed back by the sentries. The gentlemen inquired whither they were going, and were answered that the Peishwa had sent for them on some concern of his own. But all around was a deep throng of spectators, the foremost rows seated on the ground, so that those behind might see: while an outer circle occupied, as it were, reserved places on the wall of the enclosure. There, beneath a spreading lime-tree, lounged Dhoondoo Punth, the gold lace of his turban glittering in the sun-shine. There were Jwala Pershad; and Tantia Topee; and Azimoolah, the ladies' man; and Bala Rao, the twinges of whose shoulder-blade heightened his avidity for the coming show. When this concourse was noticed by our countrymen, their lips moved as if in prayer. At the gate which led into the road they were stopped by a squad of sepoys, and shot dead. Their bodies were thrown on to the grass which bordered the highway, and became the sport of the rabble; who, doubtless, pointed to them in turn, and said: "That "Sahib is the Governor of Bengal; and this is the "Governor of Madras; and this is the Governor "of Bombay." Such was the joke which during that twelvemonth went the round of Northern India.

About half-an-hour after this the woman called "the Begum" informed the captives that the Peishwa had determined to have them killed. One of the ladies went up to the native officer who commanded the guard, and told him that she learned they were all to die. To this he replied that, if such were the case, he must have heard something about it; so that she had no cause to be afraid: and a soldier said to the Begum: "Your orders will not be obeyed. "Who are you that you should give orders?" Upon this the woman fired up, and hurried off to lay the affair before the Nana. During her absence the sepoys discussed the matter, and resolved that they would never lift their weapons against the prisoners. One of them afterwards confessed to a friend that his own motive for so deciding was anxiety to stand well with the Sahibs, if ever they got back to Cawnpore. The Begum presently returned with five men, each carrying a sabre. Two were Hindoo peasants: the one thirty-five years of age, fair and tall, with long mustachios, but flat-faced and wall-eyed: the other considerably his senior, short, and of a sallow complexion. Two were butchers by calling: portly strapping fellows, both well on in life. The larger of the two was disfigured by the traces of the small-pox. They were Mahommedans, of course; as no Hindoo could adopt a trade which obliged him to spill the blood of a cow.

These four were dressed in dirty-white clothes. The fifth, likewise a Mussulman, wore the red uniform of the Maharaja's body-guard, and is reported to have been the sweetheart of the Begum. He was called Survur Khan, and passed for a native of some distant province. A bystander remarked that he had hair on his hands.

The sepoys were bidden to fall on. Half-a-dozen among them advanced, and discharged their muskets through the windows at the ceiling of the apartments. Thereupon the five men entered. It was the short gloaming of Hindostan:—the hour when ladies take their evening drive. She who had accosted the officer was standing in the doorway. With her were the native doctor, and two Hindoo menials. That much of the business might be seen from the verandah, but all else was concealed amidst the interior gloom. Shrieks and scuffling acquainted those without that the journeymen were earning their hire. Survur Khan soon emerged with his sword broken off at the hilt. He procured another from the Nana's house, and a few minutes after appeared again on the same errand. The third blade was of better temper: or perhaps the thick of the work was already over. By the time darkness had closed in, the men came forth and locked up the house for the night. Then the screams ceased: but the groans lasted till morning.

The sun rose as usual. When he had been up nearly three hours the five repaired to the scene of their labours over-night. They were attended by a few sweepers, who proceeded to transfer the contents of the house to a dry well situated behind some trees which grew hard by. "The bodies," says one who was present throughout, "were dragged out, "most of them by the hair of the head. Those who "had clothes worth taking were stripped. Some of "the women were alive. I cannot say how many: "but three could speak. They prayed for the sake of "God that an end might be put to their sufferings. "I remarked one very stout woman, an half-caste, "who was severely wounded in both arms, who "entreated to be killed. She and two or three "others were placed against the bank of the cut by "which bullocks go down in drawing water. The "dead were first thrown in. Yes: there was a great "crowd looking on: they were standing along the "walls of the compound. They were principally "city people and villagers. Yes: there were also "sepoys. Three boys were alive. They were fair "children. The eldest, I think, must have been six "or seven, and the youngest five years. They were "running round the well, (where else could they go "to?) and there was none to save them. No: none "said a word, or tried to save them."

At length the smallest of them made an infantile attempt to get away. The little thing had been frightened past bearing by the murder of one of the surviving ladies. He thus attracted the observation of a native, who flung him and his companions down the well. One deponent is of opinion that the man first took the trouble to kill the children. Others think not. The corpses of the gentlemen must have been committed to the same receptacle: for a townsman who looked over the brink fancied that there was "a Sahib uppermost." This is the history of what took place at Cawnpore, between four in the afternoon of one day and nine in the morning of another, almost under the shadow of the church-tower, and within call of the Theatre, the Assembly Rooms, and the Masonic Lodge. Long before noon on the sixteenth July there remained no living European within the circuit of the station.

But there were plenty at no great distance: for, about the turn of day, our force, after travelling five leagues, rested for a space in a hamlet buried amidst a forest of mango groves. A mile to northward lay the sepoy host, entrenched across the spot where the byway to Cawnpore branches from the Grand Trunk Road. Seven guns commanded the approaches, and behind a succession of fortified villages were gathered five thousand fighting men, prepared to strike a last blow for their necks and their booty. Havelock resolved to turn the flank of the Nana: for he was aware that, if an opponent assails a native army otherwise than as it intended to be assailed when it took up its position, the general for a certainty loses his head, and the soldiers their heart. The word was given, and our column defiled at a steady pace round the left of the hostile line. The Fusileers led, with two field-pieces in their rear. Then came the Highlanders, and the bulk of the artillery; followed by the Sixty-fourth, the Eighty-fourth, and the Sikh battalion. For some time the mutineers seemed to be unconscious of what was going on: deceived by clumps of fruit-trees, that screened our movement; and distracted by the sharp look-out which they were keeping straight ahead. But soon an evident sensation was created along their whole array. Their batteries began discharging shot and shell with greater liberality than accuracy; while a body of cavaliers pushed forward in the direction of our march, and made a demonstration that did not lead to much. As soon as the enemy's flank was completely exposed to the English attack, our troops halted, faced, and advanced in the order wherein they found themselves, covered by two companies of the Fusileers extended as skirmishers. Colonel Hamilton bade the pipes strike up, and led the Seventy-eighth against a cluster of houses defended by three guns. His horse was shot between his legs: but the kilts never stopped until they were masters of all inside the village. Three more pieces were captured by Major Stirling and the Sixty-fourth regiment. The rebel infantry were everywhere in full retreat: for the last half-hour nothing had been seen of the cavalry: and the battle appeared to be won.

Our fire had already ceased. The officers were congratulating each other on their easy victory: the privates were lighting their cheroots, and speculating on the probability of an extra allowance of rum: when of a sudden a twenty-four pounder, planted on the Cawnpore Road, opened with fatal precision upon our exhausted ranks. Two large masses of horsemen rode forward over the plain. The foot rallied, and came down with drums beating and colours flying: and the presence of a numerous staff, in gallant attire, announced that the Peishwa himself was there, bent on daring something great in defence of his tottering throne. Meanwhile our artillery cattle, tired out by continual labour over vile roads and under a burning sun, could no longer drag the cannon into action. The volunteers did whatever might be done by a dozen and a half planters mounted on untrained hunters. The insurgents grew insolent: our soldiers were falling fast: and the British general perceived that the crisis was not yet over. He despatched his son to the spot where the men of the Sixty-fourth were lying down under such cover as they could get, with an order to rise and charge.

They leapt to their feet, rejoicing to fling aside their inaction: and young Havelock placed himself at their head, and steered his horse straight for the muzzle of the gun: mindful, perhaps, how, four and forty years before, his sire, then a light-haired stripling, showed our allies on the banks of the Bidassoa that an English steed could clear a French breastwork. But our people were not Spaniards: and more than one indignant veteran asked in grumbling tones whether the corps might not be trusted to the guidance of its own officers. Nor did their major need that any one should show him the way, when once he had dismounted, and thrown to a groom the bridle of his fidgety little charger, a shapely bay Arab, on whose back, four months later, he was shot dead amidst his shattered regiment in a glorious but ineffectual attempt to retrieve a disastrous day.

And then the mutineers realized the change that a few weeks had wrought in the nature of the task which they had selected and cut out for themselves. The affair was no longer with mixed groups of invalids and civilians, without strategy or discipline, resisting desperately wherever they might chance to be brought to bay. Now from left to right extended the unbroken line of white faces, and red cloth, and sparkling steel. In front of all, the field officer stepped briskly out, doing his best to keep ahead of his people. There marched the captains, duly posted on the flank of their companies; and the subalterns, gesticulating with their swords; and the sober, bearded serjeants, each behind his respective section. Embattled in their national order, and burnng with more than their national lust of combat, on they came, the unconquerable British Infantry. The grape was flying thick and true. Files rolled over. Men stumbled, and recovered themselves, and went on for a while, and then turned and hobbled to the rear. But the Sixty-fourth was not to be denied. Closer and closer drew the measured tramp of feet: and the heart of the foe died within him, and his fire grew hasty and ill-directed. As the last volley cut the air overhead, our soldiers raised a mighty shout, and rushed forward, each at his own pace. And then every rebel thought only of himself. Those nearest the place were the first to make away: but throughout the host there were none who still aspired to stay within push of the English bayonets. Such as had any stomach left for fighting were sickened by a dose of shrapnel and canister from four light guns, which Maude, as though by an effort of volition, had driven up within point-blank range. Squadron after squadron, battalion upon battalion, these humbled Brahmins dropped their weapons, stripped off their packs, and spurred, and ran, and limped, and scrambled, back to the city that was to have been the chief and central abode of sepoy denomination.

Nanukchund was hanging about the vicinity all the while the conflict was in progress. "On the "fifteenth," he writes, "I perceived some sepoys "and troopers running away in great confusion, and "exclaiming that they would have an easy victory, "as the British were few, and would soon be de-"spatched. I was then sitting in an orchard, when I "observed a shopkeeper running up. He came, and "seated himself under a tree near me, and told me "that he was hastening to pack up his wife and "children, as the Europeans would arrive shortly, "and would spare nobody. I thought to myself, "this must be true, and the gentlemen must be very "savage. I returned to the city, and saw several "villagers with their dresses changed coming along "the banks of the Ganges, and I joined them. The "terror in the hearts of all was so great that they "asked each other no questions."

On the morrow, the day of the final struggle, Nanukchund says: "I was in the streets soon after "noon-time. People who have seen the fighting "declare that the rebels are running back, and that "the mutineers are trying to escape from the battle. "Intelligence of this sort was brought from time to "time till it got dusk. The bad people are all "crestfallen, and advising each other to quit the "town. I saw Kalka, a barber by caste, who took "service as a trooper under the Nana, running in "for his life, and trying to get something to eat "from the bazaar. A little while after it was pro-"claimed by beat of drum that the inhabitants must "not get alarmed, as there were only one hundred "Europeans remaining: and that whoever brought "in the head of an Englishman should receive a "hundred rupees. But news came that the Sahibs "were close upon the cantonments, and the man "who was beating the drum abandoned it and fled."

At nightfall Dhoondoo Punth entered Cawnpore upon a chestnut horse drenched in perspiration, and with bleeding flanks. A fresh access of terror soon dismissed him again on his way towards Bithoor, sore and weary, his head swimming and his chest heaving. He was not in condition for such a gallop, the first earnest of that hardship and degradation which was thenceforward to be his portion. Far otherwise had he been wont to return to his palace after a visit of state in the English quarter, lolling, viniagrette in hand, beneath the breath of fans, amidst the cushions of a luxurious carriage, surrounded by a moving hedge of outriders and running footmen. Once again in the home of his fathers he slept as the wicked sleep, whose sin has found them out; and, when the morrow's sun had set, he departed in craven trepidation, and was never after seen among the haunts of peaceful men. But he was true to himself, even in the crash of his falling dynasty: for, as he stepped on board the barge that was to transport him to the confines of Oude, he bethought him of the young mother who was recovering from the pains of child-birth in the recesses of the female apartments. For the first time he had practised economy in his enjoyments, and was now well repaid: for his savings had borne high interest. There were two English lives to take where a fortnight ago there had been but one. And then, having filled to overflowing the measure of his guilt, he passed away like a thief in the night, and left his wealth to the spoiler, and his halls to the owl and the snake. A curse was on those glittering saloons, and echoing colonnades;—on those dungeons conscious of crime, and frescoed chambers blazoned with ineffable vice. That house was full of silver and gold, neither was there any end of his treasures. It was full of horses, neither was there any end of his chariots. There he was given to pleasures.

There he dwelled carelessly. There he said in his heart: "I am, and none else beside me." There he said: "None seeth me." There he trusted in his idols, and in the multitude of his sorceries, and in the great abundance of his enchantments. Therefore had evil come upon him: and he knew not whence it had arisen. Therefore had mischief fallen upon him: and he was not able to put it off. Now was it for him to stand with his enchantments and his sorceries: if so be he might be able to profit: if so be he might prevail. Now was it for the astrologers, the stargazers, the monthly prognosticators to stand up and save him from these things which had come upon him. But they were as stubble, and the fire did burn them; and he was wearied in the multitude of their counsels. For the day of the Lord was upon him that was proud and lofty, and upon his high tower, and his fenced wall, and upon all his pictures of desire. In that day he cast his idols of silver and his idols of gold, which he had made to himself to worship, to the moles and to the bats; and went into the clefts of the rocks, and the tops of the ragged rocks. And they with whom he had laboured wandered every one to his quarter, and there was none to save him.

Some months subsequently two of our spies, who had been commissioned to obtain information about

Miss Wheeler, passed six days in the train of the fugitive Nana in the depths of an Oude wilderness. In the vicinity of his encampment they overtook a sepoy, with whom they got into conversation. He asked why they had come into the desert. They represented themselves as desirous of taking service with one of the Peishwa's eunuchs, and reminded the soldiers that they were old acquaintances of his own. He seems to have been a good-natured fellow: for he told them that it was a dangerous neighbourhood for strangers, but promised, since they had ventured that far, to introduce them as his fellow-villagers. They found from twelve to fifteen thousand people collected in the jungles. Everything betokened distress, disorder, and discontent. Food was scarce and dear. The Maharaja had appropriated the single pair of tents; so that his followers were fain to bivouack under the foliage, starving on rice bought at twelvepence a pound; wringing out their tattered garments, wet with the eternal rain; and sighing for the curry-pots and tight roofs of the Cawnpore cantonments. It is interesting to learn that the most poverty-stricken and dejected of all the mutineers were the troopers of the Second Cavalry. The horses had been reduced to less than a hundred, and the artillery to a couple of field-pieces. The Nana, attended by a servant with an umbrella, went daily to bathe in a river which flowed at the foot of the hill whereon his pavilion stood. A crowd regularly assembled to pay their respects as he passed. The two men especially noticed certain officers of his household: the treasurer and paymaster; the driver of his bullock-carriage; his chief baker, and chief gardener; his shampooer, his sweeper, his boatman, and his wrestlers, both Hindoo and Mahomedan. Bala was there, with the scar of an English bullet on his shoulder, which he has probably by this time carried to an obscure grave. The royal brothers were said to be very anxious to get back to ease and civilization. Their wives were disposed upon an adjoining range of heights, in company with the widows of Bajee Rao, who deserved better than to be transported about against their will in the suite of that unromantic Pretender. The ladies of the court travelled in six palanquins, and the gentlemen on as many elephants.

Yet a few weeks, and Dhoondoo Punth, stripped of even these relics of his former affluence and grandeur, escaped across the Nepaulese marches to a life of suspense, and toil, and privation amidst the Himalayan solitudes. The end of that man we know not, and may never know. Perchance, as they hover over some wild ravine or wind-swept peak, the eagles wonder at the great ruby which sparkles amidst the rags of a vagrant who perished amidst the snows of a past December. Perchance another generation will hear, not without a qualm of involuntary reverence and pity, that the world-noted malefactor is at last to expiate misdeeds already classical. He may have eluded human justice. His hemp may be still to sow. But his place in history is fixed irreversibly and for ever. The most undaunted lover of paradox would hardly undertake to wash white that ensanguined fame.

"In the month of July, a year and a half ago," so deposes a native tradesman, eighteen months after the massacre, "I was in my house at Ooghoo, "when ten or eleven persons, who had fled from "Cawnpore, came to my shop, and asked for betel-"leaf to chew. I showed them new betel-leaf; "when two of them, both Hindoos, told me to fetch "good old betel-leaf, or they would take my head off. "I accordingly went to another seller of betel-leaf, "and bought the kind they asked for, and told them "the price of the same, namely ten pice. The two "men said they would only give me two. I replied "that the betel-leaf was worth ten pice, and that "they ought at the least to give me eight pice: on "which they said that they would kill me and all "my family. I stated I was a poor man, and had "got the betel-leaf from another person. They "then said that they had shown no pity to the "ladies and children whom they had just murdered, "and who clung to their feet, and that they would "have no pity upon me. They frightened me greatly, "showing me a naked sword, covered with blood, "and said that they would cut off my head with the "same. I wept," says this weak-minded young man, "and my mother, hearing me cry, came out, "and begged of them not to hurt me, and that she "would let them have more betel-leaf. After this "they drew water from a well close to my house, "near a temple, and, conversing among themselves, "I heard their companions ask the two men how "many ladies they had killed. They replied that "they had murdered twenty-one ladies and children, "and had received a reward of twenty-one rupees; "and added that at first the Nana ordered the "sepoys to massacre the ladies; but they refused; "and that they two, with three others, carried out "the Nana's orders."

Another resident of Ooghoo thus tells his story: "The truth is that, shortly after the Nana fled, I "was sitting under a tamarind tree, where all the "men of the village assemble to talk, and was con- "versing with a few others about the massacre of "the Europeans at Cawnpore. We were saying "that the Nana ought not to have murdered the "women and children: when Souracun, Brahmin, "of Ooghoo, who is thirty-five years old, and has "a defect in his eye, stated that the officials sent "him to kill the ladies; that he struck one with his "sword, which bent, and he then felt pity, and did "not again strike. He showed us the bent sword." On this occasion Souracun seems to have sunk the twenty-one rupees: which, however, must have lasted him a good while if he made all his purchases at the same rate as he bought betel-leaf. "All the village "heard that he was one of the murderers: but, since "the British rule has been re-established, no one "speaks of it for fear he would be hung, and his "death be laid on their head."

There is good reason to believe that Souracun and his fellow met with their deserts. Mr. Batten, now in high office at Agra, was the first representative of settled government in the district of Cawnpore after the troubles began to subside. He had the honour of removing the gibbet from the ladies' well, and so tempered ferocity with common sense that those who once railed at him as squeamish have at length come to approve his conduct in spite of themselves. But he did not bear the sword in vain. There were brought before him two Hindoos, one advanced in years, and the other much his junior. These men were found guilty of having compassed the death of a Eurasian, and doomed to the gallows. No sooner had their sentence been pronounced than they poured forth a torrent of foul abuse, and were dragged from the dock shouting, and kicking, and cursing their judge and all his relatives on the maternal side.

Now, the Oriental, always polite, becomes doubly courteous when death is in immediate prospect. Then, more than ever, is he anxious to set the company at their ease, and to make away with any disagreeable sense of the false position in which the hangman stands towards the felon. A civilian at Lucknow was superintending an execution when the rope, which had doubtless borne more than one such strain, gave way, and the convict fell to the ground. As he rose, he turned to the Englishman, and said in the tone wherein men utter social conventionalities: "Sahib, the rope's broke." He felt that it was incumbent on him to do what he could towards relieving the general embarrassment arising from a pause in the proceedings, awkward for all parties, but especially for the commissioner, who was endowed with sensibility and genuine refinement.

Batten, than whom no man was more conversant with the native character, regarded the fury of his two prisoners as an extraordinary phenomenon, and requested an explanation from the bystanders.

He was told that the pair were piqued at being condemned on so paltry a charge as the murder of a half-caste, after having taken the principal part in a strange and note-worthy exploit, at which they hinted in their cups; and that, poor as they seemed, they rode fine horses, and wore gorgeous shawls, which they were accustomed to speak of as having been presented to them by the Nana in token of his esteem and satisfaction.

Few of the Cawnpore mutineers survived to boast of their enterprise. Evil hunted these violent men to their overthrow. Those whom the halter and the bayonet spared had no reason to bless their exemption. Many whom pillage had enriched were slain for the sake of that which they had about them by banditti who confidently presumed that the law would not call in question the motives of him who exterminated a sepoy. All who returned to their villages empty-handed were greeted by their indignant families with bitter and most just reproaches. They had been excellently provided for by the bounty of God and the Company. Their pay secured them all the comforts which a Brahmin may enjoy, and left the wherewithal to help less fortunate kinsmen. Yet they flung away their advantages in wilful and selfish haste. They sinned alone and for their private ends; but alone they were not to suffer. They had changed the Sahibs into demons, and had conjured up tenfold more of these demons than had hitherto been conceived to exist. They had called down untold calamities upon the quiet peasantry of their native land. And all this misery they had wrought in pursuit of the vision of a military empire. Let them return to the desert, there to feed without interruption on the contemplation of their power and pre-eminence. Such were the taunts with which they were driven forth again into the jungles: some to die by the claws of tigers on whose lair they had intruded for refuge, or beneath the clubs of herdsmen whose cattle they had pilfered in the rage of hunger: others to wander about, drenched and famished, until amidst the branches of a tree into which they had climbed to seek safety from the hyænas and the ague, or on the sandy floor of a cave whither they had crept for shelter from the tempest, they found at once their death-bed and their sepulchre. The jackals alone can tell on what bush flutter the shreds of scarlet stuff which mark the spot where one of our revolted mercenaries has expiated his broken oath.

Soon after day-break on Friday the seventeenth July, the English van was marching across the desolate plain which lay to southward of the city. Already the magical effect of the tropical rain had clothed that expanse of parched and dusty soil with luxuriant grass, in which rustled the feet of our soldiers as they pushed along, now stumbling over a hidden cannon-ball, and now kicking up the fragments of a sepoy skeleton. They traversed the deserted line of rebel posts, and halted beneath the walls of the roofless barracks, pitted with shot and blackened with flame, and beside the grave at whose mouth were scattered the bones of our people, as when one cutteth and cleaveth wood upon the earth. Three Fridays back from that very morning the treaty of surrender was being attested by a faithless signature, and sworn to with perfidious vows: and again at a like interval of time the men of the Second Cavalry were firing their stables, and saddling their horses, and buckling on the swords that were to be fleshed in unmanly strife. So much had been done and endured within a period of six weeks and a space of six miles.

"At half past six A.M." writes Nanukchund, "the British force arrived in cantonments outside the "city. Those of the citizens who were well-wishers "to the Government brought them bread, butter, "and milk. A great crowd of the town's people "assembled to see what was going on. I also, who "had not stepped out of my house for a month and "a half for fear of being murdered, now came out

" and went to cantonments. Generals Havelock, " and Neill, and a number of other officers were " standing there. Fruiterers, milkmen, buttermen, " bakers and other sellers of provisions were in " attendance with their dollies. Those who were " aware of what was coming had made preparations " on the night previous by having provisions cooked " in the bazaar. A little after eight the rebels who " had mined the magazine set fire to the powder, and " fled. The report of the explosion was so terrific, that " the doors of city-houses fell off their hinges."

Our old friend was now in high spirits. His turn had come, and he showed himself fully equal to the occasion. "I continued" he says "to " attend on the Sahibs with a view of performing " acts of loyalty. I set to work to find out what " men of the city have been loyal, and which of " them disloyal, and how some of the public officers " came to present themselves to the Nana, while " others contrived not to present themselves. I " laboured night and day at great personal incon- " venience to learn full particulars about these " people. I questioned only honourable and upright " men, and no others." He is especially disturbed at the assurance of one Narain Rao, "who, just as I " anticipated, wishes to pass himself off as a well- " wisher to the Government. But there is a great "crowd at this moment, and the Sahibs have no "time to spare. It is also very difficult to find "witnesses against him by private enquiries, and "I see no chance of filing a complaint about it "before any officer."

It seems strange if the Sahibs could not afford time to pay off an old score that had really been incurred. But the truth was that it mattered to them very little whom they killed, as long as they killed somebody. After the first outbreak of joy and welcome the inhabitants of Cawnpore began to be aware that the English were no longer the same men, if indeed they were men at all. The citizens, with their wives and children, poured forth into the country by crowds, without stopping to calculate whether they could establish their innocence. At such an assize, and in the eyes of such a jury, absence was the only defence that could avail aught. From noon till midnight, on the Lucknow and Delhi highway were to be seen immense mobs rushing eastward and westward in headlong haste. They did well both for their own security and for our honour. Of what did take place the less said is the better. Of that from which by God's mercy we were saved it were best to say nothing at all. The heat of the climate and the conflict, the scarcity of food and the constant presence of disease, the talk which they had heard at Calcutta, the deeds that they had been allowed and even enjoined to commit during their upward progress, had depraved the conscience and destroyed the self-control of our unhappy soldiers. Reckless as men who for many weeks had never known what it was to be certain of another hour's life,—half starved, and more than half intoxicated, —regarding carnage as a duty and rapine as a pleasure,—they enacted a scene into the details of which an Englishman at least will not care to inquire. Havelock, in a report to the Commander-in-Chief, thus writes: "I have ordered all the beer, wine, "spirits, and every drinkable thing at Cawnpore "to be purchased by the Commissariat. It will "then be guarded by a few men. If it remained "at Cawnpore it would require half my force to "keep it from being drunk up by the other half, "and I should not have a soldier in camp. While "I was winning a victory on the sixteenth some of "my men were plundering the Commissariat on the "line of march."

And so the general purchased all the liquor. Would that he could have bought up the blood also! It was idle to count upon the forbearance of poor ignorant privates, when the ablest among our officers had forgotten alike the age in which he lived, and the religion that he professed. This is an extract from a letter which would that Neill had never found occasion to indite!

"Whenever a rebel is caught he is immediately "tried, and, unless he can prove a defence, he is "sentenced to be hanged at once: but the chief "rebels or ringleaders I make first to clean up a "certain portion of the pool of blood, still two "inches deep, in the shed where the fearful murder "and mutilation of the women and children took "place. To touch blood is most abhorrent to the "high-caste natives. They think, by doing so, they "doom their souls to perdition. Let them think so. "My object is to inflict a fearful punishment for a "revolting, cowardly, barbarous deed, and to strike "terror into these rebels. The first I caught was a "soubahdar, or native officer, a high-caste Brahmin, "who tried to resist my order to clean up the very "blood he had helped to shed: but I made the "provost-martial do his duty, and a few lashes soon "made the miscreant accomplish his task. When "done, he was taken out and immediately hanged, "and, after death, buried in a ditch at the road-"side."

For a parallel to such an episode we must explore far back into the depths of time. Homer relates the punishment that befell those maidservants, who in the palace of Ithaca had been unmindful of what they owed to their absent lord. First they bore forth from the hall the dead bodies of their paramours, and placed them in the vestibule, staggering beneath the weight: while Ulysses urged on the work by word and gesture: and they laboured at the ungrateful task, wailing, and shedding bitter tears. And afterwards with water and sponges they washed the tables and the seats: and Telemachus and his henchmen scraped with spades the floor of the chamber. But, when they had set the house in order, the women were led out, and cooped up for a while in a corner of the well-fenced court, in a strait place, whence escape was none. And then Telemachus slung from the roof the cable of a dark-prowed ship, and made it fast to a pillar of the colonnade, stretching it high and taut, so that no foot might feel the ground. And, as when swift thrushes or doves, making for their nest, have dashed into a snare which a fowler had planted across the thicket: so these women were fastened in a row, with a halter round every neck, to die in unseemly fashion. And their feet fluttered a moment in the air: but not for long.

It is curious that an act, which the Pagan poet allows an old moss-trooper and his son to perpetrate in the flush of revenge and victory, should have been revived by a Christian warrior after the lapse of twenty-five centuries. And it must be owned that Neill surpassed his model: for apparently the primary object of Ulysses was to sweep away the traces of the butchery, and make his refectory clean and habitable: an unpleasant drudgery, which, as with the simplicity of a primitive Greek he reflected, might as well be performed by the least worthy members of his household before they were taken to execution: whereas the Englishman desired only to wound the sentiments of the doomed men, and prolong their prospect of death with a vista of eternal misery. And this, when the rallying-cry of the insurrection was the preservation of caste:— when in the wide-spread confidence that our faith did not seek to extend itself by carnal weapons lay the salvation of the British supremacy!

But there was a spectacle to be witnessed which might excuse much. Those who, straight from the contested field, wandered sobbing through the rooms of the ladies' house, saw what it were well could the outraged earth have straightway hidden. The inner apartment was ankle-deep in blood. The plaster was scored with sword-cuts: not high up, as where men have fought; but low down, and about the corners, as if a creature had crouched to avoid the blow. Strips of dresses, vainly tied round the handles of the doors, signified the contrivance to which feminine despair had resorted as a means of keeping out the murderers. Broken combs were there, and the frills of children's trousers, and torn cuffs and pinafores, and little round hats, and one or two shoes with burst latchets, and one or two daguerrotype-cases with cracked glasses. An officer picked up a few curls, preserved in a bit of card-board, and marked "Ned's hair, with love": but around were strewn locks, some near a yard in length, dissevered, not as a keepsake, by quite other scissors. All who on that day passed within the fatal doors agree positively to assert that no inscription of any sort or kind was visible on the walls. Before the month was out, the bad habit, common to low Englishmen, of scribbling where they ought not, here displaying itself in an odious form, had covered the principal buildings of Cawnpore with vulgar and disgusting forgeries, false in date, in taste, in spelling, and in fact.

There were found two slips of paper: one bearing in an unknown hand a brief but correct outline of our disasters. On the other a Miss Lindsay had kept an account of the killed and wounded in a single family. It runs thus, telling its own tale:

"Entered the barracks May 21st.

"Cavalry left June 5th.

"First shot fired June 6th.

" Aunt Lilly died June 17th.
" Uncle Willy died June 18th.
" Left barracks June 27th.
" George died June 27th.
" Alice died July 9th.
" Mamma died July 12th."

The writer, with her two surviving sisters, perished in the final massacre.

The library of the captives was small indeed: but such books as they had were to the purpose. The earliest comers discovered among the vestiges of slaughter, a treatise, entitled " Preparation for Death:" and a bible, which must have travelled in Major Vibart's barge down to Nuzzufgur and back to Cawnpore, as may be gathered from the following record:

" 27th June. Went to the boats.
" 29th. Taken out of boats.
" 30th. Taken to Sevadah Kothi. Fatal day."

Fatal indeed: for that was the day when "the " wives sat down, each by her husband;" when " the sepoys, going in, pulled them away forcibly; " but could not pull away the doctor's wife, who " there remained;" when "one Sahib rolled one " way, and one another, as they sat." That bible was a present from the dead to the dead: for on the fly-leaf appeared this address: "For darling "Mamma, from her affectionate daughter, Isabella "Blair:" the "Bella Blair," whose fate is mentioned in the letter from young Masters to his father. The list was closed by a church service, from which the cover had been stripped, and many pages at the end torn off. Unbound and incomplete, it had fulfilled its mission: for it opened of itself where, within a crumpled and crimson-sprinkled margin, might be read the concise and beautiful supplications of our Litany. It concluded, that mutilated copy, with the forty-seventh Psalm, wherein David thanks the Almighty for a victory and a saving mercy.

"O, clap your hands together, all ye people: "O, sing unto God with the voice of melody.

"He shall subdue the people under us: and the "nations under our feet.

"God is gone up with a merry noise, and the "Lord with the sound of a trump.

"God rejoiceth over the heathen: God sitteth "on his holy seat.

"God, which is very high exalted, doth defend "the earth, as it were with a shield."

Such were the printed lines which, from amidst the rent tresses, and shivered toys, and the scraps of muslin dyed in the most costly of all pigments, lay staring up to high heaven in tacit but impressive irony.

It is good that the house and the well of horror have been replaced by a fair garden and a graceful shrine. But there let piety stay her hand. A truce thenceforward to that mistaken reverence which loves to express sorrow and admiration in guineas, and rupees, and the net product of fancy bazaars! Too often already have architect and sculptor disguised the place where a notable thing was done. India still contains some sacred plots untouched by the art of the decorator,—some shapeless ruins more venerable than dedicated aisle or stately mausoleum. Still, amidst the fantastic edifices of Lucknow, hard by a shattered gateway, rise or lie prostrate the pillars of a grass-grown portico. Beneath that verandah, in the July evening, preferring the risk of the hostile missiles to the confinement of a stifling cellar, was dying Henry Lawrence, the man who tried to do his duty. It was not time and the weather that made bare of plaster the brickwork of the old gate. There from summer into winter,—until of his two hundred musketeers he had buried four-score and five, and sent to hospital three-score and sixteen,—earning his Cross in ragged flannel trousers and a jersey of dubious hue, burly Jack Aitken bore up the unequal fray. An Englishman does not require any extraneous incentives to emotion when, leaning against the beams of that archway, he recalls who have thereby gone in and out, bent on what errands, and thinking what thoughts. Between those door-posts have walked Peel, and Havelock, and gentle Outram, and stout Sir Colin, heroes who no longer tread the earth. Through the same entrance passed, but not erect, the form of a tall grey soldier, stern even in death, with a bullet-wound in the centre of his forehead, whom the orderlies announced in whispers to be Neill of the Madras Army. At Delhi still, before the police-court in the Street of Silver, may be seen the platform whereon, naked to the waist and besmeared with dirt and blood, were exposed to three autumn suns the corpses of the last descendants of Timour, slain and spoiled by one who knew neither pity nor scruple. Still, after an evening stroll along the ridge outside the battlements, as on his return he descends the slope rough with crag and brushwood, the visitor may come upon a mound of rubbish so beaten with shot that it is not easy to discern what of it is artificial rampart, and what is broken ground. The rocks coated with frequent films of lead, and the wreck of a small temple, testify that this is the famous post, known in military history as the "Sammy-house picket," which Briton, and Sikh, and Ghoorka, fighting shoulder to shoulder, hardly made good throughout the hundred days of the terrible siege. On the summit of the tottering dome, at a height of some twelve feet from the soil, presides a Hindoo idol with an elephant's head. There he sits, a stupid little god, with arms reposing on his knees, gazing across the valley at the minarets of the ancient capital, as though he had never seen any stranger sight than the tourist in his white dress and dust-coloured helmet, or heard any sounds more wild and maddening than the chirping of the grass-hoppers, and the lowing of the belated cattle as they stray homeward to their stalls. Not urn, nor monolith, nor broken column is so fit a monument for brave men as the crumbling breastwork and the battered wall. And in like manner the dire agony of Cawnpore needs not to be figured in marble, or cut into granite, or cast of bronze. There is no fear lest we should forget the story of our people. The whole place is their tomb, and the name thereof is their epitaph. When the traveller from Allahabad, rousing himself to learn at what stage of his journey he may have arrived, is aware of a voice proclaiming through the darkness of the city of melancholy fame, —then those accents, heard for the first time on the very spot itself which they designate, recall, more vividly than written or engraven eloquence, the memory of fruitless valour and unutterable woe.

THE END